COLE'S KITCHEN ARTS

# Regional French Cuisines

## FROM NORMANDY TO PROVENCE

**JANET FLETCHER**
**HALLIE HARRON**
*Writers*

**KEVIN SANCHEZ**
*Photographer*

## COLE
### GROUP

**Hallie Harron** *(left)* is Executive Chef of Premier Crew Restaurant Services and Consulting Chef for Tang's Ginger Cafe in Minneapolis. Hallie, who trained at the California Culinary Academy and at schools in France and Italy, is an accomplished chef known for her made-from-scratch, imaginative approach to restaurant food. The author of six cookbooks, previously she owned a Minnesota country inn and restaurant and a San Francisco catering company. She also has been extensively involved with the Nicollet Island Inn and the Minnesota Grille in Minneapolis, and has contributed recipes to General Mills and Chun King. She frequently travels to Indonesia and the Orient, seeking new food ideas. **Janet Fletcher** *(right)* is a food and wine writer who trained at the Culinary Institute of America and at Berkeley's celebrated Chez Panisse. She is a contributing restaurant editor to *San Francisco Focus* magazine; editor of *American Wine & Food,* the national newsletter of The American Institute of Wine & Food; and was for nine years the restaurant columnist for the *Oakland Tribune.* Her writing has appeared in *The New York Times, House Beautiful, Barron's, Bon Appetit, Food and Wine, San Francisco Chronicle,* and *National Gardening.* She has eight cookbooks to her credit, including her newest release, *Pasta Harvest.* A past president of the San Francisco Professional Food Society, she lives in Oakland, California, with her husband, a Napa Valley winemaker.

**Front Cover** A traditional favorite from Provence, Salade Niçoise can be made with fresh or canned tuna (page 93). Serve with Gratin de Courgettes for a satisfying meal (page 46).

**Title Page** There are more French cheese varieties than days of the year. Many are available in the U.S., ready to be enjoyed as the cheese course at dinner or for dessert (pages 88-89).

**Back Cover**

**Upper** Full-flavored summer vegetables and seasonings combine in Ratatouille, a colorful stew from the south of France (page 99).

**Lower** This delicious tart from the Basque region of France, Tart aux Poires à la Basquaise, features poached pears and a rich custard in a cornmeal crust (page 121).

**Special Thanks to** Molly Beverly, Cal Mart, Fabrique Delices, Guerra Meats, Laurin Guthrie, Sue Hood, Michèle Morainvillers

Cole books are available for quantity purchases for sales promotions, premiums, fund-raising, or educational use. For more information on Cole's Kitchen Arts Series or other Cole culinary titles, please write or call the publisher.

**Contributors**

*Editor*
Elaine Ratner

*Additional Photographers*
Laurie Black; Victor Budnik, front cover; Alan Copeland, pages 25, 85, and 92; Kit Morris, authors at left; Richard Tauber, pages 15, 47, and 115

*Food Stylist*
Susan Massey-Weil

*Additional Food Stylists*
Clay Wollard, pages 15, 47, and 115

*Photographic Stylist*
Liz Ross

*Calligraphers*
Keith Carlson, Chuck Wertman

*Illustrator*
Ron Hildebrand

*Designers*
Linda Hinrichs, Carol Kramer

The Cole's Kitchen Arts Series is published by the staff of Cole Group, Inc.

*Publisher*
Brete C. Harrison

*VP Publishing*
Robert G. Manley

*VP and Director of Operations*
Linda Hauck

*VP Marketing and Business Development*
John A. Morris

*VP and Associate Publisher*
James Connolly

*Senior Editor*
Annette Gooch

*Editorial Assistant*
Lynn Bell

*Production Coordinator*
Dotti Hydue

© 1995 Cole Group, Inc.

All rights reserved under international and Pan-American copyright conventions.

*Printed in Hong Kong through Mandarin Offset.*

G F E D C B A
1 0 9 8 7 6 5

ISBN 1-56426-070-4

Library of Congress Catalog Card Number 94-28048

*Address all inquiries to*
Cole Group, Inc.
1330 N. Dutton Ave., Suite 103
Santa Rosa, CA 95401
(800) 959-2717   (707) 526-2682
FAX (707) 526-2687

Distributed to the book trade by Publishers Group West.

# C O N T E N T S

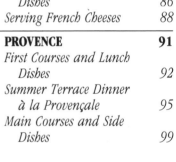

*French home cooking owes its savor to the high quality of the bountiful fresh ingredients found in local markets.*

# The Food of France

From the salt marshes of Brittany to the thyme-covered hills of Provence, France is a nation of regions. The many regional cuisines, developed over centuries, retain their distinctiveness today. Yet time is bringing change to the French home kitchen. Traditional dishes are being updated to fit a health-conscious and fast-paced life-style. This exploration of the food of contemporary France begins with an introduction to French cooking styles (see page 6), kitchen equipment (see page 9), and the most important basic ingredients (see page 10).

# FRENCH COOKING TODAY

Ah, French cooking. Those rich, complex stews simmered for hours. Sauces finished with mountains of butter and rivers of cream. Sumptuous game pâtés and elaborate, time-consuming terrines. That's the real French cooking, right? Not anymore. Today's French cooks are just as concerned about health and as pressed for time as their American counterparts.

In France, both restaurant and home cooks are looking for ways to prepare favorite dishes without the quantities of butter and cream called for in traditional recipes. This desire for more healthful food explains in part the popularity of nouvelle cuisine, which represents a dramatic departure from classic French cooking. Although it has fallen out of favor somewhat, nouvelle cuisine has left its mark: Today the most talked-about restaurant guide in France is not the venerable *Michelin* but the *Gault Millau*, champion of the lighter cooking style.

In addition, eating patterns in France are changing as women enter the work force in growing numbers. In the cities, the traditional routine of husbands returning home for lunch is less and less common. With both husband and wife working outside the home, who would prepare it? Fast-food businesses thrive in Paris and other urban areas; *le sandwich* is now a popular lunch.

The rise of two-career families is also revolutionizing the way the French cook at home. Timesaving devices such as the food processor and convenience foods such as frozen puff pastry are becoming widespread. Food is getting lighter and preparation times shorter. The classics of French cuisine will always be in style, but the preparation of these dishes is changing with the times.

# NOT ONE CUISINE BUT MANY

In France, as in every country, the way people cook and the way they eat depend in part on economic status and environment. Country people eat differently from city people; the prosperous eat differently from the poor.

Over the years, labels have evolved to differentiate styles of cooking. There's nothing snobbish or elitist about these labels; the French know that each style has its place and its merits. In large cities, for example, you can find people relishing the most rustic country specialties at neighborhood bistros; in Paris well-to-do bankers lunch on sausage and lentils with as much pleasure as they would on truffled pheasant. The branches of French cooking include the following.

**Haute cuisine**  Literally *high cuisine*, this is the cooking of the wealthy. You rarely encounter it in private homes, except where grand entertaining is common—say, in the home of a prominent diplomat or a Bordeaux château owner. Instead, haute cuisine resides primarily in expensive international restaurants. Its hallmark is refinement—precise carving and dicing techniques, elaborate garnishes, elegant sauces, subtle flavors, expensive ingredients such as truffles and foie gras, and formal presentation.

**Nouvelle cuisine**  This restaurant movement flowered in the 1970s as a reaction to the richness and excess of haute cuisine. Chefs who adhered to the principles of nouvelle cuisine aimed to lighten sauces and shorten cooking times of meats, fish, and vegetables. Portion sizes were reduced and, perhaps in compensation, elaborate (some say fussy) presentation took on new importance. Nouvelle cuisine chefs were proudly experimental, combining conventional ingredients in unconventional ways, or incorporating "exotic" ingredients from Asia or the United States. Although the 1980s brought a backlash against nouvelle cuisine for its own excesses (minuscule portions, bizarre flavor combinations, contrived presentations), the movement has altered French haute cuisine, making it lighter, less rule-bound, and more attuned to the basic flavors of the raw materials.

**Cuisine minceur**  Essentially a spa cuisine, *cuisine minceur* aims to present the diner with beautiful, tasty, low-calorie French food. It rose to prominence about the same time as did nouvelle cuisine. Chef Michel Guérard, the main proponent of this cooking style, uses fruit and vegetable purées and *fromage blanc* (see page 56) instead of butter and cream to thicken sauces, and he steams meats and vegetables in flavorful liquids instead of sautéing them.

**Cuisine bourgeoise**  Even in France this term means different things to different people. To some, it refers to classic food as prepared in orderly, well-to-do urban households, usually by a hired female cook. Others use the term to describe something more relaxed and unrefined: the cooking of provincial middle-class homes, where material comforts are highly valued and the comforts of the table are prized above all. In a traditional bourgeois household, the mother or wife shops and cooks for the family. Dishes such as *canard rôti* and *navets glacés* (roast duck and glazed turnips, see pages 75 and 76), ratatouille (see page 99), and *boeuf bourguignon* (see page 74) are classics of *cuisine bourgeoise*. They are also the dishes featured in countless bistros, the restaurants French people go to when they want good home-style cooking.

**Cuisine paysanne**  This is the cooking of the countryside, the robust fare of people who work the land or raise farm animals for market. Dishes are hearty, even somewhat fatty, and consequently full of flavor. There's nothing refined about the preparation or the presentation of such food; in a typical country home, dishes are served family style, often directly from the earthenware casseroles in which they were baked. Many of the best-loved examples of *cuisine paysanne*—such as Cassoulet (see page 109) and *garbure* (see page 108)—are dishes that simmer for a long time; they can be put on to cook, then left for hours.

Some of the most delicious dishes in the French repertoire are the inventions of resourceful peasant cooks who learned to make sausages from every part of the pig, to stretch a little meat with a lot of beans, and to make rib-sticking soups out of scraps. French people from all walks of life are fond of these soul-satisfying dishes, which are the stock-in-trade of countless French bistros. In working-class restaurants, these classics are prepared as they would be at home; in the fancier bistros of Paris, they may be refined slightly but never so much as to lose their honest, straightforward appeal.

Most of the recipes in this book belong to the last two categories. Haute cuisine and nouvelle cuisine are not well suited to home cooking, depending as they do on large kitchen staffs, expensive ingredients, and last-minute preparation. The home cook is more likely to have good results and a good time preparing the specialties of French homes and bistros.

## COOKING FROM THE MARKET

All good French cooks—whether three-star chefs or conscientious home cooks—are practitioners of *la cuisine du marché. Cooking from the market* means letting the marketplace shape your menu. It means acknowledging that most foods have a season and planning meals to take advantage of what is freshest and best. The philosophy is just good common sense: When a produce item is at its seasonal peak, its flavor and nutrition are also at their peak, and its price drops.

It is a lot easier to cook well with good ingredients. You don't have to do much to vine-ripened tomatoes or spring asparagus to make them taste good. To improve your cooking without lifting a whisk, buy the freshest seasonal produce you can afford. Where feasible, seek out sources for locally grown fruits and vegetables. The expanding network of farmers' markets can supply wonderful produce for cooks who have time to take advantage of them.

The French home cook often shops every day, making dinner from whatever is best and freshest. Daily marketing may not be practical for American cooks, but everyone can bear in mind the benefits of patronizing good merchants and buying foods at the peak of their season.

*Cooking from the market—using what is freshest and best—is the French home cook's approach to daily meal preparation.*

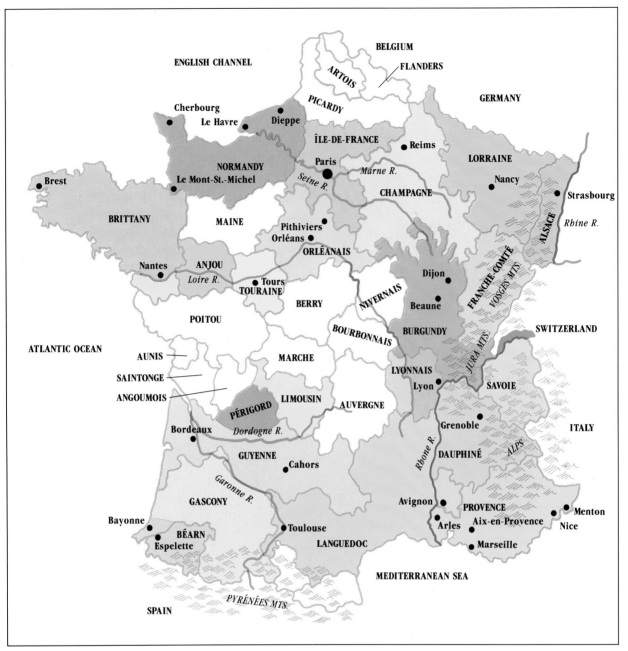

BELGIUM
ENGLISH CHANNEL
ARTOIS
FLANDERS
PICARDY
GERMANY
Cherbourg
Le Havre
Dieppe
ÎLE-DE-FRANCE
Reims
LORRAINE
Paris
Nancy
NORMANDY
Marne R.
Strasbourg
Le Mont-St.-Michel
Seine R.
CHAMPAGNE
ALSACE
Brest
Rhine R.
FRANCHE-COMTÉ
BRITTANY
MAINE
Pithiviers
VOSGES MTS.
Orléans
Dijon
Nantes
ANJOU
ORLÉANAIS
Beaune
Loire R.
Tours
NIVERNAIS
JURA MTS.
TOURAINE
BERRY
BURGUNDY
SWITZERLAND
POITOU
BOURBONNAIS
ATLANTIC OCEAN
AUNIS
MARCHE
LYONNAIS
SAVOIE
SAINTONGE
Lyon
ANGOUMOIS
PÉRIGORD
LIMOUSIN
AUVERGNE
ITALY
Bordeaux
Dordogne R.
Grenoble
ALPS
GUYENNE
DAUPHINÉ
Cahors
Rhône R.
GASCONY
Garonne R.
Avignon
PROVENCE
Menton
Bayonne
Arles
Aix-en-Provence
Nice
BÉARN
Toulouse
Espelette
LANGUEDOC
Marseille
MEDITERRANEAN SEA
PYRÉNÉES MTS.
SPAIN

---

*Although the historical regions of France have no political meaning today, they still have distinctive culinary identities and are important to an understanding of modern French cooking.*

## FRANCE, A NATION OF REGIONS

Ask a Strasbourg resident what part of France he is from and he is far more likely to say "Alsace" than "Bas-Rhin." The latter is the name of the *département*, the official political entity; the former is a historical province name that has not had official meaning since 1789.

The 32 ancient provinces still exist in the hearts and minds of the French. History and geography determined these original divisions; in many ways, they are more natural and more meaningful than today's political lines. Regional identity remains strong in many parts of the

country. Women in Brittany still wear the picturesque Breton headdress at regional celebrations; the Provençaux cling to their ancient dialect.

Nowhere are regional differences more evident than at the table. The distinctive culinary traditions of each province are based on local resources: The apples and thick cream of Normandy, the sun-ripened tomatoes of Provence, and the earthy Pinot Noir from Burgundy have given rise to the regional specialties that define French cuisine. To understand French food, the most logical approach is to consider the nation region by region.

# THE FRENCH KITCHEN

You don't need special equipment to be a good French cook, but the following items will make certain tasks easier.

**Dutch oven** For making stews and braised dishes, a large, lidded pot that can go from stovetop to oven is a wise investment. If it's a handsome one, it can go directly from stove or oven to table. In any case, it should be heavy to ensure even heating and have a tight-fitting lid.

**Earthenware baking dishes** Earthenware has qualities that make it practical for slow-cooked stews and casseroles. The porous clay surface absorbs heat slowly but thoroughly and holds heat steadily for a long time. For long-cooked dishes such as Cassoulet (see page 109) or for baked dishes such as Gratin Dauphinois (see page 88), the even heat provided by earthenware is a real advantage. Most modern earthenware has an unglazed exterior for maximum heat absorption and a glazed interior to prevent the dish from absorbing food flavors.

**Food mill** Essentially a sophisticated sieve, the food mill has a rotating blade that pushes a mixture through a perforated disk, leaving bones, skins, or seeds behind. Although any mixture that can be pressed through a food mill can also be pushed through a sieve with a spatula, the sieve requires more effort.

**Grater** A four-sided, standing hand grater should have both coarse and fine sides. The coarse holes are used for grating cheeses such as Gruyère, the fine holes for grating citrus zest and hard cheeses, such as Parmesan.

**Knives** A basic set of well-constructed knives will make kitchen work much easier. A chef's knife with a 10- or 12-inch blade, a boning knife, a serrated knife for slicing bread, and a 3- or 4-inch paring knife are most useful. A good knife has a blade that extends the length of the handle. The knife should feel balanced in your hand.

Some cooks prefer blades of carbon steel because they take an extremely sharp edge; however, carbon steel is discolored by acidic food such as tomatoes and, in turn, can discolor the food. Stainless steel blades won't discolor, but they are difficult to keep sharp. A high-carbon stainless steel alloy offers a third option: a blade that won't rust and that takes an edge almost as well as a blade made of pure carbon steel.

You will also need a sharpening stone for keeping knives well honed and a sharpening steel for quick touch-ups. When you buy knives, be sure to request instruction on how to keep them sharp.

**Mandoline** This stainless steel device, with its four cutting blades, makes it easy to slice potatoes thinly for Gratin Dauphinois (see page 88) or to make neat julienne strips for Céleri Rémoulade (see page 34) or french fries. A relatively expensive item, the mandoline is essential to professional French kitchens where speed and neatness are important but is something of a luxury in a home kitchen.

**Meat thermometer** The most accurate way to check meat for doneness is with a meat thermometer. For a true reading, the thermometer should be inserted in the thickest part of the meat and should not touch bone. An instant-read thermometer, which rises quickly to the proper reading, is an excellent investment.

**Pepper mill** For grinding whole peppercorns easily, a pepper mill is a necessity.

**Salad spinner** Nothing dilutes a good vinaigrette and ruins a good salad more quickly than wet lettuce. The plastic salad spinner, a relatively new kitchen device available at houseware shops, makes drying lettuce quick and easy.

**Sauté pan** A slope-sided, shallow sauté pan is ideal for frying chicken, liver, mushrooms, onions, or other foods, uncovered, in small amounts of fat. A straight-sided sauté pan is preferable when the dish requires more than a small amount of fat or liquid and will be cooked tightly covered. Most sauté recipes in this book call simply for a skillet; where the recipe includes a lot of liquid or requires a lid, a straight-sided skillet is preferred.

**Sieves** A coarse and a fine sieve are useful for straining sauces, stocks, soups, and other liquids. With thick mixtures, you may need to press down on the solids with a spatula to force them through the sieve. Be sure to clean sieves well after each use.

**Stockpot** A large, heavy, straight-sided pot, taller than it is wide, is useful for making stocks and soups.

**Wire whisk** A wire whisk is the best instrument for whipping egg whites or cream, incorporating oil into a vinaigrette, or incorporating melted butter into a hollandaise or béarnaise sauce (see page 115). Although a single whisk will do all these tasks, some cooks prefer to have two: a flexible balloon whisk, which has a rounded shape ideal for incorporating air into egg whites and cream, and a sturdier wire whisk, for stirring sauces and making dressings.

**Wooden spoons** Long-handled wooden spoons are helpful for stirring sauces or large pots of soup. They won't scratch pots or discolor food. However, they do absorb flavors, so it's a good idea to have at least two—one for desserts and another for savory dishes.

**Zester** This small, inexpensive device removes the zest (the colored part of the skin) of citrus fruit in long, thin slivers.

## WINE IN THE FRENCH KITCHEN

Wine is more than a beverage in France. It's a kitchen staple, as critical to many dishes as salt and pepper. As you prepare French recipes, you'll use wine in the following ways:

**To braise** Wine provides a flavorful medium for braising meats, fish, and vegetables. Poulet au Riesling (see page 61), for example, derives its character from the wine used as the braising liquid.

**To deglaze** Deglazing is a way to salvage the flavorful caramelized bits of meat stuck to the skillet after sautéing. With the pan over heat, a little wine is added, and a wooden spoon is used to scrape up clinging bits as the alcohol boils off. Cream or stock is added and simmered until slightly thickened. With the pan off the heat, nuggets of butter can be swirled in to finish the sauce.

**To flavor** Sometimes wine is used for its flavor alone. Champagne can add subtle character to a sausage mixture, for example (see page 37). In dishes like Sorbet au Gewurztraminer (see page 63) the wine predominates. There's no reason to cook with fine wine, because heat destroys its subtle flavors, but there's every reason to use good wine. A musty or acidic wine can impart those flavors to the finished dish.

**To marinate** In a marinade, wine acts as a tenderizer and flavor enhancer. Acid in the wine breaks down proteins and softens connective tissue, allowing the flavors of the marinade to penetrate the meat.

**To poach** Wine adds character to poaching liquids for meats, fish, vegetables, and fruits. Fruits poached in Sauternes, for example (see page 111), absorb the taste of the wine and in turn flavor the poaching liquid.

## INGREDIENTS

Adding a few important ingredients will turn a well-stocked American home pantry into a French pantry.

**Butter** The recipes in this book call for unsalted butter because that is the type of butter preferred in France. Salt can mask off-flavors in butter; fresh, unsalted butter has a pure, sweet, mild flavor that French cooks appreciate.

**Cider** Fermenting apple juice yields the sparkling dry cider commonly used for cooking and drinking in Normandy and Brittany. In this country, apple cider may be sweet or dry, sparkling or still (nonsparkling). For the recipes in this book, sparkling dry cider is preferred.

**Crème fraîche** This thick, velvety cream, with its subtle, nutty flavor, plays a major role in the French kitchen. Unlike American whipping cream, crème fraîche has been allowed to mature, which gives it special texture and flavor. Unlike sour cream, it can be boiled in sauces without separating. Many well-stocked supermarkets now carry crème fraîche, but it is easy to make your own (see page 22). In cold dishes, sour cream is an acceptable substitute.

**Freshly ground pepper** Once ground, pepper loses pungency quickly, which is why the recipes in this book call for pepper to be freshly ground. An inexpensive pepper mill will make grinding easy. Use black pepper unless otherwise indicated.

**Herbs** The French typically cook with fresh herbs in season and with dried herbs when fresh are unavailable. In this country, where commercial cultivation of culinary herbs in greenhouses is a growing business, many markets carry a wide variety of fresh herbs the year around. The subtle, pure aroma of fresh herbs is almost always preferable to that of dried herbs. Drying intensifies the aroma but also alters it somewhat. In general, you need only half the quantity of dried herb as fresh.

Try to buy dried herbs in small quantities. Store them in a cool, dark place and replace them when they lose their pungency. To release their aromatic oils, crush the herbs between your fingers as you add them to a dish.

**Kosher salt** A coarse-grained salt without additives, kosher salt is about half as salty as iodized table salt. Its coarse texture and its subtle salt flavor make it preferable to table salt in most French dishes. To substitute table salt in a recipe, use half as much.

**Oils** You will want to keep a variety of oils in the kitchen for French cooking. A flavorless vegetable oil such as corn oil is best for deep-frying, since it can be heated to a high temperature without burning. For sautéing and for dressing salads and cold dishes, olive oil is a good choice because of its appealing flavor. It's a good idea to have two: an inexpensive, mild olive oil for cooking and for everyday use in cold dishes, and a fruity, full-flavored extravirgin oil for special salads and cold dishes. For a flavor lift, use extravirgin olive oil to replace some of the mild oil in a vinaigrette or homemade mayonnaise (a dressing made entirely with extravirgin oil can be too strong). Expensive oils should never be heated, since heating alters their distinctive flavor. A pungent walnut oil or hazelnut oil is also delicious in vinaigrettes, although, like extravirgin olive oil, these two should be used sparingly.

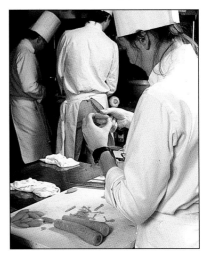

## FRENCH BREAD

Few French home cooks ever make their own bread because good bread is so readily available at nearby *boulangeries* (bread bakeries). In most homes, bread is a daily—sometimes twice daily—purchase. Because it is such a large part of the French diet, especially in poor regions, the government regulates the content, size, and price of the most basic loaves. Specialty breads—distinctive creations of a particular bakery—are unregulated.

The basic daily bread of the French is the long, slender, white-flour loaf known as a baguette. It contains nothing but flour, water, yeast, and salt and thus stays fresh for only a day. The same dough is made into other popular shapes, such as the skinny *ficelle* or the short, plump *bâtard*.

Some bakeries make a denser, chewier bread using a sourdough starter. This type of bread is generally known as *pain de campagne* (country bread); it may contain whole wheat or rye flour. Country breads are generally baked in a round shape. Thanks to the starter, these breads stay fresh for at least a couple of days.

Both baguettes and pain de campagne are suitable for serving as an accompaniment to a French meal. However, the baguette, with its mild flavor, is possibly a better choice when the meal is somewhat formal, the full-flavored pain de campagne more appropriate when the food is rustic and hearty. Either bread can be sliced and toasted for croutons; however, the long baguette makes a neat, even, round crouton that may be preferable for some appetizers, salads, and soups.

Fortunately, it is increasingly easy in this country to find good French-style breads. Most French bakeries make a long, unsliced baguette; even many supermarkets carry baguettes or bake them on the premises. A chewy country-style loaf made from a starter may be more difficult to find. Check the European bakeries in your area; if such a loaf is not readily available, a good recipe for home bakers appears on page 50.

Apples, oysters, artichokes, and berries fill the markets of Normandy and Brittany, ready to be partnered with the region's sweet butter and thick cream.

# Normandy & Brittany

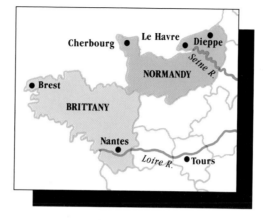

T hick fresh cream, pale sweet
butter, cider from fragrant apples,
and oysters with the briny taste
of the sea—these are the natural riches
of Normandy and Brittany. This rugged land
of dairy farmers and fishermen gives us
such specialties as Roast Chicken With Calvados
(see Poulet Rôti au Calvados, page 19) and
the famous Brittany Buckwheat Crêpes (see
Galettes Bretonnes, page 24). Lobster cooked
outdoors, another Breton favorite, is featured in
the Summer Seafood Dinner menu on page 25.

# NORMANDY AND BRITTANY

In Normandy and Brittany, the sea is never far away. The long Norman coastline faces the English Channel (*la Manche*), and Brittany is essentially a peninsula, surrounded on three sides by water. The nearness of the sea has influenced the cooking of both regions enormously.

Normandy boasts major fishing ports at Dieppe, Cherbourg, and Le Havre, which supply the Norman table with exceptional shrimp, oysters, mussels, clams, sole, and flounder. Often the shellfish are steamed in cider or grilled over coals; occasionally they are simmered or baked in cream. Norman cooks frequently pair fish and shellfish in elaborate dishes such as Filets de Sole aux Moules (see page 19).

Normandy is the premier dairy country of France. The region's cows give a milk that is particularly high in fat; the milk in turn yields famous butter, cream, and cheese. Norman cream is rich and heavy and is used lavishly by Norman cooks to sauce everything from fish to green beans. Chicken and veal are stewed in cream; oyster soup is enriched with cream; and baked apples are served in thick pools of cream. Isigny butter is sought after throughout France, and some of the country's best-known cheeses—Camembert, Pont l'Evêque, and Livarot—are Norman.

Normandy is also apple country. Its juicy apples flavor chicken and veal dishes as well as a variety of desserts—apples are stuffed in sweet omelets or crêpes, baked with butter and cream, or sliced and baked in tarts. Apples are pressed for hard cider, the favored beverage of the region, and the cider is distilled to make the fiery Calvados brandy.

Brittany is more rugged than Normandy, both on its coastline and in its interior. Breton fishermen are among the world's best and bravest sailors; they venture regularly into rough waters for lobster, scallops, herring, sardines, and sole. The Brittany coast is also France's main source of oysters, both wild and cultivated.

Sheep graze on the salt marshes of Brittany, which gives their meat a distinctive flavor prized by connoisseurs. The white Breton chicken, the product of top-grade breeding stock, is also sought after.

Market gardens—small plots of fruits and vegetables intended for the commercial market—thrive in the mild climate of the peninsula. Brittany supplies much of the country's artichokes, cauliflower, leeks, and onions, as well as quantities of carrots, peas, beans, cabbages, brussels sprouts, and new potatoes. Apples and berries do well, and the strawberries of Plougastel are superb.

Breton cooking is simple and hearty. Probably no dish is more symbolic of the region's humble ways than the famous *galette bretonne*, a rustic buckwheat crêpe traditionally made on a large round griddle (see page 24).

Hard cider is the preferred beverage at most tables in Brittany, but the region also produces some well-known wines. The fresh and lively Muscadet and the refreshing Gros Plant are excellent partners to briny oysters and other seafood.

## FIRST COURSES

In Normandy and Brittany, popular first courses include omelets made with farm-fresh eggs, salads of Breton shellfish, and simple soups enriched with thick Normandy cream.

### OMELETTE À LA MÈRE POULARD
*Basic omelet*

The real Mère Poulard died in 1931, but tourists still flock to her namesake restaurant in Mont-Saint-Michel in Normandy for puffy omelets cooked over an open fire. Countless diners have wondered what makes the restaurant's simple omelet superior. Is it the majesty of the natural setting? Or is it the quality of the famous Normandy butter and farm-fresh eggs?

> 3 *large eggs*
> 1 *teaspoon water*
>   *Kosher salt and freshly ground pepper*
> 1 *tablespoon unsalted butter, plus 1 tablespoon melted unsalted butter for brushing omelet*
> ½ *tablespoon finely minced parsley or chives, for garnish*

**1.** Crack eggs into a small mixing bowl. Add the water. Season with salt and pepper. Whisk lightly with a fork to blend.

**2.** Place warm serving plates close at hand. Heat an 8- or 9-inch omelet pan or slope-sided skillet over moderately high heat until a drop of water sizzles on its surface. Add butter and swirl to coat pan. Add beaten eggs.

**3.** Cook and fold omelet as shown on page 15.

**4.** Brush top lightly with melted butter and sprinkle with minced parsley or chives.

*Makes 1 omelet.*

**Apple and Cheese Omelet** In a small bowl combine ⅓ cup grated, unpeeled apple and 2 tablespoons grated Gruyère cheese. Before folding omelet in step 3, sprinkle apple-cheese mixture evenly over surface of omelet. Continue with recipe.

**Cheese Omelet**   Before folding omelet in step 3, sprinkle 3 tablespoons of grated Gruyère cheese evenly over the surface of the omelet. Continue with recipe.

**Fresh Pea Omelet**   In a small saucepan over moderately high heat, simmer ½ cup whipping cream until reduced to ¼ cup. Add ¾ cup fresh peas. Cover and steam over low heat until tender-crisp (5 to 7 minutes). Stir in 2 teaspoons chopped fresh mint; season to taste with kosher salt and white pepper. Before folding omelet in step 3, spoon the pea mixture evenly over the surface of the omelet. Continue with recipe.

**Goat Cheese Omelet**   In a small skillet over moderate heat, melt 1 tablespoon unsalted butter. Add one minced shallot and sauté until softened (about 3 minutes). Before folding omelet in step 3, sprinkle sautéed shallot and 3 tablespoons crumbled goat cheese evenly over surface of omelet. Continue with recipe.

**Ricotta Cheese Omelet**   In a small bowl stir together ¼ cup ricotta cheese and 1 tablespoon sugar. Before folding omelet in step 3, sprinkle sweetened ricotta evenly over surface of omelet. Continue with recipe, but omit parsley garnish; instead, sprinkle the buttered omelet lightly with sugar.

*Note*   This recipe may be multiplied to make more than one omelet. Beat eggs, the water, salt, and pepper together in a large bowl. Cook only one omelet at a time, however, measuring out a generous ½ cup of egg mixture per omelet. Omelets should be served and eaten as soon as they are made; do not try to keep the finished ones warm while you make the others.

---

*Step·by·Step*

## HOW TO COOK AN OMELET

**3.** *Tilt pan slightly away from you and fold bottom third of omelet (side closest to you) toward center.*

**1.** *Coat a hot omelet pan with butter and add beaten eggs. Swirl pan with one hand while stirring eggs in a circular motion with a fork (tines of fork should be parallel to but not touching bottom of pan).*

**2.** *When omelet begins to set, rapidly push cooked egg toward center of pan, allowing uncooked egg to run underneath. The omelet is ready when it is firm on the bottom but still moist in the center. Total cooking time is about 30 seconds.*

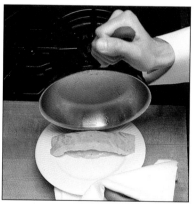

**4.** *Holding pan in one hand at a 45-degree angle and a warm serving plate in the other hand, also at a 45-degree angle, carefully slide top third of omelet onto plate.*

**5.** *Raise angle of pan even more to allow rest of omelet to roll over onto top third.*

## OMELETTE JARDINIÈRE
### Omelet with mixed spring greens

The lemony tang of fresh sorrel adds a lift to this vegetable filling. Look for sorrel in produce markets from fall through spring; if unavailable, substitute ½ cup shredded butter lettuce.

- 2 tablespoons butter
- ½ cup finely shredded spinach leaves
- ½ cup finely shredded sorrel leaves
- ½ cup finely shredded romaine
- 1 tablespoon Crème Fraîche (see page 22) or sour cream
    Freshly grated nutmeg
    Kosher salt and freshly ground pepper
    Omelette à la Mère Poulard (see page 14), batter

1. In a medium skillet over moderately low heat, melt butter. Add spinach, sorrel, and romaine, and cook, stirring often, until greens are wilted. Stir in Crème Fraîche. Season to taste with nutmeg, salt, and pepper.

2. Cook Omelette à la Mère Poulard. Before folding, spoon hot vegetable filling evenly over surface of omelet. Continue with Omelette à la Mère Poulard recipe.

*Makes 1 omelet.*


## SOUPE AUX HUÎTRES
### Oyster stew

Succulent Breton oysters and rich Norman cream are the inspiration for this buttery soup. Serve in small portions as a first course, or make it the centerpiece of a casual supper with a green salad and fruit for dessert. For best flavor, shuck the oysters yourself or ask the fishmonger to shuck them the same day you plan to use them; shucked oysters in jars are generally not fresh enough for this soup.

- 30 oysters in the shell
    Dry white wine or dry cider, as needed
- 3 tablespoons unsalted butter
- 1 large shallot, minced
- 4 cups milk
- 1 teaspoon dried thyme
- 2 sprigs parsley
- 1 bay leaf
- 1 teaspoon coarsely cracked pepper
- ½ cup whipping cream
- 2 egg yolks
    Kosher salt and freshly ground pepper
- 2 tablespoons minced chives, for garnish

### Croutons

- 6 slices (¾ in. thick, 3 to 4 in. long) day-old, best-quality French bread

1. Shuck oysters, reserving all oyster liquor. Add enough white wine to liquor to make ½ cup.

2. In a large saucepan over moderately low heat, melt 1 tablespoon of the butter. Add shallot and sauté until softened (about 4 minutes). Add milk, thyme, parsley, bay leaf, cracked pepper, and oyster liquor mixture. Raise heat to moderately high and bring to a simmer; then reduce heat and simmer 5 minutes. Remove from heat and let cool slightly. Strain through a fine sieve into a clean saucepan.

3. Add oysters to strained milk mixture and cook over moderately high heat until edges of oysters begin to curl. In a small bowl whisk together cream and egg yolks. Add to pot in a slow, steady stream, whisking constantly. Cook, stirring, until soup is hot; do not allow to boil. Season to taste with salt and pepper. Cut the remaining 2 tablespoons butter into small pieces and swirl into soup.

4. To serve, put warm Croutons in warm bowls. Ladle soup over bread and garnish with minced chives.

*Makes 6½ cups, 6 servings.*

**Croutons**    Preheat oven to 350° F. Bake bread slices on a tray until lightly browned (8 to 10 minutes). Croutons may be made up to 3 days ahead and stored in a plastic bag. Before serving, warm 5 minutes in a 350° F oven.

*Makes 6 croutons.*


## POTAGE AUX CAROTTES ET AUX PANAIS
### Carrot and parsnip soup

Making the soup with water will bring out the flavor of good, sweet carrots; if the carrots are not noticeably sweet, use chicken stock.

- 7 tablespoons unsalted butter
- 3 cups coarsely chopped carrot
- 2½ cups coarsely chopped parsnip
- 1¾ cups coarsely chopped green onion
- 1 shallot, coarsely chopped
- 4 cups cold water or Fond de Volaille (see page 32)
- 8 slices (½ in. thick) day-old French bread
    Kosher salt and freshly ground pepper
- ½ cup Fond de Volaille (see page 32) or milk or whipping cream (optional)

1. In a medium saucepan over moderately low heat, melt 3 tablespoons of the butter. Add carrots, parsnips, green onions, and shallot. Sauté 5 minutes, stirring often. Add the water. Bring to a simmer over moderately high heat; cover and reduce heat. Simmer until carrots are just tender (about 40 minutes). Parsnips will be quite soft. Remove from heat and cool slightly.

2. Preheat oven to 350° F. In a large skillet over moderate heat, melt the remaining 4 tablespoons butter. Cut French bread into ½-inch cubes and add to skillet. Toss to coat with butter, then turn cubes out onto a baking tray. Bake until golden brown (about 15 minutes); set aside.

3. Transfer soup mixture to a food processor or blender and purée until smooth. Pour into a clean saucepan, reheat, and season to taste with salt and pepper. Garnish each serving with croutons and pass extra croutons separately. For a thinner soup, add Fond de Volaille and reheat; garnish with croutons. Or, reheat purée without thinning it and serve topped with croutons. Heat cream separately and pass a pitcher of hot cream to add to soup, to taste.

*Makes about 6½ cups, 4 to 6 servings.*

## MOULES AU CITRON CONCASSÉ
### Chilled mussels with citrus relish

Diced lemon and orange make a zesty relish for cold steamed mussels. Serve mussels on the half shell for stand-up cocktail fare. Or nestle them in butter lettuce cups as a first course for lunch or dinner; garnish with additional mussels on the half shell.

> 3  dozen mussels
> 1  cup dry white wine
> 1½  cups water
> 1  bay leaf
> 1  tablespoon minced fresh thyme or 1 teaspoon dried thyme
> 2  shallots, minced
> 1  tablespoon plus 1 teaspoon grated orange zest
> 1  tablespoon plus 1 teaspoon grated lemon zest
>   Flesh of 1 small orange (pith, seeds, and membranes removed), finely diced
>   Flesh of 1 small lemon (pith, seeds, and membranes removed), finely diced
> 2  tablespoons finely minced green onion or parsley
>   Kosher salt and freshly ground pepper
>   Lemon juice and orange juice, as needed
>   Hearts of butter lettuce

**1.** Scrub mussels well; pull out the hairy beard that protrudes from shell.

**2.** In a large pot combine wine, the water, bay leaf, thyme, shallots, 1 tablespoon of the orange zest, and 1 tablespoon of the lemon zest. Bring to a boil over high heat. Add mussels and cover. Cook over high heat 1 minute, then uncover and remove any opened mussels to a separate bowl. Cover pot and continue cooking, shaking pot vigorously once or twice and uncovering every 20 to 30 seconds to check for opened mussels. Discard any mussels that refuse to open in 5 minutes.

**3.** After removing all mussels from pot, reduce liquid over high heat to ¾ cup. Strain through dampened cheesecloth into a large stainless steel, glass, or ceramic bowl. Add orange and lemon pulp, green onion, and the remaining orange and lemon zest. Remove mussels from shells, reserving 12 half shells, and add to bowl. Stir to blend, then cover and refrigerate for at least 2 hours or up to 1 day. Remove from refrigerator 20 minutes before serving. Season to taste with salt and pepper; add more lemon or orange juice if necessary.

**4.** To serve, spoon a mussel and some of its liquid into each of the 12 reserved shells. Line a large serving platter or individual salad plates with cup-shaped leaves of butter lettuce. Spoon remaining mussels into lettuce cups. Garnish platter or plates with filled mussel shells.

*Serves 6 as an appetizer, 3 as a first course.*

*A lemon and orange relish gives a lift to cold steamed mussels.*

17

*Normandy's fragrant apple brandy, Calvados, flavors a juicy roast chicken with apples.*

## MAIN DISHES AND ACCOMPANIMENTS

Normans and Bretons have famously healthy appetites, enjoying such hearty daily fare as veal stew with cream, lamb stew with white beans, or roast chicken stuffed with apples. Even the region's vegetables, such as chard and brussels sprouts, are prepared in rib-sticking ways.

### BROCHETTES DE COQUILLES SAINT-JACQUES, BEURRE NOISETTE
#### *Steamed scallop brochettes with brown butter*

These easy brochettes are a reliable choice for busy-day dinners. On their own, they make an elegant first course; with buttered noodles or steamed rice, they're the main event. Either way, a French Vouvray or a California Chardonnay would be a fine partner.

> 12 *tablespoons unsalted butter*
> 1¼ *pounds fresh sea scallops*
> 1½ *cups dry white wine*
> *Minced fresh chervil or parsley, for garnish*
> *Lemon wedges, for garnish*

**1.** In a small saucepan over low heat, melt butter. Continue cooking over low heat until butter turns hazelnut brown and begins to smell nutty; do not allow to burn. Remove from heat. Carefully spoon clear butter off dark solids in bottom of pan. Save clear butter and discard solids.

**2.** Trim away the tough white muscle on the side of each scallop. Thread scallops loosely on twelve 6-inch wooden skewers, dividing them evenly among the skewers. Arrange skewers in the top of a steamer.

**3.** Place wine in bottom of steamer and bring to a boil over high heat. Place scallops over simmering wine, cover, and steam until done (about 2 minutes).

**4.** In a small saucepan over low heat, reheat brown butter. Transfer scallop skewers to a warm serving platter. Drizzle with brown butter and garnish with minced chervil. Serve with lemon wedges.

*Serves 6.*

## FILETS DE SOLE AUX MOULES
### Sole with mussels and cider

Thin buttered noodles would be delicious with this dish, and dry cider is the perfect companion.

- 2 dozen mussels
- 2 cups sparkling apple cider
- 1 bay leaf
- 2 shallots, minced
- 1 stalk celery, coarsely chopped
- 2 sprigs thyme or 1 teaspoon dried thyme
- 3 tablespoons unsalted butter
- 1½ cups thinly sliced leeks (white and pale green part only)
- ½ cup Crème Fraîche (see page 22)
- 2 pounds fresh sole fillets Kosher salt and freshly ground pepper
- 2 tablespoons minced chives, for garnish

**1.** Scrub mussels and pull out hairy beard that protrudes from shell. In a large pot combine cider, bay leaf, shallots, celery, and thyme. Bring to a boil over high heat and boil 3 minutes. Add mussels and cover. Cook over high heat for 1 minute, then uncover and remove any opened mussels to a bowl. Cover pot and continue cooking, shaking pot vigorously once or twice and uncovering every 20 to 30 seconds to check for opened mussels. Discard any mussels that have not opened after 5 minutes.

**2.** Remove mussels from shells; discard shells and set mussels aside. Return any juices that have accumulated in bottom of mussel bowl to pot. Strain mussel liquid through a cheesecloth-lined sieve into a large skillet.

**3.** In another large skillet over moderately low heat, melt butter and add leeks. Cook, covered, until leeks are soft (about 15 minutes). Add Crème Fraîche and bring to a simmer.

**4.** Bring mussel liquid to a boil over high heat and boil until reduced to 1½ cups. Reduce heat to maintain a simmer, add sole (in two batches if necessary) and poach, uncovered, until fish barely flakes with a fork (3 to 4 minutes). Transfer fish to a warm serving platter with a slotted spatula. Raise heat to high and reduce liquid in skillet to ¼ cup. Add to leek mixture along with the mussels and bring to a simmer over high heat. Season to taste with salt and pepper. Spoon sauce and mussels over sole. Garnish with chives.

*Serves 6.*

## POULET RÔTI AU CALVADOS
### Roast chicken with Calvados

Apples inside and around the bird and a sauce made with apple brandy produce the perfect roast chicken for an autumn dinner. Leftovers would make a memorable chicken salad.

- 2 whole chickens (2½ to 3 lb each) Kosher salt and freshly ground pepper
- 2 onions, coarsely chopped
- 1½ cups unpeeled apple slices
- 2 tablespoons unsalted butter, melted
- ¼ cup apple juice
- 2 tablespoons olive or safflower oil
- 4 tablespoons Calvados or apple brandy
- 2 large red apples
- 2 tablespoons minced parsley, for garnish

**1.** Preheat oven to 350° F. Remove wing tips from chickens and reserve. Clean chickens well, removing excess fat deposits and any bloody bits inside cavities. Wash and dry thoroughly. Reserve giblets. Salt and pepper cavities lightly. Set aside half the chopped onions; stuff each chicken with half the remaining onions and half the apple slices. Truss birds with kitchen string. Season with salt and pepper.

**2.** In a small saucepan combine butter, apple juice, oil, and 2 tablespoons of the Calvados. Brush chickens with some of the butter mixture. Place on rack in roasting pan and roast 40 minutes, basting after 20 minutes with more butter mixture and any juices that accumulate on bottom of roasting pan.

**3.** While chickens are roasting, combine remaining onions with wing tips and giblets in a small saucepan. Add water just to cover. Bring to a simmer over high heat, skimming as necessary to remove any scum that rises to the surface. Reduce heat to maintain a simmer. Cook 1 hour, uncovered, then strain and reserve.

**4.** Meanwhile, quarter and core large red apples. Slice each quarter in half lengthwise. After chickens have cooked 40 minutes, baste them and add apples to roasting pan. Continue roasting. Baste both apples and chickens after 20 minutes. After 65 minutes total cooking time, check birds for doneness. Juices should run clear when a skewer is poked into meatiest part of breast. When done, remove chickens from oven and baste one last time with butter mixture. Transfer chickens to a cutting board and apple slices to a warm platter.

**5.** Let chickens rest while you prepare the sauce: Pour off any fat in roasting pan and place pan on top of stove over moderate heat. Add strained giblet stock, stirring to scrape up any brown bits stuck to bottom of pan. Add the remaining 2 tablespoons Calvados. Reduce liquid over high heat to ⅔ cup. Season to taste with salt and pepper.

**6.** To serve, untruss chicken and discard apples and onions in the cavity. Carve chicken into serving pieces, if desired. Arrange on platter with roasted apples. Spoon sauce over chicken. Garnish with parsley.

*Serves 6.*

## GRATIN DE BLETTES AUX POMMES
### Swiss chard and apple gratin

A roast ham or a platter of pork chops never had a better companion than this creamy chard and apple gratin. The word *gratin* refers to the crust formed by the buttery bread crumb topping.

- 1½ pounds Swiss chard
- 6 tablespoons unsalted butter
- ¾ cup thinly sliced red onion
- 1 teaspoon kosher salt
- ½ teaspoon freshly ground pepper
  Pinch nutmeg
- ½ cup whipping cream
- 1 large unpeeled apple, cored and grated
- ¼ cup soft bread crumbs

**1.** Preheat oven to 350° F. Cut greens away from ribs of Swiss chard. Cut ribs into 1-inch pieces. In a large pot over high heat, bring 4 quarts salted water to a boil. Blanch greens 30 seconds. Transfer with a slotted spoon or wire skimmer to ice water; when cold, drain and squeeze leaves to remove as much excess moisture as possible. Transfer to a medium bowl. Blanch ribs in same pot of boiling water until tender-crisp (about 3 minutes). Transfer with a slotted spoon or wire skimmer to ice water; when cold, drain and pat dry. Transfer to bowl with greens.

**2.** In a small skillet over moderate heat, melt 3 tablespoons of the butter. Add onion and sauté until softened (about 5 minutes). Transfer to bowl with chard and toss to blend. Add salt, pepper, and nutmeg.

**3.** Using 1 tablespoon of the butter, butter a 9-inch oval gratin dish. Spread one fourth of the chard-onion mixture over bottom of dish. Drizzle with 2 tablespoons of the cream. Top with one third of the grated apple. Repeat twice more, then end with a layer of chard-onion mixture and the

remaining 2 tablespoons cream. Top with bread crumbs; dot with the remaining 2 tablespoons butter and bake for 15 minutes. Raise oven temperature to 375° F. Bake until golden brown (about 10 more minutes). Serve from the dish.

*Serves 6.*

## GIGOT D'AGNEAU À LA BRETONNE
### Leg of lamb with white beans

Polls have shown that leg of lamb is the favorite dish of the French. Here it's prepared *à la bretonne*, a phrase that usually signals the presence of white beans. For accompaniment, consider a red Bordeaux wine or a California Zinfandel. This recipe should be started the day before you wish to serve it.

- 2½ cups dried white beans
- 1 cup diced salt pork (½-in. cubes)
  Unsalted butter, as needed
- ½ cup minced carrot
- ½ cup minced onion
- ½ cup minced celery
  Bouquet garni (1 stalk celery tied together with 1 bay leaf, 3 sprigs parsley, and 2 sprigs thyme)
- 2 cups plus 2 tablespoons dry white wine
- 3½ cups (approximately) Fond de Volaille (see page 32)
- 1 leg of lamb (5 lb), boned and butterflied
- 2 cloves garlic, peeled and thinly sliced
- 2 teaspoons kosher salt
- 1 teaspoon freshly ground pepper
- 1 teaspoon minced fresh thyme or ½ teaspoon dried thyme
- 1 bay leaf, crumbled
- 2 tablespoons olive oil
- 2 tablespoons finely minced parsley, for garnish

**1.** Put beans in a large pot; cover with 8 cups cold water and let soak overnight. (To quick-soak, bring beans and water to a boil; boil 1 minute, then cover and let stand 1 hour.) Drain beans and set aside.

**2.** In an ovenproof casserole large enough to hold both lamb and beans, render salt pork over low heat until crisp. With a slotted spoon, transfer salt pork to paper towels to drain. Pour off all but 3 tablespoons fat in pan, or add enough butter to make 3 tablespoons. Add carrots, onions, and celery, and sauté over moderately low heat until softened (about 10 minutes). Add drained beans, salt pork, bouquet garni, the 2 cups wine, and just enough Fond de Volaille to barely cover.

**3.** Bring mixture to a simmer over moderately high heat, stirring. Cover, reduce heat to maintain a simmer, and cook until beans are just tender. Depending on age of beans, cooking may take up to 3 hours.

**4.** With a small, sharp knife, cut 10 slits in the lamb about ½ inch long and ¼ inch deep. Insert a garlic sliver in each slit. In a blender combine remaining garlic, salt, pepper, thyme, bay leaf, oil, and the remaining 2 tablespoons wine. Blend to mix. Rub mixture evenly over meat. Cover lamb and marinate, refrigerated, at least 5 hours, or overnight.

**5.** Preheat oven to 350° F. Make a space in center of beans large enough to hold lamb. Transfer lamb to casserole. Sprinkle beans with just enough stock (about 1 cup) to moisten them. Roast, uncovered, until lamb is done to your liking (about 1 hour and 10 minutes for rare meat). Let stand 10 minutes before carving.

**6.** To serve, arrange sliced lamb on a warm serving platter. Serve beans in a separate dish or surround lamb with beans. Garnish beans with minced parsley.

*Serves 6.*

**Make-Ahead Tip** Beans may be prepared through step 3 up to 3 days ahead; cover and refrigerate.

## BLANQUETTE DE VEAU AUX CHAMPIGNONS
### Veal stew with oyster mushrooms

The traditional *blanquette* is thickened at the last minute with a *liaison,* a mixture of egg yolks and cream. This lighter version omits the liaison and relies instead on reduction—rapid boiling of the braising liquid to concentrate its flavors—to yield a flavorful and subtly thickened sauce. Buttered noodles or steamed rice would be a good accompaniment.

2½  pounds boneless veal shoulder, cut into 2-inch cubes

6  cups (approximately) Fond de Veau or Fond de Volaille (see pages 33 and 32)

1  onion, peeled and stuck with 6 whole cloves

8  whole, unpeeled cloves garlic

1  bay leaf

1  teaspoon dried thyme

12  black peppercorns

2  sprigs parsley

24  small shallots, peeled

1  cup julienned carrots (2- by ¼- by ¼-inch matchsticks)

1  cup julienned celery (2- by ¼- by ¼-inch matchsticks)

½  pound oyster mushrooms, halved if large

½  cup whipping cream Kosher salt and cayenne pepper

2  tablespoons parsley minced with 1 teaspoon grated lemon zest, for garnish

**1.** Preheat oven to 350° F. Place meat in a large pot and cover with cold water. Bring to a boil over high heat, drain, and refresh under cold running water. Place meat in a clean, ovenproof casserole.

**2.** Add 4 cups of the stock, onion, and garlic cloves to casserole. Tie bay leaf, thyme, peppercorns, and parsley together in a cheesecloth bag and add to casserole. Bring to a simmer over high heat. Remove from heat, cover tightly, and transfer to oven.

**3.** Add enough of the remaining 2 cups of stock to bottom of a steamer to reach depth of 1 inch. Bring to

a boil over high heat. Place shallots in steamer top and set over, not in, simmering stock. Cover and steam 3 minutes. Remove to a dish and add carrots to steamer. Cover and steam 1 minute. Remove to dish with shallots. Add celery to steamer; cover and steam 30 seconds. Add to shallots and carrots.

**4.** Uncover veal after 1¾ hours and add steamed vegetables to casserole. Cover and bake 15 minutes. Add mushrooms, cover, and bake until meat is tender, about 15 more minutes.

**5.** Drain contents of casserole in a colander or sieve set over a large, clean saucepan. Discard cheesecloth bag, onions, and garlic cloves. In the large saucepan over high heat, reduce liquid to 1½ cups. Add cream and simmer 1 minute, then add contents of colander. Season to taste with salt and pepper. Reheat. Serve blanquette on warm plates, garnishing with parsley–lemon mixture.

*Serves 6.*

**Make-Ahead Tip**  Stew may be prepared through step 4 one day ahead; cover and refrigerate.

*White beans and red wine are the traditional French partners for thick slices of rosy lamb.*

## CHOUX DE BRUXELLES ET MARRONS AUX LARDONS
### Brussels sprouts braised with bacon and chestnuts

Fresh chestnuts, which turn up in many markets in late fall, are a seasonal treat worth seeking out. Packaged chestnuts will work in this recipe, however. Just be sure to buy the bottled variety that is vacuum-packed without liquid; chestnuts in water or syrup are unsuitable.

  *½ pound fresh chestnuts or 2 cups whole, peeled, vacuum-packed chestnuts*
  *3 cups Fond de Volaille (see page 32)*
  *3 cups brussels sprouts, trimmed*
  *4 slices lean, thick-cut bacon, cut into 2-inch lengths*
  *Unsalted butter, as needed*
  *Kosher salt and freshly ground pepper*
  *Minced parsley, for garnish*

**1.** If using fresh chestnuts, make an *x* in the flat side of each nut with a small, sharp knife. Blanch chestnuts 1 minute in boiling water, then drain. Immediately peel away tough brown shell and papery brown skin underneath to reveal golden nut. Chestnuts are easier to peel when hot. If they cool too quickly, dip them in boiling water for a few seconds to make peeling easier.

**2.** Place chestnuts in a medium saucepan and add stock. Bring to a boil over high heat; then reduce heat, cover, and simmer 45 minutes. Drain, reserving stock. (Chestnuts may be cooked 3 days ahead and refrigerated with ½ cup cooking liquid.)

**3.** Bring a large pot of salted water to a boil over high heat. Add brussels sprouts and boil 3 minutes. Drain sprouts and transfer to a bowl of ice water to stop the cooking. When completely cold, drain and pat dry.

**4.** In a skillet over moderately low heat, render bacon until crisp. With a slotted spoon, transfer bacon to paper towels to drain. Chop enough bacon to yield 2 tablespoons and set aside for garnish.

**5.** Pour off all but 2 tablespoons of fat in skillet. If necessary, add butter to make 2 tablespoons fat. Add drained brussels sprouts and sauté over moderate heat for 2 minutes. Add chestnuts, rendered bacon, and 1½ cups reserved stock. Cover and bring to a simmer. Reduce heat and simmer until most of the liquid is absorbed and brussels sprouts are very tender (about 20 minutes). Season to taste with salt and pepper. Transfer to a warm serving bowl and garnish with reserved bacon and minced parsley.

*Serves 6.*

# DESSERTS

The region's best desserts are rustic—a buckwheat crêpe drizzled with crème fraîche and honey, a bowl of warm applesauce, or a slice of pound cake with seasonal berries.

## MARMELADE DE POMMES AU CALVADOS
### Warm applesauce with Calvados

For a sophisticated end to an autumn dinner, drizzle the famous apple brandy of Normandy, Calvados, over fragrant applesauce.

  *9 cups peeled, cored, and coarsely chopped apples*
  *¾ cup water*
  *¾ cup apple juice*
  *1 tablespoon grated lemon zest*
  *3 cinnamon sticks (each 2 in. long)*
  *¼ teaspoon allspice*
  *¼ teaspoon nutmeg*
  *5 tablespoons Calvados or apple brandy*
  *Honey, to taste*

**1.** In a large saucepan combine apples, the water, apple juice, lemon zest, cinnamon sticks, allspice, nutmeg, and 1 tablespoon of the Calvados. Bring to a simmer over moderate heat, reduce heat, and cook, covered, until apples are easily pierced with a knife (10 to 15 minutes). Remove cinnamon sticks.

**2.** Transfer mixture to a food processor, add honey to taste, and pulse until blended but still chunky. Or put mixture through a food mill fitted with the coarse blade, then stir in honey to taste.

**3.** Just before serving, return mixture to a clean saucepan. Bring just to a simmer over moderately low heat, stirring. Divide applesauce evenly among 4 goblets or bowls, and drizzle each serving with 1 tablespoon of the remaining Calvados.

*Serves 4.*

**Make-Ahead Tip**   Applesauce may be made through step 2 up to 2 days ahead; cover and refrigerate.

## GÂTEAU AU BEURRE
### Pound cake with berries and crème fraîche

This brown-sugar pound cake tastes better the second day; cover with plastic wrap when cool and let it stand overnight. Raspberry eau-de-vie (*framboise*) is available in most fine wine shops. Note that the Crème Fraîche must be made at least a day ahead.

  *Butter for greasing pan, plus ½ cup unsalted butter, slightly softened*
  *Granulated sugar, for dusting pan and for sweetening berries, if needed*
  *1 cup dark brown sugar*
  *4 large eggs*
  *Pinch salt*
  *1 teaspoon vanilla extract*
  *1 teaspoon grated lemon zest*
  *½ teaspoon allspice*
  *2 cups flour*
  *3 tablespoons sour cream or Crème Fraîche*
  *½ cup toasted almonds, ground medium-fine*
  *3 cups mixed summer berries (strawberries, raspberries, blackberries, blueberries)*
  *¼ cup raspberry eau-de-vie or Cognac*

#### Crème Fraîche

  *1 cup whipping cream, not ultra-pasteurized*
  *1 tablespoon buttermilk*

**1.** Preheat oven to 350° F. Lightly butter a 9-inch (6-cup capacity) loaf pan. Sprinkle bottom and sides with granulated sugar, shaking out excess.

**2.** With an electric mixer cream butter until smooth. Add brown sugar gradually and beat until light. Add eggs one at a time, beating well after each addition. Beat in salt, vanilla, lemon zest, and allspice. On lowest speed add 1 cup of the flour and beat just until blended. Add sour cream and beat to blend. Add remaining flour and almonds, beating just to blend. Batter will be very thick and sticky.

**3.** Pour batter into prepared pan and smooth the top. Bake until top is firm and a cake tester inserted in the center comes out dry (about 1¼ hours). Cool in pan 2 minutes, then remove from pan and finish cooling right side up on a rack.

**4.** In a medium bowl combine berries and eau-de-vie. Add sugar if berries are not sufficiently sweet. Let macerate at room temperature 15 minutes. Serve pound cake in thin slices with berries on the side or on top. Pass a pitcher of cold Crème Fraîche.

*Makes one 9-inch loaf cake.*

**Crème Fraîche**   In a clean glass jar, combine cream and buttermilk. Cover jar and shake 30 seconds to blend. Store at room temperature until thickened (24 to 36 hours), then refrigerate. Crème Fraîche will keep 5 to 7 days in the refrigerator.

*Makes 1 cup.*

*Sweet Normandy butter makes delectable pound cakes, like this almond and brown-sugar cake topped with mixed summer berries.*

## GALETTES BRETONNES
### *Brittany buckwheat crêpes*

Buckwheat flour in the batter and an extralarge circumference are the distinguishing characteristics of the Brittany crêpe. If you lack a 12-inch pan, however, make smaller crêpes; the crêpes won't be authentic but they'll taste just as good. To find buckwheat flour and barley malt powder or syrup, check a natural-food store.

- ½ cup buckwheat flour
- 1 cup all-purpose flour
- ½ teaspoon barley malt powder or syrup
- ½ teaspoon kosher salt
- 2 tablespoons sugar, if making dessert crêpes
- 4 large eggs
- 1 cup water
- 1 cup apple cider
- 1 cup milk
- ⅓ cup unsalted butter, melted, plus additional melted unsalted butter, for brushing pans

**1.** In a blender or food processor, combine buckwheat flour, all-purpose flour, barley malt powder (if using), and salt. If making dessert crêpes, add sugar. Pulse to blend. Add eggs, the water, barley malt syrup (if using instead of barley malt powder), cider, milk, and the ⅓ cup melted butter. Blend until smooth. Let mixture stand in blender or processor, covered, for 1 hour. Blend briefly before using.

**2.** Over moderately high heat, heat a 12-inch crêpe pan until almost smoking. Brush surface lightly with butter and add ⅓ cup batter. Quickly swirl pan to spread batter over entire bottom surface and halfway up sides of pan. Cook until crêpe is browned around the edges and set in the middle (about 1 minute and 15 seconds). If using a 5-inch crêpe pan, figure 2 tablespoons batter per crêpe; cooking time will be about the same. Invert pan to remove crêpe.

**3.** Fold crêpe in quarters and transfer to a warm serving plate.

*Makes fifteen 12-inch crêpes.*

### Applesauce-Filled Crêpes
Make Galettes Bretonnes through step 2. Spread uncooked surface of crêpe with a few tablespoons of Marmelade de Pommes au Calvados (see page 22), then fold in quarters and drizzle with Crème Fraîche (see page 22).

### Cheese and Bacon Crêpes
Make Galettes Bretonnes through step 2, but do not remove crêpe from pan. Top uncooked side with grated Gruyère cheese and crumbled bacon; fold in half and remove from pan.

### Ham and Cheese Crêpes
Make Galettes Bretonnes through step 2, but do not remove crêpe from pan. Top uncooked side of crêpe with paper-thin slices of Gruyère cheese and ham, then fold in half and remove from pan.

### Ice Cream Crêpes
Make Galettes Bretonnes through step 2. Place crêpe cooked side down on a large plate. Spoon small scoops of softened vanilla ice cream down the center of the crêpe. Fold in the sides and drizzle with hot chocolate sauce.

### Jam-Filled Crêpes
Make Galettes Bretonnes through step 2. Spread uncooked surface of crêpe with strawberry jam, apple butter, or other fruit preserve. Fold in quarters and drizzle with Crème Fraîche (see page 22).

### Lemon-Honey Butter Crêpes
Combine ½ cup soft unsalted butter, 1 teaspoon grated lemon zest, 2 tablespoons lemon juice, and 3 tablespoons best-quality aromatic honey in a food processor or blender and blend until smooth. Butter will be soft. Transfer to a serving crock and chill. Remove from refrigerator 30 minutes before using. Make Galettes Bretonnes. Put a swipe of Lemon-Honey Butter on top and drizzle with Crème Fraîche (see page 22).

### Maple Syrup Crêpes
Make Galettes Bretonnes. Top with melted butter and warm maple syrup.

### Mushroom Crêpes
Make Galettes Bretonnes through step 2, but do not remove crêpe from pan. Top uncooked side of crêpe with sliced sautéed mushrooms; fold in half, remove from pan, and drizzle with Crème Fraîche (see page 22).

### Orange-Honey Butter Crêpes
Beat softened unsalted butter with honey and grated orange zest to taste. Make Galettes Bretonnes. Top with orange-honey butter.

### Sweet Cheese–Filled Crêpes
Make Galettes Bretonnes through step 2. Spread uncooked surface with Fromage Blanc (see page 56), then fold in quarters and drizzle with honey or hot chocolate sauce.

### Toasted Almond Crêpes
Make Galettes Bretonnes. Top with sliced almonds browned in butter.

*Note* Crêpe batter may be made up to one day ahead and refrigerated. Reblend or whisk briefly just before using. Once made, crêpes should be served on warm plates and eaten as soon as possible; they cannot be successfully held. Thus, a meal of crêpes is best suited to small, informal kitchen dinners where guests or family can take turns at the stove. For an all-crêpe dinner, figure one savory and one sweet crêpe per person. For dessert, one crêpe is sufficient.

## SUMMER SEAFOOD DINNER

*Palourdes Grillées, Sauce Mignonette*

*Haricots Verts au Beurre*

*Homard Grillé aux Trois Sauces*

*Coeur à la Crème*

*California Chardonnay*

*Like a New England shore dinner, this meal of Breton seafood specialties would taste its romantic best oceanside, with the grilling done on site and picnic blankets spread right on the beach. If you lack a beach, set your dinner outside on a patio or at a backyard picnic table. Guests can gather around the barbecue for clams hot off the grill, then be seated for the main event—succulent grilled lobster with three dipping sauces. Dessert is a soft fresh cheese with a cloak of mixed summer berries. Menu serves four.*

## PALOURDES GRILLÉES, SAUCE MIGNONETTE
### Warm grilled clams with lemon-pepper vinegar

Although the clams are great stand-up cocktail fare, you can also pile them in a warm bowl and serve them as a first course at the table. Be sure to build a large enough fire to cook both clams and lobsters. The tangy Lemon-Pepper Vinegar is also delicious drizzled on raw clams or oysters on the half shell. Note that clams need to refrigerate for at least four hours.

> 24  small clams
> 2  tablespoons cornmeal
> ¼  cup unsalted butter, melted

#### Lemon-Pepper Vinegar

> 2  teaspoons grated lemon zest
> 2  teaspoons coarsely cracked black peppercorns
> 1  cup apple cider vinegar

**1.** Place clams in a stainless steel, glass, or enamel bowl. Add cornmeal and water to cover. Refrigerate at least 4 hours or up to 12 hours to allow clams to disgorge any sand.

**2.** Prepare a medium-hot charcoal fire. When coals are gray, drain clams and place directly on grate over coals, as close to coals as possible. As clams open (3 to 5 minutes), remove to a warm serving bowl and brush clam meat with melted butter. Discard any clams that do not open after 5 minutes. Serve immediately with Lemon-Pepper Vinegar.

*Serves 4 as an appetizer, 3 as a first course.*

**Lemon-Pepper Vinegar**   Whisk lemon zest, peppercorns, and vinegar together in a small bowl.

*Makes 1 cup.*

## HARICOTS VERTS AU BEURRE
### Buttered green beans

For best flavor, check a produce market or farmers' market for the slender French green beans known as *haricots verts*. If unavailable, choose the smallest, sweetest green beans you can find. For a beach party, prepare beans through step 1 and chill. Toss with ¼ cup Summer Garden Vinaigrette (see page 26) just before serving.

> ¾  pound tender young green beans, strings removed
> 2  tablespoons unsalted butter, melted
>    Kosher salt and freshly ground pepper

**1.** In the bottom of a steamer, bring a small amount of salted water to a boil over high heat. Put beans in steamer top or steamer insert and set over, not in, boiling water. Cover and steam until tender-crisp (5 to 9 minutes); taste for doneness.

**2.** Place butter in a warm serving bowl. When beans are done, pat dry, then transfer to serving bowl, season to taste with salt and pepper and toss to coat with butter. Serve beans immediately.

*Serves 4.*

## HOMARD GRILLÉ AUX TROIS SAUCES
### Grilled lobster with three sauces

A sour cream sauce, an herb butter, or a chunky vinaigrette? All three are enticing options for saucing juicy grilled lobsters and are delicious with steamed green beans as well. Why not offer the trio and invite guests to try them all?

- 2 live lobsters (2 lb each)
- ¼ cup (approximately) melted unsalted butter

### Basil Cream Sauce

- 1 cup sour cream or Crème Fraîche (see page 22)
- ¼ cup minced fresh basil
- 2 teaspoons lemon juice
  Kosher salt and freshly ground pepper

### Shallot Tarragon Butter

- 1 cup plus 1 tablespoon unsalted butter, softened
- 1 shallot, minced
- 2 tablespoons dry white wine
- 2 heaping tablespoons minced fresh tarragon
- ½ teaspoon kosher salt
- ½ teaspoon freshly cracked pepper

### Summer Garden Vinaigrette

- 2 tablespoons apple cider vinegar
- 1 tablespoon lemon juice
- 1 teaspoon Dijon mustard
- 2 tablespoons minced parsley
- ¾ cup olive oil
- ½ cup diced fresh tomato
- 2 teaspoons minced chives
  Kosher salt and freshly ground pepper

**1.** Bring a large pot of salted water to a boil over high heat. Plunge lobsters into boiling water for 2 minutes. Drain. When lobsters are cool enough to handle, split them in half lengthwise with a heavy knife. Remove and discard any viscera, including the intestinal vein in the tail.

**2.** Brush lobsters with melted butter and place them on grill, shell side up. Grill over a medium-hot fire for 8 to 10 minutes, then turn, brush with butter, and continue grilling until tails are firm and white (about 5 minutes more). Remove to a warm serving platter. Twist off claws and return the claws to grill for an additional 3 to 4 minutes. Serve on platter accompanied by three sauces.

*Serves 4.*

**Basil Cream Sauce**   In a small bowl, whisk together sour cream, basil, and lemon juice. Season to taste with salt and pepper. Cover and refrigerate at least 1 hour or up to 1 day. Remove from refrigerator 30 minutes before serving.

*Makes about 1¼ cups.*

**Shallot Tarragon Butter**

**1.** In a small skillet over moderately low heat, melt the 1 tablespoon butter. Add shallot and sauté until softened (about 5 minutes). Add wine and reduce until most of the wine has evaporated. *To make in a food processor:* Place contents of skillet in processor with the remaining 1 cup butter and tarragon. Process until smooth. *To make by hand:* Combine the remaining 1 cup butter, tarragon, and contents of skillet in a bowl; stir with a wooden spoon until smooth.

**2.** Season to taste with salt and pepper. Pack seasoned butter into serving ramekin(s) and chill at least 1 hour or up to 1 day. Bring to room temperature before serving.

*Makes about 1 cup.*

**Summer Garden Vinaigrette**
Whisk together vinegar, lemon juice, mustard, and parsley in a medium bowl. Add oil in a slow, steady stream, whisking constantly; mixture should be thick and creamy. Stir in tomatoes and chives. Season to taste with salt and pepper.

*Makes about 1¼ cups.*

## COEUR À LA CRÈME
### Heart-shaped fresh cheese with mixed summer berries

Many kitchenware stores carry the perforated, heart-shaped ceramic molds designed expressly for this dessert. The holes allow excess moisture to drain off; lining the molds with cheesecloth makes unmolding easy. Note that the mixture needs to chill at least four hours.

- 1 cup (8 oz) cream cheese
- ½ cup Crème Fraîche (see page 22)
- ¼ cup whipping cream
- ¼ cup superfine sugar, plus superfine sugar for sweetening berries
  Pinch salt
- ½ teaspoon vanilla extract
- 1 cup sliced strawberries
- 1 cup each raspberries and blackberries
- 2 tablespoons raspberry eau-de-vie
  Fresh mint sprigs, for garnish

**1.** In a medium electric mixer bowl, combine cream cheese, Crème Fraîche, whipping cream, the ¼ cup superfine sugar, salt, and vanilla. Beat until smooth.

**2.** Line a 7-inch *coeur à la crème* mold or four 3-inch molds with a double thickness of dampened cheesecloth. Spoon cheese mixture into mold, smoothing the top. Set mold on a saucer to catch any moisture that drains out, and chill at least 4 hours or up to 2 days.

**3.** Combine strawberries, raspberries, and blackberries in a stainless steel, glass, or enamel bowl. Add eau-de-vie and sweeten to taste with superfine sugar; stir to blend. Cover and refrigerate for up to 3 hours. To serve, unmold cheese onto serving platter or individual plates and spoon berries over and around it. Garnish with fresh mint.

*Serves 4.*

Lobster with three dipping
sauces and grilled clams provide
delicious summer dining,
Normandy-style.

*The woods and farms near Paris yield magnificent produce: mushrooms, potatoes, carrots, asparagus, and peas of unsurpassed quality.*

# Champagne, Orléanais & Ile-de-France

ÎLE-DE-FRANCE
Reims
Seine R.
Paris
Marne R.
CHAMPAGNE
Pithiviers
Orléans
ORLÉANAIS
Dijon
Tours

Paris is the gastronomic heart of France; delicacies from around the country flow into the city's markets and restaurants. In Paris, eating and talking about food are favorite pastimes. Among the dishes that have made Parisian bistros famous are an aromatic onion soup (see Soupe à l'Oignon, page 35) and the bittersweet chocolate Pots de Crème (see page 38). From the nearby Champagne region comes the world's finest sparkling wine; a festive Champagne Reception (see page 39) makes the most of it.

# CHAMPAGNE, ORLÉANAIS, & ÎLE-DE-FRANCE

If these three provinces of north-central France cannot claim a distinctive cooking style, they can at least boast of their contribution to French cooking in general. The bountiful gardens of the Île-de-France and the Orléanais and the vineyards of Champagne provide cooks throughout France with fine raw materials.

## The Île-de-France

The province of Île-de-France (Island of France) owes its name to the several rivers that encircle the region, nearly cutting it off from the rest of the country. Excluding the urban sprawl of Paris, it is extremely fertile country, yielding famous asparagus, carrots, peas, potatoes, watercress, strawberries, and cherries.

Paris is the cultural and culinary heart of the region, although the city is too much of a melting pot to have its own culinary style. Instead, historians credit Paris with being the birthplace of the restaurant, traceable to a clever eighteenth-century soup vendor named Boulanger.

In Boulanger's day, the arcane rules of the medieval guilds made it illegal for a food vendor to sell less than a whole cut of meat to a customer. It wasn't illegal to sell bouillon, however, so Boulanger set up shop, inviting his clients to enjoy his tasty *restaurants* (restoratives). Soon, the daring Boulanger bent the rules and served a prepared dish of sheep's feet in sauce. The guild's power to monopolize the food trade was broken, and Boulanger's precedent-setting business was eventually imitated throughout the country.

Today, the bistros, brasseries, and grand restaurants of Paris are the guardians of classic French cooking. The city's luxury establishments preserve the haute cuisine, the "high" or refined cooking based on costly ingredients and elaborate techniques.

The *cuisine bourgeoise*—informal, home-style cooking—is the province of bistros and brasseries.

Paris is indisputably a restaurant mecca, attracting lovers of fine dining from around the world. The haute cuisine restaurants are incomparable, but the average Parisian is more likely to grab a quick *croque-monsieur* (grilled ham and cheese sandwich) from a sidewalk vendor; stop for a late-night bowl of onion soup at a neighborhood cafe; order the prix fixe lunch at a working-class bistro—perhaps an assortment of marinated vegetables, a roast chicken, and a strawberry tart; or enjoy a leisurely dinner of sweetbreads and spring peas at a chic brasserie.

## Champagne

The region's rocky, infertile soil is inhospitable to vegetables but perfect for grapes. Because the vineyards are so far north, the grapes develop less sugar than they would in a warmer climate. The juice they yield is too thin and tart for a still (non-sparkling) wine but just right for a refreshing Champagne.

Apart from that major contribution to gastronomy, the region has few culinary trademarks. Sometimes local cooks use their famous sparkling wine in a sausage stuffing (see page 37) or sauce for fish, but the wine is too expensive and delicate to use often in cooking (see Wine in the French Kitchen, page 10).

## The Orléanais

The Orléanais is a fertile region to the southwest of Paris. Its woods are full of wild mushrooms and game—deer, rabbit, quail, duck, and partridge—and its farms produce some of the finest asparagus in France. The town of Orléans is a center for wine vinegar production.

## SALADS, SOUPS, AND FIRST COURSES

A creamy celery root salad, a steaming onion soup, and a colorful array of dressed vegetables are among the favored ways to begin a Parisian restaurant lunch.

---

### SOUFFLÉ AU FROMAGE DE CHÈVRE
### *Goat cheese soufflé with watercress salad*

A Sauvignon Blanc would be a good partner for this tangy soufflé.

*1 tablespoon unsalted butter, for buttering soufflé cups*
*2 tablespoons finely ground walnuts*
*4 large eggs, separated*
*3 ounces mild goat cheese, at room temperature*
*2 tablespoons minced chives Kosher salt and freshly ground pepper*
*2 bunches watercress*
*2 tablespoons lemon juice*
*6 tablespoons walnut oil*
*½ cup toasted walnut halves*

**1.** Preheat oven to 400° F. Butter six ½-cup soufflé cups and dust bottom and sides with ground nuts.

**2.** In a large bowl beat egg yolks, 2 ounces of the cheese, chives, salt, and pepper with a wire whisk until blended; cheese need not be totally smooth. Beat egg whites with a pinch of salt until stiff but not dry. Gently fold beaten whites into cheese mixture. Spoon into prepared soufflé cups. Bury a small chunk of the remaining goat cheese in the center of each soufflé. Bake until puffed and browned (about 12 minutes).

**3.** Meanwhile, wash and dry watercress and remove tough stems. In a small bowl whisk together lemon juice and walnut oil. Season to taste with salt and pepper.

**4.** When soufflés are ready, quickly toss watercress with walnuts and dressing. Put soufflé cups in the center of 6 large salad plates and surround each with watercress salad.

*Serves 6.*

## CHAMPIGNONS ET FENOUIL À LA GRECQUE
### *Marinated mushrooms and fennel*

Vegetables prepared à la grecque (Greek-style) are simmered in oil, lemon juice, and herbs, then cooled in their cooking liquid. They are a common first course in Parisian bistros, generally accompanied by a slice of ham or dried sausage. Note that this dish needs to refrigerate for at least four hours.

   1 *fennel bulb (½ lb)*
  ½ *pound mushrooms*
  ¼ *cup plus 1 tablespoon olive oil*
   1 *large leek (white part only), cleaned and coarsely chopped*
   1 *tablespoon grated lemon zest*
   1 *cup dry white wine*
   1 *cup water*
   1 *teaspoon freshly ground pepper*
   1 *bay leaf*
   2 *teaspoons fennel seed*
    *Lemon juice*
    *Kosher salt*

**1.** Cut fennel in half lengthwise. Cut away core. Place each half, cut side down, on a cutting board and slice ¼ inch thick. Clean and quarter mushrooms.

**2.** In a 2-quart saucepan over moderate heat, heat the ¼ cup olive oil. Add leeks and sauté for 2 minutes. Add lemon zest, wine, the water, pepper, bay leaf, and fennel seed. Bring to a simmer and cook 5 minutes. Add fennel and simmer 5 minutes longer. Fennel will still be crisp. Stir in mushrooms and simmer until fennel and mushrooms are tender (about 7 minutes). Remove from heat and cool 5 minutes.

**3.** Add the remaining 1 tablespoon olive oil and lemon juice to taste. Cool thoroughly, then add salt to taste. Cover and refrigerate for at least 4 hours or up to 4 days. Taste and adjust seasoning before serving. Serve at room temperature.

*Serves 6.*

## *Basics*

## VINAIGRETTE

Vinaigrette is the traditional French salad dressing. Blends of oil (usually olive, safflower, peanut, or walnut) and wine vinegar, with minced herbs added to taste, vinaigrettes dress everything from simple lettuce salads to elaborate combinations of meats and vegetables. Some cooks add a touch of cream to their vinaigrette, but creamy dressings in the American style are rare in France.

In French homes, a green salad appears on the dinner table almost every evening, served after the main course and before the cheese. Typically, the salad is nothing more than a bowl of crisp seasonal greens—endive, chicory, and the soft hearts of butter lettuce are common—tossed with a simple vinaigrette. Some cooks occasionally add a handful of home-made croutons or a chopped egg.

Leftover vinaigrette may be stored at room temperature for up to a day or refrigerated in an airtight jar for up to three days. Whisk, taste, and adjust seasoning before using.

## BASIC VINAIGRETTE

  ¼ *cup red wine vinegar*
    *Kosher salt and freshly ground pepper, to taste*
  ¾ *cup olive oil*

In a small bowl, combine vinegar, salt, and pepper. Whisk in oil and let stand 5 minutes. Whisk again, then taste and adjust seasoning.

*Makes 1 cup.*

**Garlic Vinaigrette** Cover ½ tablespoon minced garlic with ¾ cup olive oil and let stand overnight. Substitute the resulting flavored olive oil for regular olive oil.

**Lemon-Chive Vinaigrette** Substitute ¼ cup freshly squeezed lemon juice for wine vinegar. Add zest of ½ lemon and 2 tablespoons minced chives.

**Mustard Vinaigrette** Add 2 teaspoons prepared Dijon-style mustard to wine vinegar before adding oil.

**Tarragon Vinaigrette** Add 1 tablespoon minced fresh tarragon and substitute white wine vinegar for red wine vinegar.

## STOCKS: THE FOUNDATION OF FRENCH CUISINE

The ability to make a rich, clear stock is fundamental to good French cooking. Even the French word for stock—*fond*—literally means *base* or *foundation*.

The traditional family of French stocks includes chicken, veal, vegetable, and fish stocks. All are made by simmering water with flavoring elements such as raw bones, vegetables, herbs, and spices.

In the French home kitchen, stocks are used for making good soups and stews and for braising vegetables. A chicken or veal stock is a more flavorful cooking medium than water alone, although some rustic soups are traditionally made with water (see Soupe à l'Oignon, page 35). With stock on hand, soup is easy. Broccoli, cauliflower, peas, carrots, or a mixture of fresh vegetables can be simmered in stock until tender, then puréed, sieved, and reheated with cream to make a quick and tasty soup.

In restaurant kitchens, stocks are the foundation for countless sauces. A classic *sauce velouté*, for example, is made by cooking butter and flour together until smooth, then whisking in stock and cooking until the sauce is thickened.

The more modern way with stock-based sauces is to omit the butter and flour and to thicken the stock by reduction—by simmering until it is reduced in volume and concentrated in flavor. At the last minute, cream is added or solid butter is swirled in.

The principles of stock making are the same for all types of stock. For best results, pay attention to the following guidelines.

**1.** Bring cold water and flavoring ingredients to a simmer slowly to ensure maximum flavor extraction.

**2.** Never allow stock to boil. It should merely flutter on the surface. Adjust heat as necessary to keep liquid at this slow simmer.

**3.** To keep stock clear and clean in flavor, skim as necessary to remove any scum (coagulated protein) that rises to the surface.

**4.** Stocks should be cooled to room temperature quickly, preferably by setting stock container in a bowl of ice water and stirring until cool. Refrigerating a large quantity of hot stock can put a strain on a home refrigerator; be sure to cool completely before refrigerating. Stock should not be covered until cool.

---

### FOND DE VOLAILLE
*Chicken stock*

Whenever you cut up a whole chicken for sautéing or frying, freeze any bony parts—such as the wing tips, backs, and necks—that you don't plan to use. When you're ready to make stock, you can supplement the collection of bones with a few chicken wings.

> 5 pounds chicken parts (backs, necks, wing tips, wings)
> 2 carrots, coarsely chopped
> 2 cloves garlic, peeled and lightly crushed
> 1 large stalk celery
> 2 large leeks, well washed and chopped
> 1 large onion, halved
> 2 whole cloves

#### Bouquet Garni

> 4 sprigs parsley
> 1 bay leaf
> 1 teaspoon dried thyme or 4 sprigs thyme
> 10 black peppercorns, lightly crushed

Put chicken parts in a large pot and add 10 cups cold water. Bring slowly to a simmer over moderate heat, skimming as necessary with a slotted spoon to remove any scum that rises to the surface. When mixture begins to simmer, add carrots, crushed garlic, celery, leeks, and Bouquet Garni. Pierce each onion half with a clove and add to pot. Return to a simmer, then reduce heat to maintain a simmer. Cook 3 hours, uncovered. Cool to room temperature, then strain and refrigerate. When ready to use, lift off any congealed fat on the surface. Stock may be refrigerated for up to 1 week or frozen for up to 3 months.

*Makes about 8 cups.*

**Bouquet Garni**  Combine all ingredients in a cheesecloth bag and tie securely.

---

### FOND DE LEGUMES
*Vegetable stock*

When you want a delicate soup base, or when you're preparing a meatless meal, a vegetable stock comes in handy. For maximum flavor, do not peel vegetables.

> 3 onions, halved
> 6 whole cloves
> 1 bulb garlic, broken up into separate unpeeled cloves
> 3 leeks, well washed and coarsely chopped
> 1 parsnip, coarsely chopped
> 1 turnip, coarsely chopped
> 2 large carrots, coarsely chopped
> 1 pound tomatoes, quartered
> ½ pound mushrooms, thickly sliced
> 1 bunch green onions, coarsely chopped
> 2 tablespoons olive oil

Pierce each onion half with a clove. Combine all ingredients in a 1-gallon pot and stir to coat vegetables with oil. Sauté over moderate heat for 10 minutes. Add 10 cups cold water, bring slowly to a simmer, then reduce heat to maintain a simmer and cook 4 hours. Cool to room temperature, then strain and refrigerate or freeze. Stock may be refrigerated for up to 1 week or frozen for up to 3 months.

*Makes about 8 cups.*

## FOND DE VEAU
### Veal stock

Roasting the bones and vegetables thoroughly adds color and rich caramelized flavor to veal stock. Note that stock has to simmer 12 hours.

    2 pounds veal shanks
    2 pounds veal bones
    1 onion, halved
    2 whole cloves
    ½ pound carrots, coarsely
       chopped
    2 leeks, well washed and
       coarsely chopped
       Bouquet Garni (see page 32)

**1.** Preheat oven to 450° F. Place veal shanks and bones in a large roasting pan and bake 45 minutes. Pierce each onion half with a clove. Add onion, carrots, and leeks to pan, and bake an additional 30 minutes. Transfer bones and vegetables to a large stockpot.

**2.** Add 4 cups water to roasting pan and bring to a boil on top of the stove, scraping bottom of pan with a wooden spoon to release any deposits.

Pour into stockpot. Add 6 cups cold water and Bouquet Garni. Bring slowly to a simmer, skimming as necessary with a slotted spoon to remove any scum that rises to the surface. Reduce heat to maintain a simmer and cook 12 hours.

**3.** Cool stock to room temperature, then strain and refrigerate. When ready to use, lift off any congealed fat from the surface. Stock may be refrigerated for up to 1 week or frozen for up to 3 months.

*Makes about 8 cups.*

## FUMET DE POISSON
### Fish stock

For the most delicate flavor, use only bones from lean white fish.

    5 pounds fish bones and heads
    ¼ cup unsalted butter
    2 tablespoons olive oil
    3 cups coarsely chopped onion
    ⅓ cup minced shallot
    1 carrot, coarsely chopped
    1 cup dry white wine
       Bouquet Garni (see page 32)

**1.** Place fish bones in a 1-gallon stockpot. Add cold water to cover and soak for 1 hour to remove any blood.

**2.** Drain and return bones to dry pot. Add butter and olive oil and cook over moderate heat for 10 minutes, stirring to melt butter and coat bones. Add onion, shallot, and carrot; reduce heat to moderately low and sauté, stirring occasionally, for 15 minutes.

**3.** Add wine and cook until wine is almost completely evaporated. Add 8 cups cold water and Bouquet Garni. Bring slowly to a simmer, skimming as necessary with a slotted spoon to remove any scum that rises to the surface. Reduce heat to maintain a simmer and cook 30 minutes. Cool to room temperature, then strain and refrigerate. Stock may be refrigerated for up to 5 days or frozen for up to 3 months.

*Makes about 8 cups.*

*Raw shredded celery root in a creamy mustard dressing is one of the best-loved salads in France.*

## CÉLERI RÉMOULADE À LA MENTHE FRAÎCHE
### *Minted celery root salad*

You can find this creamy salad in almost every Parisian charcuterie (see page 82), where it is a suggested companion to sliced cold ham. The mustard dressing is classic, but the mint is a modern touch.

　　1　celery root (about 1 lb)
　　3　tablespoons lemon juice
　　½　cup minced red onion
　　¼　cup minced green onion
　　¼　cup Dijon-style mustard
　　½　cup olive oil
　　2　tablespoons whipping cream
　　¼　cup minced fresh mint
　　　Kosher salt and freshly
　　　ground pepper

**1.** Peel celery root; julienne with a mandoline (see page 9) or by hand, or grate coarsely. Immediately transfer to a stainless steel, glass, or enamel bowl; add lemon juice and toss. Add onions and toss again.

**2.** Place mustard in a small bowl. Whisk in olive oil in a slow, steady stream to make a thick, creamy mixture. Whisk in cream and mint. Add dressing to vegetables and toss to blend. Season to taste with salt and pepper. Chill well before serving.

*Serves 6.*

**Make-Ahead Tip** Salad may be made up to 2 days ahead. Before serving, taste and adjust seasoning.

## CRUDITÉS EN SALADE
### Marinated vegetable salad

*Crudités* means *raw vegetables* (*cru* means *raw*). Nevertheless, an order of crudités in a Paris restaurant will often include cooked beets or briefly blanched green beans. The vegetables are never served with a dip; instead, they are lightly dressed before serving and are presented in distinct mounds on a salad plate or in separate bowls. Vary the dressing to suit your taste.

- 1 large fennel bulb
- 2 small celery hearts
- 1 red or yellow bell pepper
- 1 pound green beans
- 1 bunch finger-sized baby carrots, scrubbed and trimmed
- 2 cups Lemon-Chive Vinaigrette (see page 31)
- 1 pound beets, cooked, peeled, cooled, and sliced

**1.** Halve the fennel bulb; cut away core. Cut fennel in thin slices lengthwise. Trim base of celery hearts. Cut celery ribs crosswise ¼ inch thick. Halve pepper and remove seeds and ribs; slice into thin strips.

**2.** Bring a large pot of salted water to a boil over high heat. Add green beans and cook until tender-crisp (3 to 5 minutes). Drain and run under cold water to stop cooking. Drain again and pat thoroughly dry.

**3.** Put carrots in a medium bowl and toss with ¼ cup of the Lemon-Chive Vinaigrette. Arrange carrots on a serving platter. Add fennel to bowl along with ⅓ cup vinaigrette. Toss to coat, then arrange fennel on serving platter alongside carrots. Add celery to bowl along with ¼ cup vinaigrette; toss to coat, then transfer celery to serving platter. Add pepper strips to bowl and moisten with 2 tablespoons vinaigrette. Toss to coat, then transfer to serving platter. Add beans to bowl and dress with ¼ cup vinaigrette; transfer to serving platter. Add beets to bowl and dress with ⅓ cup vinaigrette; transfer to serving platter. Reserve remaining vinaigrette for another use.

*Serves 6.*

**Make-Ahead Tip** The vegetables may be dressed up to 2 hours ahead and refrigerated in separate containers. To save space store vegetables in heavy-duty plastic bags instead of in bowls.

## SOUPE À L'OIGNON
### Light onion soup

During the heyday of Les Halles, the now-defunct wholesale produce market in the heart of Paris, onion soup was the restorative that kept buyers and sellers going. Neighboring restaurants made a specialty of it, serving it in the early morning to the rugged vendors whose workday ended at dawn. This version is lighter but no less flavorful.

- 3 tablespoons unsalted butter
- 2 cups coarsely chopped red onion
- 2 cups coarsely chopped white or yellow onion
- 2 cups coarsely chopped green onion
- 3½ cups water
- ½ cup dry white wine
  Kosher salt and freshly ground pepper
- 6 thick slices dense, day-old French bread
- ⅓ cup (approximately) olive oil
- 1½ cups grated Gruyère cheese, for garnish

**1.** In a 4-quart saucepan melt butter over low heat. Add onions, cover, and cook, stirring occasionally, for 45 minutes. Uncover and add the water and wine. Raise heat to moderately high and bring mixture to a simmer. Reduce heat to maintain a simmer and cook, uncovered, for 45 minutes. Add salt and pepper to taste.

**2.** Preheat oven to 350° F. Brush bread slices generously with olive oil, arrange on a baking sheet, and bake until golden (about 10 minutes). To serve, put a slice of bread in each of 6 warm soup bowls. Ladle soup over bread. Garnish with cheese or pass cheese separately at the table.

*Makes 6 cups, 6 servings.*

**Make-Ahead Tip** Onion soup may be made through step 1 up to 3 days ahead.

## RAGOÛT PRINTANIER
### Spring vegetable stew

The fertile region surrounding Paris is famous for delicate spring vegetables such as new potatoes, carrots, asparagus, and onions. To make a delectable vegetable stew, choose the youngest, most tender specimens and braise them whole in butter. The dish should be served as a first course, with bread to soak up the juices.

- 4 tablespoons unsalted butter
- 2 shallots, minced
- 2 cloves garlic, minced
- 6 boiling onions (about 2 in. diameter), peeled
- 4½ cups water or Fond de Legumes (see page 32)
- 6 ounces small red potatoes, cut in ½-inch dice
- 12 finger-sized young carrots, tops removed, left whole
- 8 ounces baby yellow summer squash or zucchini, quartered lengthwise
- 8 ounces pencil-thin asparagus
- 5 ounces mushrooms, quartered
- ¼ cup minced green onion
- ¼ cup minced parsley
  Kosher salt and freshly ground pepper

**1.** In a large skillet over moderately low heat, melt 2 tablespoons of the butter. Add shallots and garlic and sauté 3 minutes. Add boiling onions and 2 cups of the water. Bring to a boil over moderately high heat; reduce heat to maintain a simmer and simmer 10 minutes.

**2.** Add potatoes and cook 5 minutes. Add carrots and 1 cup of the water and cook 5 minutes. Add squash and 1 cup of the water, and cook 5 minutes. Add asparagus and mushrooms, and cook until asparagus is tender-crisp (5 to 8 minutes). Raise heat to high; add the remaining 2 tablespoons butter and ½ cup water. Bring to a boil and cook 30 seconds. Stir in green onion and parsley. Season with salt and pepper. Divide mixture among 6 warm soup bowls.

*Makes 6 servings.*

# MAIN COURSES AND SIDE DISHES

From the simplicity of a split roast chicken to the elegance of sweetbreads and spring peas, Parisian cooks excel at bringing out the best in their fine ingredients.

## POULET EN CRAPAUDINE
### Split chicken with mustard and bread crumbs

A chicken *en crapaudine* is butterflied and flattened so that it resembles a giant toad (*un crapaud*). A popular Parisian bistro dish, it is typically prepared with small chickens that are flattened, grilled, and served whole. The following recipe gives a roasting method, but you may grill the chickens if you prefer.

> 2 frying chickens (about
> 3½ lb each)
> 1½ cups dry white wine
> ⅓ cup plus 2 tablespoons
> Dijon-style mustard
> 3 cloves garlic, peeled and sliced
> 1 tablespoon dried tarragon
> 1 bay leaf
> 1 teaspoon freshly ground
> pepper
> 1 onion, thinly sliced
> ½ cup soft bread crumbs
> 1 shallot, minced
> 2 cloves garlic, minced
> 2 tablespoons minced parsley
> 1 teaspoon kosher salt

**1.** Clean chickens thoroughly inside and out; pat dry. Remove wing tips and reserve for stock (see page 32). Cut out backbone with poultry shears or a sharp, heavy knife. Reserve for stock. With the knife blade, crack the breastbone just enough to allow chickens to lie flat. Lay chickens skin side up and flatten with the palms of your hands. Tuck wings under breast.

**2.** Place chickens in a glass or enamel baking dish. Whisk together wine, the 2 tablespoons mustard, sliced garlic, tarragon, bay leaf, pepper, and onion, and pour over chickens. Cover and marinate, refrigerated, for at least 2 hours or up to 1 day.

**3.** Preheat oven to 350° F. Remove chickens from marinade and place on a rack in a roasting pan, skin side up. Spread the ⅓ cup mustard over chickens. Stir together bread crumbs, shallot, minced garlic, parsley, and salt. Pat bread crumb mixture onto chickens in an even layer. Remove ½ cup sliced onions from marinade and scatter over chickens.

**4.** Roast chickens, uncovered, until juices run clear (about 1¼ hours). Quarter each chicken and serve.

*Serves 6.*

## RIS DE VEAU AU BEURRE NOISETTE
### Sweetbreads in brown butter with capers

*Beurre noisette* (brown butter) should be cooked until it is the color of a hazelnut (*une noisette*). This brown butter and caper garnish is a classic French treatment, not only for sweetbreads, but also for brains, skate wing, poached sole, and shad roe. Note that sweetbreads need to refrigerate for at least six hours.

> 2 pounds veal sweetbreads
> 6 tablespoons unsalted butter
> Freshly ground pepper
> 6 tablespoons capers
> ¼ cup lemon juice
> Lemon wedges, for garnish

**1.** Put sweetbreads in a large bowl. Cover with cold water and refrigerate for 4 hours, changing water after 2 hours. Drain sweetbreads and transfer to a 2-quart saucepan. Add cold water to cover. Bring to a boil over high heat, then reduce heat to maintain a simmer. Simmer 3 minutes, then drain and refresh sweetbreads under cold running water.

**2.** Transfer sweetbreads to a tray lined with plastic wrap and cover with plastic wrap. Set a board on top of sweetbreads and put about 3 pounds of weights on top of the board. (Canned foods or a bowl filled with beans or rice work well.) Refrigerate at least 2 hours or up to 1 day.

**3.** Remove weights and inspect sweetbreads. Trim away visible fat and the tube that connects lobes; carefully peel away thin outer membrane. Slice sweetbreads ¼ inch thick.

**4.** In each of two large nonstick skillets over moderate heat, melt 2 tablespoons of the butter. When butter begins to brown, add sweetbreads and cook 1 minute. Turn, season with pepper, and cook 1 minute on second side. Add 3 tablespoons of the capers, 2 tablespoons of the lemon juice, and 1 tablespoon of the butter to each pan and continue cooking 2 minutes. Transfer sweetbreads to a warm platter or dinner plates with a slotted spatula; pour pan juices over. Serve with lemon wedges.

*Serves 6.*

## PETITS POIS À LA FRANÇAISE
### Braised peas and lettuce

Cooking peas and lettuce together seems to bring out the sweetness in both.

> 2 heads butter lettuce
> 3 tablespoons unsalted butter
> 1 onion, thinly sliced
> ½ cup Fond de Legumes
> (see page 32)
> 1 pound fresh peas, shelled,
> or 2 cups frozen petite peas
> 1 tablespoon whipping cream
> Kosher salt and freshly
> ground pepper

**1.** Core lettuce heads; wash and dry thoroughly. Cut heads in quarters, roll each quarter up into a log, and slice thinly crosswise to shred.

**2.** In a medium saucepan over low heat, melt butter. Add onion and sauté 10 minutes. Add stock; bring to a simmer over moderately high heat. Add peas; cover and simmer until almost done (5 to 8 minutes for fresh peas, about 3 minutes for frozen peas). Add shredded lettuce, cover, and simmer 2 minutes. Raise heat to high, add cream, and simmer, uncovered, for 1 minute. Season to taste with salt and pepper. Transfer to a warm serving bowl.

*Serves 6.*

## SAUCISSES AU CHAMPAGNE, SAUCE MOUTARDE
### Champagne sausages with mustard sauce

This highly seasoned pork mixture gets a lift from a splash of Champagne. Typically, a French cook would wrap loose sausage in caul fat—a lacy sheet of fat from the pig's stomach—to hold it together, but this mixture keeps its shape without a wrapper. Note that mixture needs to refrigerate at least four hours.

- ⅓ cup soft bread crumbs
- 2 pounds bone-in pork shoulder
- 1 shallot, peeled and halved
- 2 cloves garlic, peeled and coarsely chopped
- 1 large egg
- ½ teaspoon freshly ground pepper
- 1 teaspoon ground ginger
- 1 teaspoon ground cloves
  Pinch of nutmeg
- ½ teaspoon kosher salt
- ½ cup Champagne
- ¼ cup chopped green onion

**Sauce Moutarde**

- ¼ cup stone-ground honey mustard
- ¾ cup sour cream or Crème Fraîche (see page 22)
  Kosher salt and freshly ground pepper

**1.** Preheat oven to 350° F. Toast bread crumbs for 5 minutes, then set aside. Bone pork and cut meat into 2-inch cubes; do not trim away fat.

**2.** *To make in a food processor:* Combine bread crumbs, pork, shallot, garlic, egg, pepper, ginger, cloves, nutmeg, salt, and Champagne. Process until meat is well chopped but not pasty. Add green onion and process 2 seconds just to blend. *To make by hand:* Put pork through the medium blade of a meat grinder. Mince shallot and garlic. In a medium bowl combine bread crumbs, ground pork, shallot, garlic, egg, pepper, ginger, cloves, nutmeg, salt, Champagne, and green onion. Blend lightly but thoroughly with your hands.

**3.** Form mixture into 6 patties. Transfer to a large plate, cover with plastic wrap, and refrigerate at least 4 hours or up to 8 hours.

**4.** Prepare a medium-hot charcoal fire. Grill patties, turning once, until done throughout (about 15 minutes total cooking time). Serve on a warm platter with a small bowl of Sauce Moutarde in the center.

*Serves 6.*

**Sauce Moutarde** Whisk together mustard and sour cream. Season to taste with salt and pepper.

*Makes 1 cup.*

*Teamed with a green salad, a wedge of cheese, and fresh fruit for dessert, grilled Champagne sausages make a satisfying winter dinner.*

# DESSERTS

At home, French cooks rarely make desserts, but that doesn't mean the French don't eat them. At noon, many diners end their lunch with a dainty *pot de crème*; in the evening, they might stop at a favorite pastry shop for a tart to take home.

## POTS DE CRÈME AU CHOCOLAT
### Bittersweet chocolate custard

A silky smooth *pot de crème* (baked egg custard) is a popular ending to a Parisian bistro meal. This easy version of the classic dessert does not need to be baked. Note that the custard needs at least two hours to chill.

> ¾ cup Crème Fraîche (see page 22) or whipping cream
> ½ teaspoon kosher salt
> 8 ounces bittersweet or semisweet chocolate
> 8 large egg yolks
> 2 teaspoons vanilla extract
> ¼ cup pistachios, finely minced, for garnish (optional)
> 2 ounces bittersweet or semisweet chocolate, for garnish (optional)

**1.** In a small saucepan combine Crème Fraîche and salt. Heat slightly over low heat and keep warm. Place the 8 ounces of chocolate in the top of a double boiler; set over, not in, simmering water. Stir occasionally until chocolate is melted and smooth. Whisk egg yolks until light, then add to chocolate and whisk 30 seconds. Add warm Crème Fraîche and cook, stirring occasionally, until thick (5 to 7 minutes).

**2.** Divide mixture among 6 custard cups. Chill at least 2 hours or up to 2 days. Just before serving, garnish with pistachios or with curls of shaved chocolate (if desired). To make chocolate curls, use a sharp vegetable peeler to shave off thin sheets from a smooth, flat side of a chunk of chocolate.

*Serves 6.*

## TARTE AUX FRAISES
### Strawberry tart

This classic fresh fruit tart is found all over France but is at its most handsome in the elegant pastry shops of Paris. In the afternoon, weary Parisians like to pause at a *pâtisserie* (pastry shop) or a *salon de thé* (tea shop) for a pot of tea and a slice of strawberry tart. The dessert is easy to make at home with storebought frozen puff pastry.

> ½ pound frozen puff pastry
> 1 cup milk
> ½ vanilla bean, split lengthwise; or 1 teaspoon vanilla extract
> 3 large egg yolks
> ¼ cup sugar, plus 2 to 3 teaspoons sugar for sweetening berries
> 1 tablespoon cornstarch
> 3 tablespoons orange liqueur
> 1 tablespoon Crème Fraîche (see page 22) or sour cream
> 3 cups strawberries, cleaned, cored, and halved

**1.** Allow puff pastry to thaw at room temperature for 1 hour. Preheat oven to 450° F. On a lightly floured surface, roll pastry into a rectangle approximately 7 by 18 inches and ⅛ inch thick. Transfer to a heavy baking sheet. Using a small, sharp knife, gently trace a rectangle 1 inch from edge of dough. Bake pastry until puffed and browned (12 to 15 minutes). Carefully transfer to a rack to cool.

**2.** Place milk in a medium saucepan. If using vanilla bean, scrape seeds into milk, then add pod. Bring to a boil over moderately low heat, stirring; cover and remove from heat.

**3.** With a wire whisk or with an electric mixer, beat yolks and the ¼ cup sugar until pale and thick. Add cornstarch and beat to blend. Transfer mixture to saucepan with milk and return to moderate heat. Cook, whisking constantly, until mixture comes to a boil. Remove from heat and whisk briskly for 5 seconds. Cool slightly; stir in 2 tablespoons of the liqueur, Crème Fraîche, and vanilla extract (if using). Remove vanilla bean (if used). Transfer to a bowl and lay a sheet of plastic wrap directly on the surface of the filling. Chill thoroughly.

**4.** Place berries in a medium bowl. Add the 2 to 3 teaspoons sugar, depending on sweetness of berries. Add the remaining 1 tablespoon liqueur and toss to blend.

**5.** To assemble tart, carefully cut out the rectangle traced on tart shell in step 1; lift off and set aside. With your fingers, pull out and discard the soft, doughy interior. Spread chilled filling evenly in tart shell. Arrange berries neatly over the filling. Replace rectangular pastry "hat." Serve within 1 hour.

*Serves 6.*

**Make-Ahead Tip**   Pastry may be baked up to 4 hours ahead. Filling may be made 2 days ahead and refrigerated. Berries may be sugared up to 2 hours ahead.

## CHAMPAGNE RECEPTION

*Galettes de Pommes de
Terre et Champignons*

*Rillettes de Saumon*

*Pointes d'Asperge à la
Sauce Gribiche*

*Croque-Mademoiselle*

*Champagne*

*Guests will know it's
an important day when
sparkling wine is on the
menu. To fête a bride
and groom, to honor a
distinguished guest, or to
inaugurate a new home,
consider this Champagne
Reception with passed trays
of tempting hors d'oeuvres.
Most of the following menu
can be made ahead. The
potato and mushroom
pancakes need to be fried
at the last minute, but a
hired helper or a friend can
be recruited for that duty.
Menu serves 16.*

### GALETTES DE POMMES DE TERRE ET CHAMPIGNONS
*Potato and mushroom pancakes*

The French are great fans of wild mushrooms; the fleshy cèpe (*Boletus edulis*) is especially prized. On weekends, many Parisians head for the woods surrounding the city to forage for these edible treasures. Here, dried cèpes flavor a crisp potato pancake, an elegant hors d'oeuvre to serve with a glass of Champagne. On another occasion, make the pancakes larger and serve as an accompaniment to roast beef. Look for dried cèpes (known as *porcini* in Italian) in French or Italian markets.

  1½  *ounces dried cèpe mushrooms*
   3  *tablespoons dry white wine*
   2  *cloves garlic, peeled*
   2  *shallots, peeled*
   2  *large baking potatoes
     (about 12 oz each)*
   3  *egg yolks*
  ⅓  *cup sour cream or Crème
     Fraîche (see page 22)*
   1  *teaspoon kosher salt*
  1½  *teaspoons freshly ground
     pepper*
  1⅓  *cups flour*
   1  *tablespoon baking powder*
   3  *tablespoons butter*
   1  *cup sour cream or Crème
     Fraîche (see page 22) mixed
     with ¼ cup minced chives,
     for garnish*

**1.** Place mushrooms in a medium bowl and add warm water to cover. Soak until softened, about 30 minutes, then lift mushrooms out of soaking liquid with a slotted spoon. Inspect mushrooms carefully, wash away any grit, then transfer to a medium saucepan. To remove any remaining grit, strain soaking liquid through a double thickness of dampened cheesecloth into the saucepan. Add wine. Bring mixture to a simmer over moderate heat and simmer until no liquid remains (about 10 minutes). Cool slightly.

**2.** *To make in a food processor:* Put garlic and shallots in work bowl fitted with steel blade and process until finely minced. Add cooked mushrooms and process until chopped but not puréed (about 3 seconds). Leave mixture in bowl, but change blade to grater attachment. Grate baking potatoes into work bowl. Transfer mixture to a large mixing bowl and stir in egg yolks, sour cream or Crème Fraîche, salt, pepper, flour, and baking powder. *To make by hand:* Mince garlic and shallots until fine. Mince cooked mushrooms. Grate potatoes into a mixing bowl, then add garlic, shallots, mushrooms, egg yolks, sour cream or Crème Fraîche, salt, pepper, flour, and baking powder. Stir to blend all ingredients.

**3.** To make pancakes: In a nonstick skillet over moderate heat, melt 1 tablespoon of the butter. When butter foams, put 1 heaping tablespoon of potato mixture in pan. Flatten with a metal spatula. Cook until golden brown on both sides (3 to 4 minutes per side). Transfer immediately to a warm serving platter and keep warm in a low oven. Repeat with remaining batter, adding butter to the skillet as necessary. To serve, garnish each pancake with a teaspoon of sour cream or crème fraîche with chives.

*Makes about forty-five 2½-inch pancakes.*

## RILLETTES DE SAUMON
### Fresh and smoked salmon spread

For a less rich appetizer, serve the cured salmon on its own. Make the recipe through step 1, thinly slice the cured salmon, and accompany with buttered bread. Note that the salmon needs to cure for at least one day.

    1½   pounds fresh salmon fillet
     6   tablespoons Cognac or
         brandy
     6   tablespoons lemon juice
         Grated zest of 2 large lemons
     2   tablespoons sugar
     2   tablespoons dill seed
     2   tablespoons kosher salt
     2   large egg yolks
     ¼   cup unsalted butter, softened
     2   tablespoons olive oil
         Pinch of nutmeg
     ½   pound boneless smoked
         salmon
     2   tablespoons sour cream
         Kosher salt and freshly
         ground pepper
         Dill sprigs, for garnish
    48   bread rounds (¼ in. thick)
         cut from French-style baguette,
         for accompaniment

**1.** Use tweezers to remove any bones from salmon fillet. Whisk together Cognac, lemon juice, lemon zest, sugar, dill seed, and the 2 tablespoons salt. Put salmon fillet on a large rimmed plate or in a glass or enamel baking dish. Pour lemon mixture over fillet, pressing dill seed onto fish with your fingers. Cover fish with plastic wrap. Place a plate or tray with a 3-pound weight on top of the fish. (Canned foods or a bowl filled with beans or rice work well.) Refrigerate for at least a day or up to 4 days.

**2.** Cut fish in cubes, and place in food processor with egg yolks, butter, olive oil, nutmeg, and any marinade juices. Process until smooth.

**3.** Cut smoked salmon into strips about 2 inches long and ¼ inch wide. Add to processor along with sour cream and pulse two or three times. Smoked salmon should not be fully blended into mixture but should remain in small visible pieces. Season mixture to taste with salt and pepper.

**4.** Pack into one large or several small crocks. Cover with plastic wrap and refrigerate up to 3 days. To serve, garnish with dill sprigs and accompany with bread rounds. For a stand-up cocktail party, spread the mixture on bread rounds yourself and pass on trays. Serve cool but not cold.

*Makes about 3 cups.*

## POINTES D'ASPERGE À LA SAUCE GRIBICHE
### Asparagus tips with caper and tarragon mayonnaise

The tangy Sauce Gribiche is also an excellent choice with cold salmon or shellfish, cold sliced tongue, or a steamed artichoke.

     4   pounds medium-thick
         asparagus

### Sauce Gribiche

     4   eggs
     ¼   cup white wine vinegar
     2   teaspoons prepared
         horseradish
    1½   tablespoons dried tarragon
    1½   cups olive oil
     1   tablespoon capers
     6   tablespoons minced
         Cornichons (tiny pickles,
         see page 70)
     1   teaspoon freshly ground
         pepper
         Kosher salt

**1.** Cut off top 3 inches of each asparagus spear. Save stalks for soup, if desired. In a large saucepan over high heat, bring a small amount of salted water to boil. Put as many asparagus tips in a steamer rack as will comfortably fit; place over boiling water, cover, and steam until tender-crisp (4 to 5 minutes). Remove steamer and run under cold water to cool quickly. Drain and set tips aside. Repeat with remaining asparagus. Cover and refrigerate for up to 4 hours. Remove from refrigerator 30 minutes before serving.

**2.** To serve, pat asparagus dry in a clean dish towel, then arrange neatly on a serving platter. Accompany with a bowl of Sauce Gribiche.

*Serves 16.*

**Sauce Gribiche**   Place eggs in a medium saucepan, cover with lightly salted water, and bring to a boil over high heat. Cover pan and remove from heat; let stand 10 minutes. Drain eggs, rinse under cold water, and shell. Put yolks in a small mixing bowl; chop whites and set aside. Add vinegar, horseradish, and tarragon to yolks; whisk to blend. Add oil in a thin stream, whisking constantly to form a thick, creamy sauce. Whisk in capers, Cornichons, pepper, and salt to taste. Let stand 30 minutes or refrigerate overnight. Before using, bring to room temperature, stir in chopped egg whites and adjust seasoning.

*Makes 2 cups.*

## CROQUE-MADEMOISELLE
### Cocktail cheese toasts

The streets of Paris are lined with sidewalk vendors and small cafés serving *croque-monsieur* (a grilled ham and cheese sandwich) and *croque-madame* (a grilled chicken and cheese sandwich). Here is an open-faced cocktail version, a two-bite morsel to accompany a glass of red or white wine. Start this dish the day before your party.

     1   pound Gruyère cheese, grated
     1   tablespoon dry white wine
     ¼   cup plain yogurt
     ¼   cup minced green onion
     1   teaspoon minced garlic
     3   teaspoons grated lemon zest
     ¼   cup finely minced red onion
     ¼   cup finely minced parsley
    48   bread rounds (¼ in. thick)
         cut from a French-style
         baguette

**1.** In a medium bowl combine cheese, wine, yogurt, green onion, garlic, and 2 teaspoons lemon zest. Cover and chill overnight or up to 2 days.

**2.** Preheat broiler. In a small bowl combine the remaining 1 teaspoon lemon zest, red onion, and parsley. Arrange bread rounds on a baking sheet and spread liberally with cheese mixture. Broil until cheese browns and bubbles (2 to 3 minutes). Garnish with parsley mixture. Serve hot.

*Makes 4 dozen cocktail-sized toasts.*

*A glass of Champagne is the perfect companion for salmon spread, mushroom and potato pancakes, asparagus with Sauce Gribiche, and cheese toasts.*

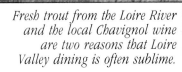

*Fresh trout from the Loire River and the local Chavignol wine are two reasons that Loire Valley dining is often sublime.*

# The Loire Valley

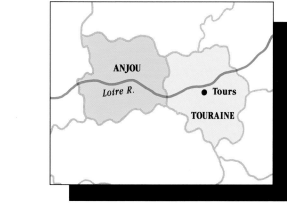

F ertile farmland and well-stocked streams provide materials for Loire Valley cooks. From the farms come radishes, beans, sorrel, peas, leeks, and herbs for salads; the rivers yield trout and salmon to sauce with a delicate beurre blanc (see page 47). One of the best-loved desserts of France, the upside-down apple tart (see Tarte Tatin, page 53), is a Loire Valley specialty. Other regional favorites—cold roast pork stuffed with wine-plumped prunes (see Longe de Porc aux Pruneaux, page 50), cucumbers in minted sour cream (see Concombres à la Crème, page 49), marinated goat cheese (see Fromage de Chèvre Mariné, page 50), and crusty bread (see Pain de Campagne, page 50)—make wonderful picnic fare.

# THE LOIRE VALLEY: TOURAINE AND ANJOU

The Loire River runs through the provinces of Touraine and Anjou, creating a lush valley known as the garden of France. From the prolific Anjou orchards come meaty prunes, the russet apples known as *reinettes*, and the Williams pear (which Americans call a Bartlett). The mild Touraine climate is perfect for growing delicate vegetables such as lettuces, peas, leeks, shallots, and sorrel, as well as radishes, string beans, and shell beans. The woods yield abundant wild mushrooms, but mushroom cultivation is also big business. The Loire River itself is home to delectable salmon, pike, and trout. With such lovely freshwater fish at hand, it's not surprising that Loire cooks developed one of the world's most subtle and sophisticated fish sauces—beurre blanc, or white butter sauce.

Charcuterie (see page 82) is also a Loire specialty. The famous *rillettes de Tours* is a smooth, highly seasoned pork spread enjoyed as an appetizer on country bread. *Andouille* (large smoked tripe sausage) and *andouillette* (smaller fresh tripe sausage) are regional favorites, as is *boudin blanc*, a plump white-meat sausage.

The famous goat cheeses of the Loire Valley—Sainte-Maure, Valençay, Selles-sur-Cher, Chavignol—are proudly offered in the region's restaurants, often alongside unnamed goat cheeses from small local farms. The region's white wines, particularly Sancerre and Pouilly-Fumé, are ideal companions for this cheese.

## SOUPS AND SALADS

The delicate greens from Loire Valley gardens enhance simple spring soups. When the market yields crisp young radishes, tender beans, and mild green onions, they're likely to be partnered with cold poached chicken or salmon for a light, fresh meal.

## SOUPE JARDINIÈRE
### Summer garden soup

Take advantage of what's freshest in the market or garden to make this quick and easy soup. Young sorrel leaves, butter lettuce, chicory, hearts of romaine, tender dandelion greens, or hearts of leaf lettuce would be suitable.

- 6 cups Fond de Volaille (see page 32)
- 4 cups mixed greens (tender leaves only), tough stems or ribs removed
- ¼ cup minced fresh herbs (a mixture of dill, parsley, chives, and chervil) Kosher salt and freshly ground pepper
- ⅓ cup minced green onion, for garnish Croutons à l'Ail (see page 114)

In a medium stockpot over moderately high heat, bring stock to a simmer. Add greens and cook until wilted (about 3 minutes). Stir in herbs and simmer 2 minutes. Season to taste with salt and pepper. Serve soup in warm bowls, garnished with green onion. Pass warm croutons separately.

*Makes 7 cups, 6 servings.*

## SALADE DE POULET AUX RADIS
### Chicken salad with spring radishes

Chicken roasted on the bone has more flavor than poached chicken and yields a more flavorful chicken salad. This spring combination of chicken and radishes couldn't be easier. Take it on a picnic or serve it for a light party lunch with rye bread and a bowl of fresh cherries.

- ¼ cup Fond de Volaille (see page 32)
- 3 pounds chicken legs and thighs, skinned Kosher salt and freshly ground pepper
- ⅓ cup Crème Fraîche (see page 22)
- 2 bunches radishes, trimmed and sliced ⅛ inch thick
- ¾ cup minced green onion

**Homemade Mayonnaise**

- 2 large egg yolks
- 1 teaspoon kosher salt
- ¼ teaspoon freshly ground pepper
- 2 teaspoons lemon juice, plus lemon juice to taste
- ½ teaspoon dry mustard
- ¾ cup safflower oil
- ¼ cup olive oil

**1.** In a small bowl whisk together ¾ cup Homemade Mayonnaise and Fond de Volaille. Cover and refrigerate for at least 2 hours or up to 1 day.

**2.** Preheat oven to 350° F. Season chicken parts lightly with salt and pepper. Transfer to a large baking or roasting pan. Coat with Crème Fraîche. Bake until juices run clear when meat is pierced with a knife (about 40 minutes). Set aside to cool.

**3.** Remove chicken meat from bones in large pieces. Transfer meat to a mixing bowl and add half the radishes and ½ cup of the onion.

**4.** Taste sauce and adjust seasoning with salt and pepper. Add to chicken and radishes and mix gently. Transfer salad to a serving platter and garnish with remaining radish slices and the remaining green onion. Serve cool but not cold.

*Serves 6.*

**Homemade Mayonnaise** In the work bowl of a food processor or in a blender, combine egg yolks, salt, pepper, the 2 teaspoons lemon juice, and mustard. Process or blend to mix. With motor running, add oil drop by drop until mixture is thick, then add remaining oil faster until all is used. Taste and add more salt, pepper, or lemon juice if needed. Mayonnaise will keep for up to 10 days in the refrigerator.

*Makes about 1 cup.*

## SALADE DE SAUMON AUX HARICOTS VERTS
### *Warm salmon salad with green beans*

To get neat, pretty pieces of salmon for this salad, slice a large fillet into thick fingers and poach them unskinned. After cooking, the skin peels off easily. Arranged on a platter with green beans and drizzled with a creamy green-onion dressing, the salmon makes a lovely summer lunch or light dinner. For best flavor, check a specialty produce market or farmers' market for the slender French beans known as *haricots verts*.

- 1 egg yolk
  Juice of 1 lime
- 2 tablespoons white wine vinegar
- 6 green onions (white and pale green part only), coarsely chopped
- 1 cup olive oil
  Kosher salt and freshly ground pepper
- 1 salmon fillet (2½ lb), skin attached
- 2 cups dry white wine
- ½ pound green beans, ends trimmed, halved if large
- 1 heart (pale inner leaves only) romaine lettuce
- 1 green onion, minced, for garnish

*A creamy green-onion sauce puts the finishing touch on a poached salmon and green bean salad.*

**1.** In a blender or food processor, combine egg yolk, lime juice, vinegar, and chopped green onions. Blend until smooth. With motor running, add oil drop by drop until sauce thickens, then add oil faster until all is used. Sauce should be thick and green. Remove to a bowl; stir in salt and pepper to taste. Sauce may be made up to 1 day ahead, covered, and refrigerated.

**2.** Cut salmon crosswise into strips about 1 inch wide. Season with salt and pepper. In each of two 9-inch skillets over moderate heat, bring 1 cup wine to a simmer. Divide salmon between the skillets, return to a simmer, then adjust heat to maintain a simmer. Cover and cook 3 minutes. Turn fillets over, cover, and cook an additional 3 minutes. Check for doneness; fish should be bright pink and firm but still moist in the center. With a slotted flat spatula, transfer fillets to clean kitchen towels to drain.

**3.** While fish is cooking, steam green beans over, not in, boiling salted water until tender-crisp (6 to 10 minutes, depending on size). On a large serving platter or on individual plates, arrange poached salmon, bundles of green beans, and heart of romaine lettuce. Garnish platter with minced green onion. Pass sauce separately or drizzle some of the sauce over the salad and pass remaining sauce separately.

*Serves 6.*

## HARICOTS EN SALADE
### Four-bean salad

Shell beans and snap beans thrive in the Loire Valley. In this recipe they're combined with vinaigrette to make a cool and colorful salad for summer picnics or buffets. Note that the dried beans need to be soaked overnight.

- ½ cup dried white beans
- 2 teaspoons minced garlic
- 1 teaspoon dried thyme
- 1 teaspoon kosher salt, or more to taste
- 1 teaspoon freshly ground pepper, or more to taste
- 1 tablespoon Dijon-style mustard
- ¼ cup white wine vinegar
- 1 cup olive oil
- 1 can (15 oz) chick-peas, rinsed and drained
- ½ white onion, peeled and sliced paper-thin
- 4 ounces green beans
- 4 ounces yellow wax beans
- 2 tablespoons lemon juice
- ¼ cup minced fresh chervil

**1.** Soak white beans overnight in cold water. Drain and place in small saucepan with 2 cups water. Bring to a boil over high heat, then reduce heat to maintain a simmer. Cook until beans are tender (about 1½ hours), adding water as necessary to keep beans covered at all times.

**2.** In a medium mixing bowl, whisk together garlic, thyme, 1 teaspoon salt, 1 teaspoon pepper, mustard, and vinegar. Slowly whisk in ¾ cup oil. Stir in chick-peas and onion.

**3.** Pinch off tips of green beans and wax beans. String if necessary. Cut large beans in half; leave small ones whole. Bring a large pot of salted water to a boil over high heat. Add green beans and cook until tender-crisp (5 to 7 minutes). Remove beans with a strainer to a bowl of ice water to stop cooking, then drain, pat dry, and add to chick-peas. Return water to a boil, add wax beans and

cook until tender-crisp (5 to 7 minutes). Drain beans, then transfer immediately to a bowl of ice water to stop cooking. Drain again, pat dry, and add to chick-peas.

**4.** Add lemon juice, white beans, and the remaining ¼ cup olive oil to beans. Stir to blend. Let stand at room temperature 30 minutes before serving. Just before serving, season to taste with salt and pepper and stir in chervil.

*Serves 6.*

## MAIN COURSES AND SIDE DISHES

Loire Valley cooks know that good fresh fish doesn't need complicated treatment. Trout are grilled or baked simply and topped with an herb butter; salmon is poached and paired with a silky butter sauce. To flavor a plump chicken, home cooks look to the aromatic ingredients that thrive in their region, such as wild cèpe mushrooms and mild leeks. Side dishes are generally uncomplicated. Boiled new potatoes might accompany a sauced poached fish; a crusty zucchini or leek gratin might partner a roast.

## TRUITE GRILLÉE, BEURRE D'OSEILLE
### Grilled trout with composed sorrel butter

A tangy sorrel butter is the perfect partner for sweet-fleshed trout. Grilling the fish over charcoal imparts a subtle smoky flavor, but you can bake the trout if you prefer.

- ¾ cup unsalted butter, softened
- 4 ounces (about 1 cup) fresh sorrel leaves, stems removed
  Kosher salt and freshly ground pepper
  Oil, for brushing grill and fish
- 6 boneless, butterflied trout (about 8 oz each)
  Lemon wedges, for garnish

**1.** Combine butter and sorrel in a food processor or blender. Blend until sorrel is well chopped and thoroughly combined. Add salt and pepper to taste and blend again. Set seasoned butter aside or cover and refrigerate for up to 1 day.

**2.** Prepare a medium-hot charcoal fire. Lightly oil grill and preheat over coals 5 minutes to prevent fish from sticking. Lightly oil skin side of trout. Arrange trout, skin side down, on grill and dot surface of each fish with 1 tablespoon of the sorrel butter. Cover and grill 5 minutes. Uncover and check for doneness; fish should be firm and white but still moist. If not, cover and continue cooking until done. To serve, transfer trout carefully with a flat spatula to warm plates. Garnish each portion with an additional tablespoon sorrel butter and a lemon wedge.

*Serves 6.*

## GRATIN DE COURGETTES
### Baked zucchini casserole

This summer side dish would be delicious with grilled lamb chops or a roast chicken.

- 5 tablespoons peanut or safflower oil, plus oil for baking dish
- 2 tablespoons unsalted butter
- 1 large red onion, thinly sliced
- 1 tablespoon finely minced garlic
- 2 pounds zucchini or yellow crookneck squash, coarsely grated
- 3 slices stale sandwich bread
- 2 eggs, lightly beaten
- 1 teaspoon freshly ground pepper
  Kosher salt
- ¼ cup coarse bread crumbs, made from day-old bread

**1.** Preheat oven to 350° F. Lightly oil a 6-cup oval earthenware baking dish. In a medium skillet over moderate heat, heat 3 tablespoons of the oil and 1 tablespoon of the butter. Add onion and garlic and sauté until softened (about 5 minutes). Add zucchini and stir to coat with oil.

2. Crumble stale bread into small pieces by hand and add to skillet. Stir to combine. Remove from heat and let cool 5 minutes. Stir in beaten eggs. Add pepper and season to taste with salt. Transfer mixture to prepared baking dish. Sprinkle top with bread crumbs and dot with the remaining 1 tablespoon butter. Drizzle with the remaining 2 tablespoons oil. Bake until top is golden brown and zucchini is hot thoughout (about 20 minutes). Let stand 5 minutes, then serve directly from the baking dish.

*Serves 6.*

### SAUMON POCHÉ, BEURRE BLANC TOMATÉ À L'ESTRAGON
*Poached salmon with tomato-tarragon butter sauce*

Salmon and pike from the Loire River never taste better than when gently poached and served with beurre blanc, a creamy shallot butter sauce (see right). Dill or Red-Wine Butter Sauce are also excellent with salmon.

- 6 *tablespoons peeled, seeded, and chopped tomato*
- 1 *tablespoon minced fresh tarragon*
- 1½ *cups Fumet de Poisson (see page 33)*
- 1 *cup dry white wine*
- 1 *bay leaf*
- 3 *sprigs parsley*
- 1 *tablespoon black peppercorns, lightly crushed*
- 2 *sprigs thyme or ½ teaspoon dried thyme*
- 6 *fresh salmon steaks (about 8 oz each)*

#### Beurre Blanc Tomaté à l'Estragon

- 1 *large shallot, minced*
- 5 *tablespoons tarragon vinegar*
- 5 *tablespoons dry white wine*
- 2 *tablespoons Crème Fraîche (see page 22)*
- 10 *tablespoons very cold butter, cut in 10 pieces*
- ¼ *cup peeled, seeded, and chopped tomato*
- 2 *tablespoons minced fresh tarragon*
  *Kosher salt and freshly ground pepper*

1. Combine tomato and tarragon and set aside. In two 14-inch skillets or in a fish poacher, combine stock, wine, bay leaf, parsley, peppercorns, and thyme. Bring to a simmer over high heat. Add salmon, reduce heat so that stock barely simmers, and poach, turning steaks over halfway through. Salmon tastes best when still moist in the center. Total cooking time will be about 8 minutes.

2. Using a slotted flat spatula, transfer salmon steaks to a clean dish towel to drain briefly. Spoon some Beurre Blanc Tomaté à l'Estragon onto each dinner plate, then top with a salmon steak. Garnish each steak with a tablespoon of tomato-tarragon mixture.

*Serves 6.*

#### Beurre Blanc Tomaté à l'Estragon

1. In a medium saucepan combine shallot, vinegar, and wine. Bring to a simmer over high heat and reduce to 1 tablespoon. Add Crème Fraîche and cook until reduced to 2 tablespoons.

2. Reduce heat to low. Add butter piece by piece, whisking until each is incorporated. Remove pan from heat as necessary to keep butter from melting too quickly.

3. When all butter is incorporated, sauce should look creamy and slightly thick. Remove from heat and stir in tomato and tarragon. Season to taste with salt and pepper.

*Makes 1 cup.*

**Basic Beurre Blanc** Substitute white wine vinegar for tarragon vinegar. Omit tomato and tarragon.

**Dill Butter Sauce** Substitute white wine vinegar for tarragon vinegar. Omit tomato. Substitute 1 tablespoon minced fresh dill for minced tarragon.

**Red-Wine Butter Sauce** Substitute red wine vinegar for tarragon vinegar, and red wine for white wine. Omit tomato and tarragon.

### Step-by-Step

### BEURRE BLANC

**1.** *Reduce shallot, vinegar, and wine. Add Crème Fraîche and reduce.*

**2.** *Add butter piece by piece, whisking constantly. Remove pan from heat as necessary to keep butter from melting too quickly.*

**3.** *When all butter is fully incorporated, sauce should be creamy and slightly thick.*

*A mix of wild and culti-vated mushrooms imparts a woodsy flavor to a roast baby chicken or game hen.*

### POUSSINS RÔTIS AUX CHAMPIGNONS
**Roasted Cornish hens with mushrooms**

Poussins are baby chickens, usually weighing about a pound. They are occasionally available in this country in specialty markets, but Rock Cornish hens make a fine substitute. Because half a Cornish hen is a small dinner serving, you might accompany this dish with a generous portion of Nouilles à l'Alsacienne (see page 64) or Petits Pois à la Française (see page 36). The dried mushrooms called for in this recipe are *Boletus edulis*, known as *cèpes* in French markets and *porcini* in Italian markets. Note that the hens need to marinate at least four hours before roasting.

    *2 ounces dried cèpe mushrooms*
    *3 Rock Cornish hens (about 22 oz each)*
    *3 tablespoons unsalted butter, softened*

    *2 tablespoons minced fresh thyme or 2 teaspoons dried thyme*
*1½ tablespoons kosher salt*
    *2 teaspoons freshly ground pepper*
    *½ teaspoon ground bay leaf*
    *1 tablespoon minced garlic*
    *1 cup dry white wine*
    *3 tablespoons olive oil*
    *1 pound mushrooms, sliced ¼ inch thick*

**1.** Soak dried cèpes in warm water to cover for 20 minutes. Meanwhile, wash hens inside and out; pat dry. Remove wing tips.

**2.** Lift mushrooms out of water with a slotted spoon and check carefully for any grit. Strain soaking liquid through a double thickness of dampened cheesecloth into a small saucepan. Add dried mushrooms and 1 table-spoon of the butter. Simmer over moderately low heat until all liquid evaporates (about 7 minutes). Divide mushroom mixture among hen cavities.

**3.** In a small bowl make a paste of the remaining 2 tablespoons butter, thyme, salt, pepper, and ground bay leaf. Rub mixture over birds. Cover with plastic wrap and refrigerate at least 4 hours, or overnight.

**4.** Preheat oven to 375° F. Bring birds to room temperature and place on a rack in a roasting pan. Whisk together garlic, wine, and olive oil. Roast birds, basting with wine mix-ture and pan drippings every 15 minutes. Add sliced mushrooms to pan after 25 minutes and stir to coat with pan juices. Continue roasting, basting mushrooms and hens, until hens are golden brown and juices run clear when birds are pierced with a knife (about 25 more minutes). Remove from oven and let stand 5 minutes. Using a sharp, heavy knife or a cleaver, cut hens in half. Trans-fer to warm serving plates. Surround each half with fresh and dried mushrooms.

*Serves 6.*

## POULET AUX POIREAUX
### Chicken with leeks and tarragon

Fresh tarragon with its pungent lemon-anise flavor has a special affinity with chicken. Loire Valley cooks often pair the two, adding the region's delicate leeks as an accompaniment. Here, the three ingredients are combined in an easy braised dish to serve with steamed rice or buttered noodles.

> 2  large leeks
>    Kosher salt and freshly ground pepper
> 6  chicken half breasts, bone-in
> 2  tablespoons unsalted butter
> 2  tablespoons olive oil
> 4  cups Fond de Volaille (see page 32)
> 1  tablespoon minced fresh tarragon

**1.** Trim away tough, dark green ends and bearded root end of leeks. Slit leeks in half lengthwise. Clean under cold running water, taking care to remove any dirt trapped between the leaves. Slice leeks thinly.

**2.** Lightly salt and pepper chicken breasts. In a dutch oven or large skillet over moderate heat, heat butter and oil. Add chicken, skin side down, and cook 10 minutes. Turn and cook 5 minutes. Transfer chicken to a plate and add leeks to pan. Sauté until slightly softened (about 5 minutes). Add 2½ cups of the stock and tarragon. Bring to a simmer and cook until stock is reduced by half (about 5 minutes).

**3.** Return chicken to pan and add the remaining 1½ cups stock. Bring to a simmer, reduce heat to medium-low, and cover. Cook until chicken tests done (about 20 more minutes), basting with pan juices after 10 minutes. Transfer chicken to a warm serving platter or to individual plates. With a slotted spoon, spoon leeks over and around each breast. Stock in pan should have reduced to a near glaze. If it is still too liquid, return pan to high heat and cook until sauce is reduced to a syrupy consistency. Spoon over chicken and serve.

*Serves 6.*

---

## menu

### A SPRING PICNIC

*Concombres à la Crème*

*Longe de Porc aux Pruneaux*

*Pain de Campagne*

*Fromage de Chèvre Mariné*

*Cerises (Fresh Cherries)*

*Pouilly-Fumé or Vouvray*

---

*Spread your picnic blanket in a warm, grassy spot and unpack a delectable meal of cucumbers in minted sour cream, cold roast pork stuffed with wine-plumped prunes, marinated goat cheese, and a crusty home-baked bread. Fresh cherries make a satisfying dessert, but storebought oatmeal cookies or lemon bars could be added for picnic-goers with a sweet tooth. The Loire Valley specialties in this menu would be flattered by a wine from the region, such as a chilled Pouilly-Fumé or Vouvray. Add a jar of Dijon-style mustard to the picnic basket and a serrated knife for slicing bread so guests can make roast pork sandwiches if they like.*

*Menu serves 12.*

---

## CONCOMBRES À LA CRÈME
### Cucumbers in cream

Throughout France, fresh cucumbers in thick sour cream are a favorite partner for cold salmon or ham. Here they make a quick picnic salad that flatters the cold roast pork. For a variation, substitute minced dill or chervil for the mint. The cucumbers need to drain for four hours and the dish can be held for up to a day. It is best, though, when freshly made.

> 6  pounds (about 8 large) cucumbers, peeled
> ¼  cup kosher salt, plus salt to taste
> ½  cup Crème Fraîche (see page 22) or sour cream
> ½  cup chopped fresh mint, plus 2 tablespoons mint for garnish
> 2  shallots, minced
> 2  teaspoons freshly ground pepper, plus pepper to taste
> 2  tablespoons lemon juice

**1.** Cut cucumbers in half lengthwise and remove seeds with a small spoon. Cut crosswise into ¼-inch-thick slices. Place in a strainer and sprinkle with the ¼ cup salt. Toss well. Set strainer over a bowl or in sink and let drain 4 hours.

**2.** Up to one day ahead, combine Crème Fraîche, the ½ cup mint, shallots, and the 2 teaspoons pepper.

**3.** Rinse cucumbers and drain thoroughly. Pat dry with clean dish towels. Combine cucumbers with minted Crème Fraîche and refrigerate for up to 1 day. Just before packing food for a picnic, stir in lemon juice. Taste and add more salt and pepper if needed. Transfer to a covered plastic container and garnish with remaining chopped mint.

*Serves 12.*

## LONGE DE PORC AUX PRUNEAUX
### Cold roast pork with prunes

The fine, fat prunes of the Touraine are often plumped in wine and stuffed inside a butterflied pork loin. For a picnic, chill the cooked roast, then slice it just before you're ready to leave. Form the slices back into a loin shape, wrap tightly in plastic wrap, and overwrap with aluminum foil. The roast can also be served hot for a dinner at home; accompany it with Purée de Céleri-Rave (see page 74) and a bottle of Chenin Blanc or a light-bodied Pinot Noir. It is best to begin this recipe two days before the picnic.

- ½ pound large pitted prunes
- 2 cups slightly sweet white wine
- 2 teaspoons dried thyme
- 2 tablespoons paprika
- 1 tablespoon dried savory
- 2 bay leaves, coarsely crumbled, or 1 teaspoon ground bay leaf
- 1 tablespoon kosher salt
- 2 teaspoons black peppercorns
- 5 pounds center-cut pork loin, boned but not tied
- 4 large cloves garlic, peeled and thinly sliced

**1.** Soak prunes in wine overnight. Drain, reserving wine.

**2.** *To prepare in a spice grinder:* Combine thyme, paprika, savory, bay, salt, and peppercorns and grind to a fine powder. *To prepare by hand:* Use ground bay leaf and freshly ground black pepper and simply combine herbs and spices in a bowl.

**3.** Trim away all but ⅛ inch fat on surface of pork. Butterfly roast by making a long, lengthwise cut through the center, almost but not all the way through. The loin should open like a book. Rub cut surfaces with 2 teaspoons of the spice mix, then cover with prunes. Using kitchen string, tie roast at 1-inch intervals. With a small, sharp knife, cut slits about ½ inch deep in fat side of pork. Roll garlic slivers in spice mix and insert in slits. Coat roast with any remaining spice mix. Place on a plate, cover with plastic wrap, and refrigerate 12 hours.

**4.** Preheat oven to 350° F. Transfer roast to a rack in a roasting pan and cook until meat thermometer registers 160° F (about 2 hours), basting every 25 minutes with reserved wine. Remove roast from oven, cool to room temperature, then cover and refrigerate. Slice thinly to serve.

*Serves 12.*

## PAIN DE CAMPAGNE
### Whole-grain country bread

To get a good, chewy texture in a loaf of bread requires several hours of rising time. This hearty, whole-grain loaf is easy to make, but you'll need to start it a day ahead.

- 1 cup whole wheat flour
- 1 teaspoon active dry yeast
- 2¾ cups warm (105° F) water
- 1½ cups rye flour
- 5 cups bread flour
- 1 tablespoon kosher salt
- 2 tablespoons olive oil
- 2 tablespoons cornmeal, for coating baking sheets
- 1 egg yolk, lightly beaten

**1.** Make a starter by combining whole wheat flour, yeast, and 1 cup of the water in a large bowl. Stir to blend, then cover with plastic wrap and let stand at room temperature at least 12 hours, or overnight.

**2.** The following day, add 1¼ cups of the water, 1 cup of the rye flour, and 1½ cups of the bread flour to bowl. Mix well and cover with plastic wrap. Let stand for 6 hours.

**3.** Stir in the remaining ½ cup water, the remaining ½ cup rye flour, and salt. Mix well. Gradually add the remaining 3½ cups bread flour, 1 cup at a time. When dough becomes too stiff to stir, transfer to a lightly floured surface and knead until dough is shiny and elastic (about 10 minutes), adding just enough flour to keep dough from sticking to surface.

**4.** Coat a large bowl with olive oil. Transfer dough to bowl and turn to coat with oil. Cover bowl with a dish towel and let stand in a warm place for 45 minutes. Punch dough down and divide in half. Form each half into a round loaf. Scatter cornmeal onto a large, heavy baking sheet. Place dough rounds on sheet. Cover with a towel and let rise in a warm place for 30 minutes.

**5.** Preheat oven to 400° F. Brush tops of loaves with egg yolk. Bake until bread sounds hollow when tapped on the bottom (35 to 40 minutes). Cool loaves completely on a rack before slicing.

*Makes 2 large loaves.*

## FROMAGE DE CHÈVRE MARINÉ
### Marinated goat cheese

An herbed olive oil marinade enhances the flavor of mild goat cheeses. Small 4-ounce rounds of goat cheese are easiest to use in this dish, but you can buy a large log and cut it into smaller pieces for marinating. The soft cheese is delicious with a crusty bread. Note that the cheese needs to marinate at least three hours before serving.

- 1½ pounds soft but sliceable goat cheese, rind removed
- 1 cup olive oil
- 2 tablespoons lemon juice
- 2 teaspoons freshly ground pepper
- 2 bay leaves, broken into pieces
- 5 sprigs thyme
- 2 cloves garlic, peeled and sliced

Cut goat cheese into 4-ounce pieces. In a small bowl whisk together oil, lemon juice, and pepper. Layer goat cheese in a widemouthed canning jar, tucking bay, thyme, and garlic between layers. Pour marinade over and around cheese. Cover and marinate at room temperature for 3 hours, or refrigerate for up to 2 days. Rotate jar occasionally to distribute marinade. Bring to room temperature before serving. To serve, transfer cheese to a serving platter and drizzle with marinade.

*Serves 12.*

*A spring picnic in the Loire Valley might include prune-stuffed pork loin, cucumbers in cream, marinated goat cheese, and fresh cherries.*

*The famous Tarte Tatin—
warm, caramelized apples
on a crisp pastry base—
needs just a dollop of soft-
whipped cream to top it off.*

## DESSERTS

Two of the best-loved pastries in
France—the almond-filled *pithiviers*
and the upside-down apple tart
known as *tarte Tatin*—are native to
the Loire Valley region. Local cooks
also turn the prunes and pears from
their bountiful orchards into simple
yet satisfying desserts.

### PITHIVIERS
**Almond-filled puff pastry cake**

Originally a specialty of the town of
Pithiviers, this delectable cake is now
made in pastry shops all over France.
For many French provincial families,
Sunday wouldn't be Sunday without
a stop at the *pâtisserie* for a *pithiviers*
to take home after Mass. A glass of
Sauternes is delightful with this warm
almond pastry. Note that the cake
should be frozen for at least four
hours before baking.

> ½ cup Crème Anglaise (see
>    page 53), without cinnamon
> 7 ounces almond paste
> 2 large eggs
>    Flour, for dusting
> 2 packages (12.4 oz each)
>    frozen puff pastry, thawed

**1.** To make filling combine Crème
Anglaise, almond paste, and 1 egg in
blender or food processor. Blend until
smooth. Refrigerate 1 hour.

**2.** On a lightly floured surface, roll
each package of puff pastry into a
10-inch circle, about ⅛ inch thick.
Transfer one circle to an ungreased
baking sheet. In a small bowl beat
the remaining egg lightly with a fork.
With a pastry brush, paint a 1-inch
border of beaten egg around edge of
pastry circle on baking sheet. Spread
chilled filling evenly on pastry within
that border. Top with remaining
pastry circle and press edges together
to seal. With a small, sharp knife, cut
5 or 6 long slits in top crust, from the
center almost to the edge. Brush top
with beaten egg. Freeze overnight or
at least 4 hours.

**3.** Preheat oven to 450° F. Transfer
pastry to oven directly from freezer
and bake 15 minutes. Reduce oven
to 400° F and bake until puffy and
golden brown (about 20 minutes
more). Serve warm (not hot) or at
room temperature in wedges; do not
refrigerate. Pithiviers is best the day
it is made.

*Serves 6.*

### PRUNEAUX ET POIRES À LA CRÈME ANGLAISE
**Prunes and pears with cinnamon custard sauce**

Here *crème anglaise*, the classic
French custard sauce, is spiced with
cinnamon and used to top warm
baked fruits. When placed under the
broiler, the custard will brown attractively but it must not be allowed to
get too hot or the sauce will break.
Cold crème anglaise is also delicious
with berries, an unfrosted chocolate
cake, or a steamed pudding.

> 12 large pitted prunes
> 1 cinnamon stick
> 1 cup water
> 2 tablespoons orange liqueur
> 3 very ripe pears, preferably
>    Bosc
> 2 tablespoons unsalted butter,
>    softened

### Crème Anglaise

¼ cup sugar
1 cinnamon stick (3 in. long)
  or 2 teaspoons ground
  cinnamon
½ vanilla bean
1½ cups milk
4 large egg yolks
⅛ teaspoon kosher salt

**1.** In a medium saucepan combine prunes, cinnamon stick, and the water. Bring to a simmer over moderate heat and simmer until liquid evaporates (about 12 minutes). Cool slightly, then add liqueur.

**2.** Preheat broiler. Quarter, core, and peel pears, and slice them lengthwise ¼ inch thick. Spread butter over bottom of a shallow baking dish just large enough to hold prunes and sliced pears in one layer. Arrange pears and prunes in buttered dish. Coat with Crème Anglaise. Broil on uppermost rack until custard browns and bubbles (about 5 minutes). Watch carefully to prevent burning. Serve immediately.

*Serves 6.*

### Crème Anglaise

**1.** *To prepare in a spice grinder:* Combine sugar and cinnamon stick in spice grinder and blend until cinnamon is finely ground. Split vanilla bean and scrape seeds into sugar mixture; pulse to blend. Reserve vanilla pod. *To prepare by hand:* In a small bowl combine sugar, ground cinnamon, and seeds scraped from vanilla bean and stir to blend. Reserve vanilla pod.

**2.** In a medium saucepan combine milk and vanilla pod and bring to a simmer over moderate heat. Cover and remove from heat.

**3.** With an electric mixer or by hand, whisk yolks, spiced sugar, and salt until very thick and pale. Remove vanilla pod from milk and discard. Whisk milk into yolks, then transfer mixture to a clean saucepan and cook over moderately low heat, stirring constantly with a wooden spoon,

until mixture reaches 175° F and is visibly thickened (about 10 minutes). Do not allow mixture to boil. Strain through a sieve into a bowl and cool to room temperature. Cover with plastic wrap and refrigerate. Sauce may be made up to 2 days ahead.

*Serves 6.*

## TARTE TATIN
### Caramelized apple tart

This upside-down apple tart was invented, the story goes, by two spinster sisters who ran their family's Hotel Tatin in the town of Lamotte-Beuvron. Sugared apples go on the bottom and pastry on top. After cooking, the tart is inverted to reveal the softened caramelized apples. Traditionally, the apples are peeled, but a mixture of unpeeled green and red apples makes a pretty rendition.

1½ pounds (5 to 6) apples
  (preferably pippins, Granny
  Smiths, or Jonathans)
¼ cup unsalted butter, plus
  butter for greasing pan
1½ cups sugar
2 tablespoons lemon juice
  Zest of 1 lemon removed with
  lemon zester or grater
½ cup water
  Flour, for dusting
  Whipped cream, sweetened
  lightly (optional)

### Pâte Brisée

1¼ cups flour
1½ tablespoons sugar
  Pinch salt
  Grated zest of ½ lemon
½ cup chilled unsalted butter,
  cut in 8 pieces
1 large egg yolk
2 tablespoons water

**1.** Preheat oven to 425° F. Core apples and cut each into 6 slices.

**2.** In a large skillet over moderate heat, melt butter. Add ½ cup of the sugar, lemon juice, and lemon zest. Add apple slices and stir to coat with butter. Cook, uncovered, for 5 minutes. Remove from heat.

**3.** In a small, heavy saucepan, combine remaining sugar and the water. Cook over moderate heat, without stirring, until sugar turns golden brown. Immediately pour caramel into a greased 9-inch cake pan. Swirl cake pan quickly to coat bottom with caramel.

**4.** Arrange apple slices in neat concentric circles on top of caramel. Any remaining apple slices can be piled randomly on top. Reduce liquid remaining in skillet to ¼ cup and spoon over apples. On a lightly floured surface, roll Pâte Brisée into a circle large enough to cover pie plate and about ⅛ inch thick. Cover apples with pastry. Bake until crust is golden brown (about 25 minutes). Cool pie on a rack 15 minutes. Unmold onto a serving dish. Serve in wedges with cream (if desired).

*Makes one 9-inch tart.*

### Pâte Brisée

**1.** *To make in a food processor:* Combine flour, sugar, salt, and lemon zest in work bowl. Process 2 seconds. Add butter and process until mixture resembles coarse cornmeal. In a separate bowl combine egg yolk and the water. With motor running, add egg mixture through feed tube and process until dough almost forms a ball. Remove from work bowl and gather into a ball with lightly floured hands. *To make by hand:* Stir together flour, sugar, salt, and lemon zest. Cut in butter until mixture resembles coarse crumbs. Combine egg yolk and the water. Add to mixture, tossing gently with a fork to blend. With lightly floured hands, knead mixture just until it forms a ball.

**2.** Pat dough into a 5-inch disk. Cover with plastic wrap and refrigerate up to 3 days or freeze for up to 1 month. Remove from refrigerator 10 minutes before rolling.

*Makes enough pastry for one 9-inch tart.*

*Alsatian cooks work wonders with cabbage and pork; with the local pears and stone fruits, they make tarts, compotes, and fruit brandies.*

# Alsace & Lorraine

Map showing Reims, LORRAINE, Nancy, Strasbourg, ALSACE, with Marne R., Seine R., and Rhine R.

T he delicate, flowery Rieslings and spicy Gewurztraminers of Alsace are the perfect match for the region's fare: creamy quiches with local Munster cheese (see Quiche au Munster, page 56), bowls of hearty split pea soup (see Soupe de Pois Cassés, page 58), and steaming platters of sausage and choucroute (see page 61). All of these rustic favorites are easy to prepare in a home kitchen. For a truly dazzling Christmas feast, treat your family to an Alsatian dinner with its traditional centerpiece: a succulent roast goose robed in apricot glaze (see Oie Rôtie aux Abricots, page 64).

# ALSACE AND LORRAINE

For centuries Alsace and Lorraine were tossed back and forth between France and Germany as spoils of battle. That unsettled history accounts for a strong German influence in the region, especially in Alsace, where the cooking is in many ways more German than French.

Alsatians, like Germans, are avid consumers of cabbage. This hardy vegetable lasts well through the region's rugged winters, when other fresh vegetables are scarce. Alsatian cooks shred it for salads, add it to soups and stews, stuff and braise the leaves, or salt it and allow it to ferment to make their famous choucroute (sauerkraut).

The pig and the goose are the principal food animals, and the frugal Alsatians let almost nothing get away. Pork is eaten both fresh and smoked and is made into a vast array of sausages, hams, and pâtés. Bacon flavors choucroute and is diced and sprinkled atop the Alsatian version of pizza, the *flammekueche* (see right).

The goose, too, is valued for every part, from its fat to its feathers. Alsatians spread goose fat on dark bread or use it to fry potatoes. They enjoy the whole roast bird at Christmas or they cut it up and preserve it in its own fat. But the prize is the unctuous liver, known as foie gras, from specially fattened geese. Sliced, sautéed, and served hot or made into a cold *pâté de foie gras*, it is one of France's greatest culinary delicacies.

The cooking of Lorraine is less recognizably regional than the cooking of Alsace. Whereas Alsace shows the indelible mark of German occupation, Lorraine is more obviously French—a largely rural area of grain fields, fruit orchards, and hog farms. Although it can't claim a major contribution to French gastronomy, Lorraine does get the credit for one of the most popular French dishes in the United States. Quiche Lorraine, a creamy egg-and-bacon tart, may be better known in the United States than abroad.

The orchards of Alsace and Lorraine produce excellent cherries, pears, and plums. What isn't eaten fresh is trucked to the local distillery where it's turned into fragrant eaux-de-vie, clear brandies that capture the essence of the fruit.

Grapes are another major product of Alsatian soil. Riesling, Tokay d'Alsace, Gewurztraminer, and Pinot Blanc are pressed and fermented to make the world-famous white wines that are the best possible match for the region's cuisine. Lorraine's few wines are not well known outside the region, but its beers are enjoyed throughout France. Even better known, perhaps, are two of its mineral waters—Contrexeville and the widely exported Vittel.

## FIRST COURSES

First courses tend to be hearty in Alsace: sturdy soups made from dried peas, creamy cheese custard tarts served in thin slivers, or the irresistible pizza-like specialty known as *flammekueche* (flaming tart).

### QUICHE AU MUNSTER
### *Munster-caraway quiche*

Alsatians often serve caraway seed with their Munster cheese, just one more indication of German influence on the region's table. Here, Munster and caraway are combined in a creamy quiche, a delicious partner to a glass of Gewurztraminer.

- 3 tablespoons unsalted butter
- 1 tablespoon vegetable oil
- 4 large leeks (white part only), minced
- ½ cup whipping cream
- 1½ cups half-and-half
- ½ teaspoon kosher salt
- ½ teaspoon freshly ground pepper
- ¼ teaspoon ground nutmeg
- 4 large eggs
- 1 tablespoon caraway seed
- 1 recipe Pâte Brisée (see page 53), made with 1 teaspoon sugar
  Flour, for dusting
- 1 cup grated Alsatian Munster cheese
- 6 chive stems, for garnish

1. Preheat oven to 350° F. In a large skillet over moderate heat, heat butter and oil. Add leeks and sauté until softened (about 5 minutes). In a medium mixing bowl, stir together cream, half-and-half, salt, pepper, nutmeg, eggs, and half the caraway seed. Whisk to blend.

2. Roll Pâte Brisée to ⅛ inch thick on a lightly floured surface. Line a 10-inch tart tin with dough, trimming away excess. Fill with sautéed leeks. Top with egg-cream mixture. Sprinkle surface with cheese and remaining caraway seed. Arrange chive stems decoratively on top. Place tart on a heavy baking sheet and bake until golden (about 35 minutes). Remove to a rack. Serve warm.

*Serves 8.*

### FLAMMEKUECHE
### *Alsatian bacon and fresh cheese tart*

The *flammekueche*, or "flaming tart," is the Alsatian version of pizza. Throughout the region, you'll find rustic restaurants that make a specialty of the dish. The floppy tarts are brought out from the wood-burning oven on a wooden peel, slid directly onto the table, and devoured while they are almost too hot to handle. Note that the Fromage Blanc needs to chill for 12 hours.

- 1 package active dry yeast
- ½ cup warm (105° F) water
- 4 cups bread flour, plus flour for dusting
- 1½ cups cold water
- 1 tablespoon kosher salt
  Oil, for bowl
- ¼ pound slab bacon, cubed
- 1 tablespoon olive oil
- 1½ cups thinly sliced yellow onion
- 3 tablespoons yellow cornmeal, for dusting pan
- 1 large egg
- 1 tablespoon all-purpose flour
- ¼ cup grated Gruyère cheese
- 2 tablespoons water

#### Fromage Blanc

- ¾ cup whole milk ricotta cheese
- 3 tablespoons plain yogurt
  Pinch of salt

**1.** In a large mixing bowl, combine yeast and the warm water. Let stand 5 minutes. Stir with a fork to blend. Add ½ cup of the bread flour and blend well. Cover and let stand 45 minutes.

**2.** Add the cold water and salt. Begin adding bread flour 1 cup at a time, stirring well after each addition. When dough becomes too stiff to stir, transfer to a lightly floured surface and knead until smooth and shiny (7 to 10 minutes). Place in a lightly oiled bowl and turn to coat dough with oil. Cover and let rise until doubled in bulk, about 1¾ hours.

**3.** In a medium skillet over moderate heat, render bacon in olive oil until bacon fat is melted and bacon is browned. Transfer bacon to a plate with a slotted spoon and add onion to skillet. Sauté until slightly softened (about 5 minutes). Cool to room temperature.

**4.** Preheat oven to 425° F. Dust a pizza stone or heavy baking sheet with cornmeal. Whisk together Fromage Blanc, egg, and the 1 tablespoon flour.

**5.** Punch down dough and roll into as large a circle or rectangle as will fit on the baking sheet. Transfer to prepared baking sheet. Spread with Fromage Blanc mixture to within ¾ inch of edge. Top with onions and rendered bacon and sprinkle with grated cheese. Brush edge of dough with the 2 tablespoons water. Bake until golden brown (15 to 20 minutes). Serve hot from the oven.

*Serves 6.*

**Fromage Blanc**   Combine all ingredients in a blender and blend 30 seconds. Chill 12 hours before using.

*A giant Alsatian flammekueche topped with fresh cheese, bacon, and onions will please all pizza lovers.*

## SOUPE DE POIS CASSÉS
### Split pea soup

Rugged Alsatian winters demand warming fare, such as this hearty pea soup. In Alsace it might be served for a simple family supper, with apples and a slice of Munster cheese for dessert. Note that the dried peas need to soak at least three hours.

- 1½ cups dried split peas
- ¼ cup chicken fat or butter
- 2 cups finely chopped onion
- 1 cup finely chopped carrot
- 1 cup finely chopped celery
- 1 parsnip, peeled and finely chopped
- 8 cups Fond de Volaille (see page 32)
- 1 teaspoon dried thyme
- 3 sprigs parsley
- 2 bay leaves
  Kosher salt and freshly ground pepper
- ½ cup Crème Fraîche (see page 22), for garnish
  Croutons à l'Ail (see page 114), for garnish

**1.** Soak peas in cold water to cover at least 3 hours, or overnight. Drain.

**2.** In a 6-quart stockpot over moderate heat, melt chicken fat. Add onions, carrots, celery, and parsnips. Sauté 5 minutes. Add peas and sauté 3 minutes. Stir in stock, thyme, parsley, and bay leaves. Bring mixture to a boil, then adjust heat to maintain a simmer and cook until peas are quite soft (about 1½ hours). Remove bay leaves.

**3.** Transfer all but 2 cups of the soup to a blender, food processor, or food mill, and purée, in batches if necessary. Return purée to pot with remaining soup. Season to taste with salt and pepper. Reheat to serve. Garnish each serving with a spoonful of Crème Fraîche and a few croutons. Pass extra croutons.

*Makes about 12 cups, 6 main-course servings.*

## MAIN COURSES

Good appetites are required to appreciate the robust fare of Alsace: platters of sauerkraut liberally garnished with pork chops and sausages or smoked fish, plump chickens braised in Riesling, fat sausages simmered in beer or stewed with cabbage and lentils, and grain-stuffed cabbage leaves.

## CHOU ROUGE FARCI
### Stuffed cabbage with grains

Alsatian stuffed cabbage is made with as many different fillings as there are cooks. In this meatless version, a savory mixture of grains and vegetables is rolled up in softened cabbage leaves and braised until tender—just one more example of the regional talent for turning humble ingredients into memorable meals. Begin with a platter of sliced dried sausage and thinly sliced fennel in vinaigrette, and finish with a prune and pear compote (see page 52) for a delectable meal.

- ⅓ cup soft bread crumbs
- 2 medium-sized red cabbages
- ½ cup unsalted butter
- ¼ cup finely minced shallot
- 1½ cups finely minced carrot
- ½ cup long-grain white rice
- ½ cup buckwheat groats
- 4½ cups Fond de Volaille (see page 32)
- 1 cup tomato purée
- 2 teaspoons kosher salt
- 1 teaspoon freshly ground pepper
- 1 cup minced parsley
- 2 tablespoons olive oil
- 2 onions, minced
- 1 cup minced celery
- 3 cups dry white wine
- 2 tablespoons red wine vinegar

**1.** Preheat oven to 350° F. Toast bread crumbs on a baking sheet until lightly browned (about 10 minutes). Set aside.

**2.** Raise oven temperature to 375° F. Remove large outer leaves from cabbage heads. Set aside 12 pretty leaves. Quarter remaining cabbage and core. Shred enough of the cored cabbage to yield 2 cups.

**3.** In a medium saucepan over moderate heat, melt 4 tablespoons of the butter. Add shallot and ½ cup of the carrot and sauté 1 minute. Add shredded cabbage and sauté 3 minutes. Add rice and buckwheat groats. Sauté 2 minutes. Add 2½ cups stock, tomato purée, salt, and pepper. Bring to a boil, then cover, reduce heat to low and cook 15 minutes. Grains will be almost tender. Cool slightly, then stir in ¾ cup of the parsley. Taste and adjust seasoning.

**4.** In a roasting pan or straight-sided skillet just large enough to hold 12 cabbage rolls side by side, heat 2 tablespoons of the butter with olive oil over moderate heat. Add onion, celery, and the remaining 1 cup carrot, and sauté 5 minutes. Add wine and the remaining 2 cups stock and bring to a simmer. Cook 15 minutes, then remove from heat.

**5.** Bring a large pot of salted water to a boil over high heat. Add wine vinegar. Parboil reserved cabbage leaves until slightly softened (about 5 to 7 minutes). Remove with a slotted spoon. When cool enough to handle, cut away the center rib of each leaf to make them easier to roll.

**6.** Place ¼ to ⅓ cup stuffing near bottom of each leaf. Roll up partway, then fold in sides and continue rolling to make a short, plump log. Place seam side down in roasting pan.

**7.** Melt the remaining 2 tablespoons butter and brush over surface of cabbage rolls. Sprinkle with bread crumbs. Cover and bake 15 minutes. Uncover and bake 15 minutes more. Serve piping hot, garnished with remaining parsley.

*Serves 6.*

**Make-Ahead Tip** Recipe may be prepared completely or through step 3 up to 2 days ahead and refrigerated. If made completely ahead, reheat covered in a 375° F oven until hot throughout (about 25 minutes).

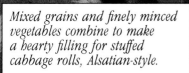
*Mixed grains and finely minced vegetables combine to make a hearty filling for stuffed cabbage rolls, Alsatian-style.*

## CHOUCROUTE AUX POISSONS FUMÉS
### Smoked fish with braised sauerkraut

This modern variation on a classic Alsatian dish uses smoked fish in place of the sausage and pork chops of a traditional choucroute. Choose smoked salmon, trout, or whitefish in any combination, and accompany the dish as the Alsatians do—with dilled mustard, crème fraîche, and a bottle of Riesling.

> 2 ounces salt pork, diced
> 2 tablespoons unsalted butter
> ½ cup minced shallot
> 1 teaspoon quatre-épices (see Note, page 61)
> 2 bay leaves
> ¼ cup plus 1 tablespoon minced fresh dill
> 1 tablespoon minced garlic
> 2 pounds sauerkraut, homemade (see left) or storebought
> 1 cup Fumet de Poisson (see page 33)
> 1 cup dry white wine
> 3 celery hearts, halved
> 3 large carrots, peeled and cut in 2-inch chunks
> 2 large parsnips, peeled and cut in 2-inch chunks
> 1½ pounds mixed smoked fish, cut in 2-ounce pieces
> 1 cup Dijon-style mustard White pepper and cayenne pepper, to taste
> ½ cup Crème Fraîche (see page 22) or sour cream, optional

**1.** In a dutch oven over moderately low heat, render salt pork until browned on all sides. Pour off all but 1 tablespoon of fat and add butter. Add shallot and sauté until softened (about 3 minutes). Add quatre-épices, bay leaves, the 1 tablespoon dill, and garlic and sauté 1 minute. Add sauerkraut, stock, and wine and bring to a simmer. Add celery hearts, carrots, and parsnips; cover, reduce heat to low, and cook 25 minutes. Add fish, cover and simmer an additional 20 minutes.

---

*Special Feature*

## MAKING YOUR OWN SAUERKRAUT

With a large crock and a cool storage place, it's easy to make delectable sauerkraut. A basement or garage is the best place for fermentation, since the fermenting cabbage can give off a strong odor.

> 10 pounds green cabbage, halved, cored, and shredded
> ½ cup plus 4 teaspoons noniodized salt

**1.** Combine 4 cups cabbage and ¼ cup of the salt in a stainless steel bowl. Let stand 1 hour.

**2.** Transfer salted cabbage to a large earthenware crock. Add remaining cabbage and salt in layers, leaving at least 3 to 4 inches of space at top of crock. Put a small plate directly on surface of cabbage, then put a 2-pound weight on the plate. Cover crock well with plastic wrap, making sure it is sealed tightly.

**3.** Set crock in a cool, dark place, no warmer than 68° F. Cabbage will begin to ferment after 7 to 10 days. Allow it to ferment 4 to 6 weeks.

**4.** Transfer fermented cabbage and any liquid to a large stockpot. Bring to a simmer over moderately high heat. Pack sauerkraut into sterilized canning jars and cover with a little juice. Cover with lids and rings and process in a boiling water bath for 20 minutes. Store sauerkraut in a cool place for up to 1 year.

*Makes 4 quarts.*

**2.** Combine 2 tablespoons of the remaining dill and mustard; place in a small serving bowl. Let stand 20 minutes to allow flavors to mingle, then season to taste with white pepper and cayenne pepper. Transfer sauerkraut and fish to a warm serving platter. Garnish with the remaining 2 tablespoons dill. Serve immediately with dilled mustard sauce and Crème Fraîche (if desired).

*Serves 6.*

**Make-Ahead Tip**    This dish may be made up to 2 days in advance and refrigerated.

*Note*    Quatre-épices is a blend of four spices (usually nutmeg, clove, black pepper, and cinnamon). It is available in most supermarkets.

## CHOUCROUTE GARNIE À L'ALSACIENNE
### Sauerkraut with pork chops, ham hocks, and sausages

The most famous Alsatian dish is undoubtedly *choucroute garnie*, a mountainous platter of well-seasoned sauerkraut topped with sausages and pork products of all kinds. Boiled potatoes can be tucked into the casserole for the final 15 minutes to heat through, or they can be cooked separately and arrayed on the platter when the choucroute is served. Beer or a dry Riesling is the traditional accompaniment to this hearty dish.

> 2 *tablespoons corn oil*
> 2 *tablespoons butter*
> 3 *meaty smoked ham hocks*
> 2 *onions, chopped*
> 2 *bay leaves*
> 1 *tablespoon juniper berries*
> 2 *teaspoons quatre-épices (see Note, above)*
> 2 *pounds sauerkraut, homemade (see page 60) or storebought*
> 2 *pounds pork loin chops*
> 2 *cups Fond de Volaille (see page 32)*
> ½ *cup dry white wine*
> 2 *pounds smoked garlic sausage links*
>    *White pepper*
> 3 *tablespoons minced parsley, for garnish*

**1.** In a dutch oven over moderate heat, heat oil and butter. Add ham hocks and brown on both sides. Transfer hocks to a plate. Add onions to dutch oven and sauté until slightly softened (about 5 minutes). Add bay leaves, juniper berries, and quatre-épices. Cook 1 minute, then add sauerkraut. Bury pork chops and ham hocks in sauerkraut and add stock and wine. Bring to a simmer, cover, and reduce heat to maintain a simmer. Cook 45 minutes.

**2.** Add sausages and cook until chops are tender (about 1 more hour). Season to taste with pepper. Transfer sauerkraut to a warm platter; top with meats and garnish with parsley. Serve immediately.

*Serves 6.*

**Make-Ahead Tip**    This dish may be made up to 2 days in advance, covered and refrigerated, and reheated just before serving.

## SAUCISSONS À LA BIÈRE
### Sausages and onions in beer

You can use either links of about 5 to 6 ounces each or a long sausage cut into sections. Serve piping hot with strong mustard, boiled potatoes, and mugs of beer.

> 5 *tablespoons unsalted butter*
> 6 *cups thinly sliced onions*
> 1 *teaspoon coarsely ground pepper*
> 12 *ounces beer*
> 2 *pounds smoked pork sausages, cut in 6 portions*
> 3 *tablespoons minced parsley, for garnish*

In a large skillet over moderate heat, melt butter. Add onions and sauté 5 minutes. Add pepper and beer. Bring to a simmer, then cover and reduce heat to low. Simmer 15 minutes. Bury sausages in onions. Cover and cook until sausages are hot throughout (about 15 more minutes). Transfer to a warm platter or individual plates and garnish with parsley.

*Serves 6.*

## POULET AU RIESLING
### Chicken in Riesling

The local Riesling makes an ideal braising liquid for the plump farm chickens of Alsace. The wine tenderizes and flavors the birds during cooking. When the chicken is done, the flavorful pan juices are thickened with cream to make a quick pan sauce. Nouilles à l'Alsacienne (see page 64) would be a delicious accompaniment.

> 2 *small chickens (about 3 lb each), quartered*
> ¼ *cup lemon juice*
> 1½ *teaspoons kosher salt*
> 1 *teaspoon ground pepper*
> 4 *tablespoons unsalted butter*
> 1 *tablespoon corn oil*
> ¼ *cup minced shallot*
> 1 *cup Riesling*
> ½ *cup Fond de Volaille (see page 32)*
> ¼ *cup whipping cream*
> ¼ *cup finely minced green onion*

**1.** Sprinkle chicken with lemon juice. Season with salt and pepper. Let marinate at room temperature 20 minutes.

**2.** In a dutch oven over moderately high heat, melt 2 tablespoons of the butter with corn oil. Brown chicken pieces on all sides, transferring to a plate as they are browned.

**3.** Reduce heat to moderate; pour off fat in pan, then add the remaining butter. Add shallot and sauté until softened (about 3 minutes). Add ¾ cup of the wine and stock. Bring to a simmer and cook until liquid is reduced by half (about 10 minutes). Return chicken to pan, cover, and simmer until juices run clear when chicken is pierced with a knife (about 20 minutes).

**4.** Transfer chicken to a warm platter. Raise heat to high and add the remaining wine to pan; whisk to scrape up any meaty bits clinging to bottom of the pan. Add cream and 2 tablespoons green onion and cook, whisking, until thickened (2 to 3 minutes). Season to taste with salt and pepper. Spoon sauce over chicken. Garnish with remaining green onion. Serve immediately.

*Serves 6.*

## RAGOÛT DE PORC AUX LENTILLES ET AU CHOU VERT
### Lentil, cabbage, and smoked pork stew

To keep their families well fed through the long Alsatian winters, the region's cooks depend on hearty stews made from ingredients that can be stored for a long time. The following recipe is just one example, a rustic one-dish dinner that needs only good beer and fresh fruit for dessert to make it a meal.

1   tablespoon unsalted butter
2   tablespoons olive oil
2   cups leeks (white part only), cut in ½-inch lengths
1   tablespoon minced garlic
1   cup dried lentils
1½  pounds smoked pork butt, cut in 2½-inch cubes
6   cups coarsely shredded green cabbage
2   cups Fond de Volaille (see page 32)
1   cup dry white wine
1   teaspoon kosher salt
1½  teaspoons freshly ground pepper
1   bay leaf

In a large, straight-sided skillet over moderate heat, heat butter and olive oil. Add leeks and sauté 3 minutes. Add garlic and sauté 2 minutes. Add lentils and cook 1 minute. Add pork and sauté until browned (about 5 minutes). Add cabbage, stock, wine, salt, pepper, and bay leaf. Bring to a simmer, then reduce heat to maintain a simmer, cover, and cook until lentils are very tender (about 1½ hours). Liquid will be mostly absorbed. Serve in a large, rustic, round dish.

*Serves 6.*

**Make-Ahead Tip**   Stew may be made up to 2 days ahead and refrigerated. Reheat on top of the stove or in the oven at moderate heat.

## DESSERTS

The fruits of Alsace and Lorraine inspire cooks to create all manner of luscious desserts—tarts of dark purple plums, compotes of firm cherries, even sorbets made from the local Gewurztraminer wine.

## BABAS AUX CERISES
### Yeast-risen cakes with cherry compote

The baba, which is Polish in origin, first took root in France in the Lorraine region, which was ruled by the Polish court from 1737 until 1766. Traditionally, the baba is studded with raisins and soaked in rum syrup; this variation substitutes a wine syrup and pairs the spongy golden cakes with a sweet cherry compote.

1½  packages active dry yeast
½   cup plus 1 teaspoon sugar
2   tablespoons warm water (105° to 115° F)
¼   cup lukewarm milk (90° F)
½   teaspoon kosher salt
2   large eggs, lightly beaten
¼   cup unsalted butter, softened, plus butter for greasing
1   cup all-purpose flour, plus flour for kneading
¾   cup sweet white wine
¾   cup water
1   cinnamon stick (3 in. long) Whipped cream, sweetened lightly (optional)

### Cherry Compote

2   tablespoons lemon juice
½   cup Riesling
½   cup water
½   cup sugar
½   teaspoon cinnamon
¼   teaspoon nutmeg
1   pound ripe cherries, stems attached
1   tablespoon kirsch
1   teaspoon vanilla extract

**1.** In a medium bowl sprinkle yeast and the 1 teaspoon sugar over the warm water. Stir with a fork to dissolve yeast. Add milk, salt, eggs, and butter. Mix well. Gradually add the 1 cup flour, stirring until well blended. Turn out onto a lightly floured surface and knead gently for 5 minutes, adding enough flour to keep dough from sticking. Dough will become shiny and elastic.

**2.** Transfer dough to a buttered bowl and turn to coat with butter; cover and let rest 10 minutes. Punch dough down and let stand 10 minutes more.

**3.** Generously butter a muffin tin or individual baba molds. Divide dough into 6 pieces and roll each piece into a ball. Place balls in muffin tins or baba molds. Cover with a clean dish towel and let rise until dough just reaches edges of molds (about 35 minutes).

**4.** Preheat oven to 400° F. Bake babas until they are golden brown and sound hollow when tapped on bottom (12 to 15 minutes). Invert babas onto a rack and allow to cool 15 minutes.

**5.** In a small saucepan combine wine, the ¾ cup water, the remaining ½ cup sugar, and cinnamon stick. Bring to a simmer over high heat, reduce heat to maintain a simmer, and cook 3 minutes. Prick babas in several places with a sharp fork or skewer. Dip babas, one at a time, into syrup, turn to coat with syrup, then return to rack. To serve, place babas on dessert plates and spoon Cherry Compote over and around. Garnish with cream (if desired).

*Serves 6.*

**Cherry Compote**   In a medium saucepan combine lemon juice, Riesling, the water, sugar, cinnamon, and nutmeg. Bring to a simmer over moderate heat. Add cherries and simmer 5 minutes. Remove from heat and let cool. Stir in kirsch and vanilla. Compote may be made 2 days in advance and refrigerated. Rewarm before serving.

*Makes about 4 cups.*

## SORBET AU GEWURZTRAMINER
### Gewurztraminer sorbet

Serve after a rich Choucroute Garnie (see page 61) or, in summer, with sliced and sugared peaches in place of grapes.

- *1 cup sugar*
- *2 cups water*
- *2 cups Gewürztraminer*
- *6 small grape clusters, for garnish*

Combine sugar and water in a small saucepan. Bring to a boil over high heat, reduce heat to maintain a simmer, and cook 5 minutes. Cool to room temperature. Stir in wine. Refrigerate 2 hours. Transfer to an ice cream freezer and freeze according to manufacturer's directions. Garnish each serving with a cluster of grapes.

*Makes about 4 cups, 6 servings.*

## TARTE AUX QUETSCHES
### Plum tart

The French use the small purple plums known as *quetsches* for this tart, but any firm, ripe plums will do.

- *1 recipe Pâte Brisée (see page 53) Flour, for dusting*
- *2 pounds ripe plums*
- *½ cup Crème Fraîche (see page 22)*
- *½ cup confectioners' sugar*
- *2 teaspoons cinnamon*
- *2 tablespoons granulated sugar*

**1.** Roll dough out on a lightly floured surface. Transfer to a 10-inch tart tin, trimming away excess. Prick all over with a fork and chill 30 minutes.

**2.** Preheat oven to 375° F. Halve plums, remove pits, then halve again. Spread Crème Fraîche evenly over bottom of tart shell. Arrange plum sections over Crème Fraîche in concentric circles, skin side down. Sprinkle with confectioners' sugar. Bake until sugar browns and Crème Fraîche bubbles slightly (20 to 25 minutes). Remove to a rack and cool 30 minutes. Serve with cinnamon and granulated sugar sprinkled on tart.

*Serves 8.*

---

*menu*

### AN ALSATIAN CHRISTMAS

*Consommé aux Quenelles de Foie*

*Oie Rôtie aux Abricots*

*Nouilles à l'Alsacienne*

*Salade d'Endives (Endive Salad)*

*Kugelhopf*

*Fruits d'Hiver au Kirsch (Fruits With Kirsch)*

*Burgundy and Kirsch*

---

*At Christmastime, the French pull out all the gastronomic stops. Even the most frugal cooks allow themselves an extravagance—a bottle of Champagne, a tiny truffle to flavor the chicken, or a coveted pastry from the local shop. In Alsace, the indulgence is likely to take the shape of a fat roast goose. In this menu, the goose is preceded by consommé with homemade dumplings and followed by an endive salad dressed with vinaigrette. With the regal, golden Kugelhopf, offer sliced ripe pears or oranges sprinkled with kirsch. Serve the Burgundy with the main course and kirsch with dessert. Menu serves eight.*

---

## CONSOMMÉ AUX QUENELLES DE FOIE
### Consommé with liver and herb dumplings

Delicate liver dumplings may be served in clear consommé or on a mound of Choucroute Garnie (see page 61).

- *3 tablespoons unsalted butter*
- *1 pound pork liver, in one piece*
- *1½ cups soft bread crumbs*
- *4 large eggs plus 2 whites*
- *1¾ cups half-and-half*
- *2 tablespoons minced garlic*
- *¼ cup minced parsley*
- *1 tablespoon minced fresh sage leaves*
- *2 teaspoons kosher salt*
- *1 teaspoon freshly ground pepper*
- *8 cups Fond de Volaille (see page 32)*

**1.** In a medium skillet over moderate heat, melt butter. Brown liver on both sides (about 5 minutes each side). Cool slightly, then mince finely.

**2.** Combine bread crumbs, whole eggs, and half-and-half and let stand 10 minutes. Stir in garlic, parsley, sage, liver, salt, and pepper.

**3.** Using two spoons, form mixture into 1-inch balls. In a medium pot over high heat, bring 4 cups of the stock to a boil, then reduce heat to maintain a simmer. Add dumplings and poach 12 minutes. Transfer with a slotted spoon to a tray. Add the remaining stock to pot and bring to a simmer. Beat egg whites until frothy and add to pot. Simmer 5 minutes. Strain stock through a double thickness of damp cheesecloth. Season to taste with salt and pepper.

**4.** To serve, bring consommé to a bare simmer; add dumplings and cook until hot, about 2 minutes.

*Makes about 8 cups, 8 servings.*

**Make-Ahead Tip** Dumplings may be poached up to 6 hours in advance. Cover and refrigerate, but bring to room temperature before reheating. Consommé may be prepared through step 3 up to 2 days in advance.

## OIE RÔTIE AUX ABRICOTS
### Roast goose with apricots

Tart fruit flavors complement the rich, sweet meat of goose. Here, minced apricots and apple help to flavor the bird from the inside, and a winy apricot glaze caramelizes and colors the skin.

- 1½ cups dried apricots, minced
- 1½ cups Riesling
- 2 tablespoons unsalted butter
- 3 tablespoons minced shallot
- 1 goose (about 10 lb)
  Kosher salt and freshly ground pepper
- 1 unpeeled red apple, quartered, cored, and coarsely grated
- ¾ cup minced onion

**1.** Preheat oven to 375° F. Combine apricots and Riesling in a saucepan. Bring to a simmer over low heat.

**2.** In a small sauté pan over moderate heat, melt 1 tablespoon of the butter. Add shallot and sauté 3 minutes. Add to apricots.

**3.** Wash goose inside and out, and pat dry. Season with salt and pepper. Combine apple, onion, and ¼ cup apricot mixture. Spoon mixture inside goose. Tie legs together with kitchen string. Tuck wings under breasts. Prick goose all over with a fork. Place on rack in roasting pan. Rub lightly all over with the remaining 1 tablespoon butter and baste with apricot mixture.

**4.** Add one inch of water to roasting pan and transfer to oven. Roast 1 hour and 10 minutes, basting with apricot mixture every 20 minutes and turning the goose to brown on all sides. At the end of the cooking time, goose should be golden brown and legs should move freely. Remove from oven but keep on rack. Using a sharp knife, make a slit at each wing joint and allow fat to drain off. Remove string, cut goose into serving pieces, and transfer to a warm platter.

*Serves 8.*

## NOUILLES À L' ALSACIENNE
### Alsatian poppy seed noodles

Fresh noodles are popular in Alsace and are often made at home. The presence of poppy seeds in the sauce marks this as a dish unlikely to be found outside the region.

- 6 tablespoons unsalted butter
- 2 heaping tablespoons Dijon-style mustard
- 4 tablespoons Crème Fraîche (see page 22) or whipping cream
- 2 tablespoons poppy seed
  Kosher salt and freshly ground pepper
- 2 pounds fresh or dried fettuccine

**1.** In a 12-inch skillet over moderately low heat, melt butter. Add mustard and whisk to blend. Whisk in Crème Fraîche, 1 tablespoon plus 1 teaspoon poppy seed, and salt and pepper to taste. Bring to a simmer and cook until well blended and slightly thickened (about 1 minute). Remove from heat.

**2.** Bring a large pot of salted water to a boil over high heat. Add noodles and cook until just tender; drain. Add noodles to mustard sauce and stir to coat. Return skillet to moderately high heat and cook, stirring constantly, until hot throughout (about 1 minute). Transfer to a warm platter and top with the remaining poppy seed. Serve immediately.

*Serves 8.*

## KUGELHOPF
### Sweet Alsatian yeast bread

The rich *Kugelhopf* is a special-occasion bread, served after dinner with a fluff of whipped cream or toasted for breakfast. Note that the bread needs to rise for over 2 hours.

- ½ cup golden raisins
- ¼ cup Cognac
- 1 package active dry yeast
- ⅓ cup warm water (105° F)
- ⅓ cup buttermilk
- 3 large eggs
- ½ cup unsalted butter, softened, plus butter for greasing
- ¼ cup confectioners' sugar
- 1½ teaspoons kosher salt
- 4¼ cups (approximately) all-purpose flour
- ½ cup whole almonds

**1.** Soak raisins in Cognac until all liquid is absorbed (about 30 minutes). In a large bowl dissolve yeast in the warm water and let stand 5 minutes. Add buttermilk and eggs. Mix well. Add butter and beat well. Add sugar, salt, and raisins.

**2.** Add flour 1 cup at a time, beating well after each addition. When dough leaves sides of bowl, transfer to a lightly floured surface; knead, adding flour as necessary to keep dough from sticking, until dough is smooth and silky (about 10 minutes). Place in a lightly buttered bowl and coat all sides with butter. Cover and let rise in a warm place until doubled in bulk (about 1½ hours).

**3.** Punch dough down. Generously butter an 8-inch Kugelhopf or bundt pan. Scatter almonds in bottom of pan. Roll dough into a ball and use your thumb to make a hole in the center. Place dough in pan. Let rise, covered, until dough reaches top of pan (about 45 minutes).

**4.** Preheat oven to 350° F. Bake Kugelhopf until golden brown (about 45 minutes). Cool in pan on rack 10 minutes, then remove from pan and finish cooling on rack.

*Serves 8.*

*Celebrate Christmas with an Alsatian dinner of roast goose and poppy seed noodles, followed by winter fruit and an almond-studded Kugelhopf.*

*Snails in garlic butter (see page 70) and beef in Burgundy wine (see page 74) are two of the dishes that have earned renown for the cooking of Burgundy.*

# Burgundy

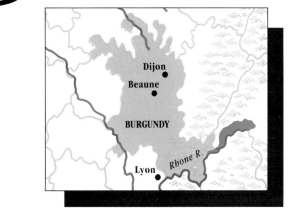

T he cooking of Burgundy marks it as a region where wine holds sway. The province's best-known dishes— Boeuf Bourguignon (see page 74) and Coq au Vin (see page 77)—depend on a well-made wine for their deep, rich flavor. Other wine-inspired Burgundian dishes include the feather-light cheese puff called Gougère (see page 68) and a quick and refreshing dessert of fresh peaches in Beaujolais (see Pêches au Beaujolais, page 77). The Bistro Menu on page 72 features time-honored favorites from Burgundy's neighborhood restaurants.

## BURGUNDY

It is hard to know whether Burgundy's wine shaped the region's cuisine or vice versa. Either way, it's clear that the two are perfect for each other: There's no better match for red Burgundy than the region's famous Charolais beef, no better partner for Morvan ham than a rich white Burgundy.

Wine is used generously in Burgundian stews, such as the famous Coq au Vin (see page 77) and Boeuf Bourguignon (see page 74). It inspires such creations as Gougère (see right), an aromatic cheese puff that flatters red wine. In Burgundy, wine even stars at dessert, when a waiter slices a ripe peach into the last of a glass of Beaujolais (see page 77).

Plump snails are another famous product of Burgundian soil. After being laboriously washed and cooked, the snails are typically tucked back into their shells with a pungent blend of butter, parsley, and garlic, then baked. Fortunately, canned snails make such dishes easy. Combined with garlicky white beans and baked with bread crumbs (see page 70), snails make a delicious first course.

Any springtime visitor to Burgundy will see fields carpeted with mustard flowers, the pretty precursors of one of the region's most important products. The mustard made in the city of Dijon is exported worldwide and is fundamental to the region's cuisine. Vinaigrettes and marinades are seasoned with mustard; rabbits and chickens are rubbed with mustard before roasting. Some bakers even add dry mustard to the famous spice bread of the area (see page 77).

Burgundy provides a striking contrast to the visible wealth of Bordeaux, the other famous wine-producing region of France. Although there are well-to-do Burgundian wine shippers, many of the most prestigious vineyards are broken up into tiny parcels tended by middle-class farming families. The stereotypical Burgundian winemaker is a hardworking, salt-of-the-earth farmer whose simple tastes explain the unpretentious nature of most Burgundian cooking.

## HORS D'OEUVRES AND SALADS

First courses in Burgundy can be as old-fashioned as a slice of coarse-textured country pâté (see page 70) or as new and creative as a combination of white beans and snails (see page 70).

### GOUGÈRE
### *Burgundy cheese puff*

Red Burgundy wine and cheese are a match made in heaven, and Burgundian winemakers know it. When buyers stop to taste the wines, the savvy vineyard owner sets out a portion of this crusty cheese puff.

- ½  cup unsalted butter
- ¾  cup water
- ¾  cup plus 2 tablespoons milk
- 1  teaspoon kosher salt
- 1  teaspoon freshly ground pepper
- ½  teaspoon cayenne pepper
- ½  teaspoon nutmeg
- 2  cups flour
- 5  large eggs
- 1  cup finely grated Gruyère cheese
- 1  tablespoon Dijon-style mustard

**1.** Preheat oven to 400° F. In a medium saucepan combine 7 tablespoons of the butter, the water, the ¾ cup milk, salt, pepper, cayenne, and nutmeg. Bring to a boil over moderately high heat. Remove saucepan from heat and add flour all at once. Stir with a wooden spoon until smooth. Add eggs, one at a time, beating well after each addition. Stir in ¾ cup of the cheese.

**2.** Butter a heavy baking sheet with the remaining 1 tablespoon butter. Drop rounded tablespoons of dough onto sheet in the shape of a wreath; the mounds should be barely touching. Whisk together mustard and the 2 tablespoons milk. Brush each mound with mustard glaze. Sprinkle with the remaining ¼ cup cheese. Bake 30 minutes, then turn oven off and leave Gougère in oven 5 minutes. Transfer to a rack to cool slightly. Serve warm.

*Serves 6.*

## A TREASURY OF FRENCH WINES

In the centuries since grapes were first introduced to Gaul (ancient France) by the Romans, the French have refined their wine-making techniques, learning which grapes thrive in which areas. Today, the best wine-growing areas of France are clearly defined. Each produces wine in a distinctive style; to a connoisseur, a red Burgundy is as different from a red Bordeaux as a watermelon is from a cantaloupe.

The following is a guide to the major French wine regions. Knowing what style to expect from each region should make buying wine easier; and knowing what foods are compatible with each style should increase your enjoyment of French wines at home.

**Alsace**  The Riesling, Tokay, and Gewurztraminer grapes dominate in Alsace, yielding dry, aromatic white wines. The Riesling is the most delicate; it makes a delicious apéritif. The Tokay, which is more full-bodied, flatters ham, fish, and chicken. Alsatian Gewurztraminer can have a powerful aroma of rose petals and a spicy flavor; try it with roast pork, pork chops, ham, or quiche. A small amount of Pinot Noir is made in Alsace but is not widely exported.

**Beaujolais**  Some consider this region part of Burgundy, but Beaujolais merits a separate consideration because its wines are made from a different grape: the Gamay. The grape and unusual wine-making techniques produce a very fruity, short-lived red wine to enjoy with hors d'oeuvres, vegetable dishes, sausage of all kinds, and grilled chicken.

**Bordeaux**  The best-known wines of the Bordeaux region are red, made primarily from Cabernet Sauvignon and Merlot grapes. Cabernet Franc, Malbec, and Petit Verdot may be added in varying proportions. The best red Bordeaux are elegant wines. Although they can be tannic and hard to like when young, with age they soften and develop a seductive perfume. These are excellent wines to accompany roast lamb or beef.

White Bordeaux wines may be sweet or dry. The best dry whites come from the Graves district and are made from Sauvignon Blanc and Sémillon grapes. They are good wines but rarely great; enjoy them with simple fish dishes. The sweet white wines, however, can be magnificent. The best is Sauternes, a honeyed wine with an aroma of apricots and peaches. Sauternes can be served alone for dessert or paired with apricots, cherries, pears, figs, a fruit tart, or a plain cake.

**Burgundy** This region produces some of the most sought-after and expensive wines of France. Production is often extremely limited. The northernmost part of Burgundy includes the region of Chablis, famous for dry, steely white wines that go well with shellfish. Chablis wines are made from the Chardonnay grape.

Pinot Noir is the grape responsible for red Burgundies. These wines are fruity when young, with the fresh aroma of raspberries and cherries. As they age, they typically develop a more earthy bouquet. Red Burgundy is delicious with game, roast chicken, duck, mushroom dishes, and creamy cheeses such as Camembert and Brie.

White Burgundies, made from the Chardonnay grape, have a rich, creamy texture and an aroma that may be slightly smoky or nutty. They pair well with mushroom dishes, chicken or fish in cream sauce, ham, and pâtés.

**Champagne** The sparkling wines made in this region from the Pinot Noir, Chardonnay, and Pinot Meunier grapes are the most famous sparkling wines in the world. Each producer has a different style: Some Champagnes are lean and crisp; others are full-bodied, rich, and toasty. The lighter ones make excellent apéritifs

and partners for shellfish; the fuller-bodied Champagnes are delicious with pâté, ham, and chicken.

**Loire Valley** This river valley produces charming wines, both red and white. At the western end, the Muscadet grape yields a light, very dry white wine that goes well with oysters and mussels. The Chenin Blanc grape comes to the fore as one travels east; on the bottle, look for such names as Savennières, Vouvray, and Anjou. These fresh and highly scented white wines are delicious with salmon, trout, and pork. Farther east, the white grape of choice is the Sauvignon Blanc; the crisp wines made from it, such as Pouilly-Fumé and Sancerre, are excellent partners for grilled fish and goat cheese.

The best-known Loire Valley reds are made from the Cabernet Franc

grape and bear the names Chinon and Bourgeuil. These delicate, fruity wines are best drunk young and slightly cool; they flatter pork, goat cheese, and chicken.

**Rhône** The Rhône region is best known for its full-bodied, peppery red wines. The Syrah grape predominates, but Rhône wines may be made from as many as 13 different grapes. Côtes-du-Rhône, Châteauneuf-du-Pape, Hermitage, and Côte Rôtie are among the better-known names. Try them with roast or grilled lamb well seasoned with garlic and herbs. White Rhône wines are generally full-bodied and suited to grilled fish or spicy shellfish preparations.

**Other regions** Although exported in smaller quantities, the rosé wines of Provence, the sturdy red wines of Cahors and the Languedoc, and the delicate whites of Savoy and Jura are worth seeking out. They are uncomplicated wines for casual meals.

## PÂTÉ DE CAMPAGNE
### Country pâté

Caul fat, the lacy white membrane that surrounds a pig's stomach, is often used in France to line pâté molds. The caul keeps the pâté moist and gives the finished dish an attractive appearance. The following coarse country pâté makes an excellent do-ahead first course for a large dinner party or buffet; leftovers will keep for one week and make delicious sandwiches. Note that the pâté needs to be started three days ahead.

- 1 veal breast (about 2 lb)
- 2½ pounds boneless pork butt, cut in 1-inch cubes
- ¼ pound salt pork, rinsed and coarsely chopped
- ¼ pound chicken liver
- 1½ pounds onion
- ½ cup dry white wine
- ¼ cup Cognac or brandy
- 3 eggs, lightly beaten
- ½ teaspoon ground cloves
- 2 teaspoons kosher salt
- 2 teaspoons freshly ground pepper
- 2 teaspoons minced fresh thyme
- ½ teaspoon nutmeg
- ½ pound caul fat (optional; see Note)
- 2 bay leaves
- 1 heart of butter lettuce Cornichons (at right), for garnish

**1.** Cut veal away from bones and reserve bones for stock (see page 33). Cut veal into small pieces. In a food processor or meat grinder fitted with a medium blade, coarsely grind veal, pork butt, and salt pork, in batches as necessary. Transfer to a large bowl. Purée or grind livers and add to meat. Chop onions very fine in food processor or by hand and add to bowl along with wine, Cognac, eggs, cloves, salt, pepper, thyme, and nutmeg. Mix lightly but well. Cover and refrigerate 24 hours.

**2.** Preheat oven to 350° F. Line two 5- by 9-inch loaf pans with caul fat (if using), trimming caul fat so that it hangs over edges of pan by about 3 inches. Divide pâté mixture between pans. Top each with a bay leaf. Fold caul fat over top. If not using caul fat, simply divide mixture between pans and top each with a bay leaf.

**3.** Cover pans with aluminum foil. Using a sharp knife, cut 4 slits in each foil top to allow steam to escape. Set both pans in a large roasting pan and place in oven. Add boiling water to come 2 inches up sides of pans. Bake 1 hour and 35 minutes. Remove from oven and cool on racks. Refrigerate when cool.

**4.** When pâtés are thoroughly chilled, unmold and cover with plastic wrap. Set pâtés on a baking sheet and top with another baking sheet or a cutting board. Set about 2 pounds of weights on top (canned foods or a bowl filled with rice or beans work well). Refrigerate 36 to 48 hours. To serve, arrange a pale green lettuce leaf on each serving plate. Top with a ⅓-inch-thick slice of pâté and garnish each portion with 2 Cornichons.

*Makes two 9-inch loaves.*

*Note* Caul fat is available from some French markets and specialty butchers. It may need to be ordered several days ahead.

## CORNICHONS
### Tarragon-flavored cucumber pickles

These tiny, nonsweet pickles are the traditional accompaniment to all kinds of pâté. Note that Cornichons should cure at least three weeks before serving.

- 3 pounds tiny pickling cucumbers (about 1½ in. long)
- ⅔ cup kosher salt
- 16 whole cloves
- 1 medium onion, peeled and quartered
- 2 ounces tarragon sprigs
- 1 cup loosely packed fresh dill
- 8 teaspoons mustard seed
- 8 teaspoons black peppercorns
- 8 shallots, peeled and halved
- 6 cups (approximately) white wine vinegar

**1.** Rub cucumbers with a moist paper towel, being careful not to damage skin. Place in a large glass bowl and add salt. Toss with your hands to distribute salt evenly. Cover bowl with plastic wrap and let stand in a cool spot for 12 hours. Transfer cucumbers to a sieve or colander and rinse well with cold water.

**2.** Put 4 cloves in each onion quarter, then put an onion quarter in each of 4 sterilized pint jars. Layer cucumbers, tarragon, and dill in each jar, dividing them equally among the jars. Add 2 teaspoons mustard seed, 2 teaspoons peppercorns, and 2 halved shallots to each jar. Add white wine vinegar to cover cucumbers by at least 2 inches. Cover with airtight lids and store in a cool place for at least 3 weeks or up to 3 months. Refrigerate jars after opening.

*Makes four 1-pint jars.*

## GRATIN DE HARICOTS AUX ESCARGOTS
### Casserole of white beans and snails

Delicate *petit gris* (small gray) snails are raised in California and can be found in cans in specialty stores. Larger imported Burgundian snails are also fine for this recipe. Note that the beans need to soak overnight.

- 2 cups dried Great Northern white beans
- 1½ teaspoons kosher salt, plus salt to taste
- 1 carrot, peeled and coarsely cut up
- 1 bay leaf
- 1 small onion, peeled and halved
- 1 teaspoon dried thyme
- 13 tablespoons unsalted butter
- ¼ cup minced garlic
- 2 shallots, minced
- 2 cans (7¼ oz each) petit gris snails
- ½ cup minced parsley
- ¼ cup lemon juice
- 2 teaspoons freshly ground pepper
- ¾ cup bread crumbs, made from day-old bread

**1.** Soak beans overnight in water to cover. Drain and place beans in a medium stockpot with 5 cups fresh water. Add the 1½ teaspoons salt, carrot, bay leaf, onion, and thyme. Bring to a boil over moderate heat, reduce heat to maintain a simmer, and cook until beans are tender (about 1½ hours). Drain beans and discard carrot, bay leaf, and onion.

**2.** Preheat oven to 375° F. In a large saucepan over moderate heat, melt 8 tablespoons of the butter. Add garlic and shallots and sauté 3 minutes. Add snails and sauté 2 minutes. Add drained beans and reduce heat to moderately low. Cook until beans are warm throughout (about 3 minutes). Stir in parsley and lemon juice. Add pepper and season to taste with salt.

**3.** Using 2 tablespoons of the butter, butter six 1-cup soufflé dishes. Divide bean-snail mixture evenly among dishes. Top each dish with 2 tablespoons bread crumbs. Dot each with ½ tablespoon butter. Bake until bread crumbs are lightly browned (12 to 15 minutes).

*Serves 6.*

**Make-Ahead Tip**  Beans may be cooked through step 1 up to 3 days ahead and refrigerated. Store beans in their cooking liquid; drain before proceeding with recipe.

## SALADE DE LENTILLES AU JAMBON
### Lentil salad with sliced ham

Lentils are a popular side dish with Burgundy's famous hams and pork products. *Petit salé aux lentilles* (salt pork with lentils) is a bistro classic. This variation pairs cold marinated lentils with thin-sliced ham.

    2  cups dried lentils
    1  onion, quartered
    1  bay leaf
    1  carrot, cut in 2-inch chunks
    3  sprigs parsley
    8  cups water
    2  teaspoons kosher salt, plus
       salt to taste
    1  tablespoon minced garlic
    1  tablespoon Dijon-style
       mustard
    ¼  cup red wine vinegar
    ¾  cup olive oil
       Freshly ground pepper
    1  cup diced red onion
    ¾  cup grated carrot
    2  tablespoons minced parsley
    1½ pounds best-quality ham,
       thinly sliced
    3  tablespoons minced chives,
       for garnish

**1.** In a large saucepan combine lentils, onion, bay leaf, carrot, parsley, the water, and 2 teaspoons salt. Bring to a simmer over moderate heat, then reduce heat to maintain a simmer and cook until lentils are just tender (about 35 minutes). Cool to room temperature, then discard onion, bay leaf, carrots, and parsley. Drain lentils.

**2.** In a small bowl whisk together garlic, mustard, and red wine vinegar. Slowly whisk in olive oil. Add salt and pepper to taste. Place drained lentils in another bowl. Add red onion, grated carrot, minced parsley, and vinaigrette. Toss gently to blend.

**3.** To serve, arrange slices of ham along one side of a serving platter. Arrange lentils on other side. Garnish lentils with minced chives.

*Serves 6.*

**Make-Ahead Tip**  Lentil salad may be made up to 12 hours in advance and refrigerated. Bring to room temperature and adjust seasoning before serving.

## LANGUE DE BOEUF EN SALADE
### Beef tongue salad

This hearty meat-based salad in a mustard vinaigrette is the sort of first course one is likely to find in inexpensive Burgundian bistros. Consider serving it for lunch as a main course, accompanied by a warm baguette and a bottle of Beaujolais.

    1½ pounds smoked beef
       tongue, in one piece
    1  cup diced celery
    3  tablespoons minced shallot
    ½  cup minced parsley
    3  hard-cooked eggs
    2  teaspoons Dijon-style mustard
    ¼  cup red wine vinegar
    1  teaspoon freshly ground
       pepper
    ¾  cup olive oil
       Kosher salt
       Hearts of butter lettuce

**1.** Skin tongue. Cut meat into 2- by ¼- by ¼-inch strips. Place tongue in a salad bowl. Add celery, 1 tablespoon of the shallot, and 2 tablespoons of the parsley.

**2.** Chop eggs coarsely, then press them through a sieve or ricer. In a small mixing bowl, combine the remaining 2 tablespoons shallot, ¼ cup of the sieved eggs, mustard, vinegar, and pepper. Whisk to blend. Slowly add olive oil and whisk to make a creamy dressing. Stir in ¼ cup of the parsley and salt to taste.

**3.** To serve, arrange butter lettuce on a platter or on individual serving plates. Add dressing to tongue and toss gently. Top butter lettuce with tongue salad and garnish with remaining sieved egg and parsley.

*Serves 6.*

## POIREAUX VINAIGRETTE
### Leeks vinaigrette

Marinated leeks make a simple but lovely first course. To dress up the following version, top the leeks with crumbled goat cheese or sieved hard-cooked egg.

- 6 large or 9 medium leeks (white and pale green part only)
- 2 tablespoons lemon juice Zest of 1 lemon, grated
- 2 teaspoons Dijon-style mustard
- ⅔ cup olive oil Kosher salt and freshly ground pepper
- ¼ cup minced chives, for garnish

**1.** Halve leeks, cutting down to, but not all the way through, the root. Wash leeks well, allowing water to run down between the leaves where dirt may be trapped.

**2.** In a large saucepan over high heat, bring 2 quarts salted water to a boil. Add leeks and return to a boil. Cook until leeks are barely tender (about 8 minutes for medium leeks, 10 minutes for large leeks). Test for doneness by piercing the white part near root with a paring knife; knife should slip in and out easily. As they are done, remove leeks to a colander to drain. Cool slightly, then pat dry.

**3.** In a small bowl whisk together lemon juice, lemon zest, mustard, and olive oil. Season to taste with salt and pepper. Pour vinaigrette over leeks and let marinate at least 1 hour at room temperature or in the refrigerator for up to 24 hours. Bring to room temperature before serving. To serve, trim away root ends and cut leeks in half. Arrange halves on a serving plate or platter and spoon vinaigrette over. Garnish with chives.

*Serves 6.*

### BISTRO MENU

*Salade Paysanne*

*Lapin à la Moutarde*

*Purée de Céleri-Rave*

*Fromages de Campagne (Farmhouse Cheeses)*

*Poires (Fresh Pears)*

*Burgundy or Beaujolais*

*Throughout France, the neighborhood bistro is a gathering place for people looking for a home-style meal at a moderate price. Many are family-run, with the husband or wife working in the kitchen and the other partner in the dining room. Good bistro fare is unpretentious, made with fresh local ingredients simply prepared. The following bistro menu is typical of the Burgundy region: a warm salad of potatoes, bacon, and curly endive, followed by an aromatic baked rabbit with mustard. A sweet dessert is omitted in favor of a platter of local cheeses such as Époisses and Chaource and a basket of ripe pears.*
*Menu serves six.*

## SALADE PAYSANNE
### Warm potato and bacon salad

A warm, mustard-thickened dressing based on bacon fat ties the elements of this salad together.

- 3 pounds small boiling potatoes, cut in ½-inch cubes
- ½ pound bacon, cut in 2-inch lengths
- 1 cup thinly sliced red onion
- 1 large shallot, minced
- 1 teaspoon minced garlic
- 2 tablespoons Dijon-style mustard
- 3 tablespoons white wine vinegar
- ½ cup peanut or olive oil
- 3 tablespoons cold water Kosher salt and freshly ground pepper
- 1 head curly endive, washed, dried, and torn into bite-sized pieces
- 3 tablespoons minced chives, for garnish

**1.** Place potatoes in a large pot, add salted water to cover, and bring to a boil over high heat. Boil until potatoes are tender (about 12 minutes). Drain and transfer potatoes to a large bowl.

**2.** In a medium skillet over moderately low heat, render bacon until crisp. Transfer with a slotted spoon to paper towels to drain. Add half the bacon to bowl with potatoes. Add red onion.

**3.** Add shallot and garlic to bacon fat in skillet and sauté over moderate heat until fragrant (about 1 minute). Whisk in mustard and vinegar. Whisk in oil slowly. Mixture may appear curdled. Whisk in the water and mixture will come together. Season to taste with salt and pepper.

**4.** Add dressing to warm potatoes and toss gently. Add endive and toss to coat. Serve on a platter or on individual plates; top with remaining bacon and minced chives.

*Serves 6.*

## LAPIN À LA MOUTARDE
### *Rabbit baked with mustard*

You can tell where you are in France by the way the rabbit is prepared: with prunes in the southwest, with tomatoes in Provence, and with mustard in the Dijon region. Note that the rabbit must marinate at least four hours.

 ⅓ cup Dijon-style mustard
 ¾ cup Crème Fraîche
   (see page 22)
 1 teaspoon kosher salt
 1 teaspoon freshly ground
   pepper
 2 rabbits, cut into serving pieces
 2 tablespoons minced parsley,
   for garnish

**1.** In a large bowl, whisk together mustard, Crème Fraîche, salt, and pepper. Add rabbit pieces to bowl and toss to coat. Cover and marinate in the refrigerator at least 4 hours or up to 8 hours. Bring to room temperature before baking.

**2.** Preheat oven to 350° F. Transfer rabbit to a roasting pan. Bake until juices run clear when legs are pierced in thickest part (about 65 minutes). Mustard coating should be a deep glazed brown. Transfer rabbit to a warm serving platter or individual plates and garnish with parsley.

*Serves 6.*

*Rabbit baked with mustard, a warm potato and curly endive salad, and celery root purée are classics of French bistro cooking.*

## PURÉE DE CÉLERI-RAVE
### Celery root purée

This smooth, creamy side dish is a purée of celery root, cooked rice, cream, and butter. The subtle, celerylike flavor is delicious with goose, ham, or duck.

> 1 large celery root (about ½ lb), peeled and cut in 1-inch dice
> 1 cup half-and-half
> 4 cups Fond de Volaille (see page 32)
> ⅔ cup long-grain white rice
> 2 tablespoons unsalted butter
> 2 tablespoons Crème Fraîche (see page 22) or sour cream
> Kosher salt and freshly ground pepper

**1.** In a large saucepan over high heat, bring celery root, half-and-half, and stock to a boil; reduce heat to maintain a simmer. Cover and cook 10 minutes. Add rice and cook, uncovered, until celery root and rice are tender (about 20 minutes). Drain, reserving liquid.

**2.** Transfer contents of saucepan to a food processor or blender and purée. Return to saucepan. Add butter, Crème Fraîche, and just enough of the reserved cooking liquid to make a thick purée. Season to taste with salt and pepper. Reheat to serve.

*Serves 6.*

**Make-Ahead Tip**  Recipe may be made up to 6 hours ahead. Reheat purée slowly in a double boiler, stirring well.

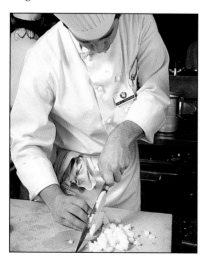

## MAIN COURSES AND ACCOMPANIMENTS

It's not surprising that Burgundian cooks have developed a repertoire of dishes that flatter the region's wines. Chicken simmered in a rich wine sauce (see page 77) or quail roasted with mustard and herbs (see below) are excellent partners for the elegant Burgundy reds. Such full-flavored main courses demand simple accompaniments, such as endive braised in butter (see page 76) or a silky purée of celery root (at left).

## CAILLES RÔTIES AUX HERBES
### Herbed roast quail

This easy preparation of herb-infused quail would bring out the best in a red Burgundy. Accompany the quail with Purée de Céleri-Rave (at left), Petits Pois à la Française (see page 36), or Navets Glacés (see page 76). Note that the quail needs to marinate for at least two hours.

> 12 quail
> 2 tablespoons minced garlic
> 1 teaspoon minced fresh thyme
> ½ teaspoon ground bay leaf
> ½ teaspoon ground rosemary
> 1 tablespoon kosher salt
> 1 tablespoon freshly ground pepper
> ¼ cup lemon juice
> 1 cup olive oil
> 1 tablespoon Dijon-style mustard
> 4 tablespoons unsalted butter
> 6 lemon wedges, for garnish

**1.** Remove wing tips from quail and discard or save for stock. Make an incision in the skin on both sides of each breast and tuck legs into slits.

**2.** In a large bowl combine garlic, thyme, bay leaf, rosemary, salt, pepper, lemon juice, olive oil, and mustard. Whisk to blend. Add quail and turn to coat with marinade. Cover and refrigerate 2 to 6 hours.

**3.** Preheat oven to 450° F. In each of 2 large skillets over moderate heat, melt 2 tablespoons of the butter. Brown quail over moderately high

heat for 2 to 3 minutes on each side. Transfer quail to a roasting pan and roast until breasts feel slightly springy when touched (5 to 7 minutes). Transfer to a warm platter or individual dinner plates and serve with lemon wedges.

*Serves 6.*

## BOEUF BOURGUIGNON
### Beef braised in Burgundy wine

*Boeuf bourguignon* is the quintessential French stew. Although the French repertoire includes many variations on this theme, it is this version that has a worldwide reputation. Beef braised in red wine and garnished with pearl onions, mushrooms, and salt pork is a rich and warming dish for cool weather. Note that the beef needs to marinate at least one day before cooking.

> 3 pounds beef chuck roast, cut in 1½-inch cubes
> 2 large leeks (white part only), cleaned and cut into ½-inch lengths
> 2 tablespoons olive oil
> 2 teaspoons minced fresh thyme
> 2 bay leaves
> 1 teaspoon crushed peppercorns
> ½ cup dry red wine, plus ½ cup wine if needed
> 2 tablespoons Cognac or brandy
> 3 ounces lean salt pork or slab bacon, cut in ¼-inch cubes
> 1½ ounces dried cèpe mushrooms
> 1 cup carrots, cut in ½-inch chunks
> 10 ounces pearl onions, blanched 30 seconds in boiling water then peeled
> 8 cloves garlic, peeled and left whole
> 3 tablespoons unsalted butter
> ¾ pound mushrooms, halved if large
> Salt and freshly ground pepper

**1.** In a large mixing bowl combine meat, leeks, olive oil, thyme, bay leaves, peppercorns, ½ cup of the wine, and Cognac. Cover bowl with plastic wrap and refrigerate 24 to 48 hours.

**2.** In a dutch oven or large skillet over moderately low heat, render pork until browned. Transfer pork to a plate with a slotted spoon. Raise heat to moderately high; add beef in small batches, brown on all sides, and remove.

**3.** Return all browned beef to dutch oven; add rendered pork and marinade. Bring to a simmer over moderately high heat, then reduce heat to barely maintain a simmer and cook 2 hours.

**4.** Soak dried mushrooms in 1 cup warm water for 20 minutes, then lift mushrooms out of liquid with a slotted spoon. Check them over carefully for grit, then add to dutch oven along with carrots, pearl onions, and garlic. Simmer until beef is fork-tender (1 to 1½ hours more), adding more red wine and water if necessary.

**5.** In a medium skillet over moderately high heat, melt butter. Add fresh mushrooms and sauté until lightly browned (about 5 minutes). Add mushrooms to stew and continue to cook 10 minutes. Remove bay leaves. Season to taste with salt and pepper.

*Serves 6.*

**Make-Ahead Tip**   Dish may be made up to 2 days ahead and refrigerated. Remove any congealed fat from surface of stew before reheating.

### CANARD RÔTI
*Roast duck*

A crisp roast duck with Navets Glacés (see page 76) or Endives Braisées (see page 76) makes an easy dinner for company. To flatter the duck, choose a young red Burgundy. This recipe doubles easily.

>    1 *duck (4 to 5 lb)*
>    2 *teaspoons kosher salt*
>    1 *teaspoon freshly ground pepper*
>    ½ *lemon*
>    2 *sprigs thyme*
>    4 *sprigs parsley*
>    ⅓ *cup dry white wine*

**1.** Preheat oven to 425° F. Remove any extra fat from neck and body cavity of duck and prick all over with a fork. Sprinkle with salt and pepper both inside and out. Squeeze lemon half into cavity, then leave it in cavity with thyme and parsley. Tuck wing tips under body and tie legs together with string. Place on a rack in a roasting pan. Add 1 cup water to pan and place in oven.

**2.** Roast, breast side up, for 15 minutes. Brush with wine, then turn duck on its side and reduce heat to 375° F. Roast 30 minutes, basting once with wine. Turn duck onto other side. Roast 30 minutes, basting once with wine. Turn duck on its back. Roast until duck is tender and juices run clear when thigh is pierced with a knife (about 30 more minutes). Remove from oven and let stand 5 minutes. Untruss and discard lemon and herbs. To carve, remove legs at thigh joint, then cut legs in half. Carve breasts off carcass. Serve immediately. Alternatively, cut the duck open along the backbone, cut away and discard backbone, cut the duck in half through breastbone, and serve each person half a duck.

*Serves 2 or 3.*

*A bronzed roast duck knows no better companions than glazed turnips and a bottle of young red Burgundy.*

In a skillet just large enough to hold endive in one layer, melt butter over moderate heat. Add shallots and sauté 2 minutes. Add endive and salt and pepper to taste, and turn to coat with butter. Add stock. Bring to a boil; reduce heat to maintain a simmer, cover, and simmer until endive is tender when pierced with a knife (about 20 minutes). Transfer to a serving platter with a slotted spoon and garnish with minced chives.

*Serves 6.*

## NAVETS GLACÉS
### *Glazed turnips*

Turnips are a harbinger of spring in France. As soon as they appear in the market, roast duckling goes on the menu in countless bistros and homes, to be accompanied by sweet young turnips. A young red Burgundy would complement the natural sweetness of the duck.

- 4 *tablespoons unsalted butter*
- 1 *tablespoon vegetable oil*
- 3 *tablespoons minced shallot*
- 4 *medium* or 6 *small turnips, cut in ½-inch cubes*
- 2½ *cups Fond de Volaille (see page 32)*
- 1 *teaspoon sugar*
- 2 *teaspoons lemon juice Kosher salt and freshly ground pepper*

In a large skillet over moderate heat, melt 2 tablespoons of the butter with oil. Add shallot and sauté 5 minutes. Add turnips and sauté 3 minutes. Add stock and sugar; bring to a boil, then reduce heat to maintain a simmer and cook, uncovered, for 45 minutes. Most of the liquid should evaporate, and turnips should be meltingly tender. Add lemon juice. Raise heat to high and cook until liquid in skillet is reduced to 2 to 3 tablespoons. Remove from heat and whisk in the remaining 2 tablespoons butter. Season to taste with salt and pepper. Serve immediately.

*Serves 6.*

*Pain d'épice, Dijon's honey and almond spice bread, is a holiday treat throughout France.*

## ENDIVES BRAISÉES
### *Braised Belgian endive*

The name may say Belgian, but this member of the chicory family is widely cultivated in France. The French love its slightly bitter flavor and its handsome tapered shape, and they enjoy it both raw and cooked. Serve this dish with roast poultry, pork, or game.

- 3 *tablespoons unsalted butter*
- 2 *large shallots, peeled and thinly sliced*
- 6 *whole Belgian endives, ends trimmed, halved Kosher salt and freshly ground pepper*
- 1½ *cups Fond de Volaille (see page 32)*
- 2 *tablespoons minced chives, for garnish*

## COQ AU VIN
### Chicken in red wine with bacon and mushrooms

The classic Burgundian coq au vin is one of the world's great chicken stews. A straight translation—chicken in wine—doesn't begin to convey the allure of the silky red wine sauce and the appetizing garnish of pearl onions, mushrooms, and bacon.

> ½ pound thick-sliced bacon, cut in 2-inch lengths
> 2 chickens (3 lb each), cut in 8 pieces
> 1½ onions, minced
> 16 cloves garlic, peeled and left whole
> 10 ounces pearl onions, boiled for 30 seconds then peeled
> 4 cups dry red wine
> 1 cup Fond de Volaille (see page 32)
> 2 teaspoons dried thyme
> 2 bay leaves
> 8 ounces fresh mushrooms, halved if large
> 2 tablespoons cold unsalted butter
> Kosher salt and freshly ground pepper

**1.** In a large skillet over moderate heat, render bacon until crisp. Drain on paper towels. In fat remaining in skillet, brown chicken parts in batches. Transfer chicken to a plate as it browns.

**2.** Add minced onion and garlic to pan and sauté 5 minutes. Add pearl onions and sauté 3 minutes. Add wine, stock, thyme, and bay leaves, and bring to a boil. Add chicken and bacon to pan. Cover. Reduce heat to maintain a simmer and cook 45 minutes.

**3.** Add mushrooms and cook until chicken is fork-tender (about 45 more minutes). With a slotted spoon, transfer chicken and pearl onions to a warm serving platter. Remove bay leaves from sauce. Raise heat to high and cook until sauce is reduced to 2 cups. Remove pan from heat and swirl in butter. Season to taste with salt and pepper. Spoon sauce over and around chicken.

*Serves 6.*

## DESSERTS

Desserts are simple in Burgundian homes—typically a platter of regional cheeses followed by a bowl of fruit. In a bistro, a housemade walnut bread might accompany the cheeses, and the fruit might take the form of sugared peaches floating in cool Beaujolais.

## PAIN D'ÉPICE
### Holiday spice bread

Dijon is famous for its fragrant *pain d'épice*, a dark spice bread that is delicious with coffee or wine. Although this honey-sweetened, heavily spiced loaf is atypical of French baking, it has long been a Christmas specialty of the region. Note that the bread should age for two to three days before serving.

> 2 tablespoons unsalted butter, melted
> Flour, for dusting pan
> 1 cup coarsely chopped almonds
> ½ cup golden raisins
> ½ teaspoon kosher salt
> ¼ teaspoon nutmeg
> 1 teaspoon ground ginger
> 1½ teaspoons cinnamon
> 1 teaspoon anise seed
> Pinch ground cloves
> 1½ teaspoons minced dried orange peel (see Note)
> 1 teaspoon baking powder
> 2 teaspoons baking soda
> 1 cup water
> 1 cup honey
> ¼ cup brown sugar
> 1 large egg, lightly beaten
> ⅓ cup dark rum
> 1 cup rye flour
> 1 cup whole wheat flour
> 1 cup bread flour

**1.** Preheat oven to 400° F. Use butter to grease one 8-cup loaf pan (6 by 10 inches) or two 4½-cup loaf pans (3 by 7 inches). Dust bottom and sides with flour, shaking out excess.

**2.** In a large mixing bowl, combine almonds, raisins, salt, nutmeg, ginger, cinnamon, anise seed, cloves, orange peel, baking powder, and baking soda. In a medium saucepan over moderate heat, bring the water to a boil. Add honey and stir to dissolve. Add brown sugar and stir to dissolve. Remove from heat; allow to cool 5 minutes.

**3.** Add egg and rum to honey-sugar mixture and whisk to blend. Add to spice mixture and stir to blend. Add flours and stir just until flour is absorbed (about 50 strokes). Transfer batter to prepared pan and bake 10 minutes. Reduce heat to 350° F and bake until a cake tester inserted in center comes out dry (about 30 more minutes for one large pan, 20 to 25 more minutes for smaller pans). Bread will be very dark.

**4.** Let bread cool in pan on a rack for 5 minutes. Unmold and finish cooling on rack. Wrap tightly with plastic wrap and store at room temperature for 2 to 3 days before serving. Slice thin to serve.

*Makes one 6- by 10-inch loaf or two 3- by 7-inch loaves.*

<u>Note</u>  Dried orange peel is available on many supermarket spice racks.

## PÊCHES AU BEAUJOLAIS
### Peaches in Beaujolais

No dessert could be easier or more symbolic of bistro fare than this delicious, artless marriage of peaches and wine.

> 6 large ripe freestone peaches, peeled, halved, and thinly sliced
> Zest of ½ lemon, grated
> 2 tablespoons lemon juice
> 1 to 3 teaspoons sugar
> 1 bottle (750 ml) Beaujolais

In a small bowl combine sliced peaches, lemon zest, and lemon juice. Add sugar to taste and toss gently to blend. Refrigerate until 30 minutes before serving. Just before serving, divide peaches among 6 wineglasses and pour ½ cup wine into each glass.

*Serves 6.*

*Cabbage, sausage, and potatoes fortify residents of the Alps and the Jura; valley dwellers enjoy Rhône River salmon and orchard fruits.*

# The Jura, the Alps & the Rhône Valley

I n the rugged mountains of southeast France, cooks appease large appetites with side-dish casseroles of creamy Gratin Dauphinois (see page 88) and platters of Pot-au-Feu (see page 87), the colorful boiled dinner of meats and vegetables. Cabbage, potatoes, and cheese sustain the residents of the Jura and Alps. In the nearby Rhône Valley, however, food is more refined. There, a strong restaurant tradition prevails, with bistro dishes such as sautéed calves' liver (see Foie de Veau à la Lyonnaise, page 86) and sausages with warm potato salad (see Saucissons Chauds à la Lyonnaise, page 80) among the favorites.

# THE JURA, THE ALPS, AND THE RHÔNE VALLEY

The harsh mountain climate of eastern France and the rigors of mountain living are reflected in the hardy cuisine of the region. Potatoes and cabbages are among the few vegetables that thrive in the rugged weather; they turn up often in rustic soups and stews. Cows graze in the lush mountain pasturage, producing some of the best milk in France. The rich local milk may be baked with sliced potatoes to make the famous *gratin dauphinois*, or it may be preserved in the form of cheese. *Reblochon,* Morbier, Comté, Vacherin, Gruyère, and Emmenthal are just a few of the cheeses that owe their savor to these well-fed cows.

From the mountain streams come fat trout and salmon. Freshwater crayfish, although not as plentiful as they used to be, are still featured on the menus of the regions' fancy restaurants—in bisques and sauces and as a luxurious garnish for chicken and chicken liver dishes. Many of the restaurant chickens come from the region of Bresse in the western lowlands, which produces the most prized chickens in France. Bresse chickens, which come to market with special leg bands to identify them, fetch a premium price.

Eastern France is not entirely a region of mountains. The Rhône River, which originates in Switzerland at Lake Geneva and flows south through Lyon to the Mediterranean, is the wellspring of the fertile Rhône Valley. Cherry, apricot, pear, peach, and walnut orchards thrive here. As one travels south toward Provence, the fruit orchards give way to almonds, olives, and artichokes, which frequently find their way into Rhône Valley kitchens.

The region's major city is Lyon, which has a long-standing reputation as the gastronomic capital of France. Although the famous *Mères Lyonnaises*—women restaurateurs responsible for many of the town's best restaurants in the early twentieth century—are no longer living, their culinary spirit survives in the countless Lyonnais bistros, where one can dine simply but extraordinarily well.

## FIRST COURSES

Dainty eaters are almost unheard of in the mountainous Jura and Alps regions and in the gastronomic heartland around Lyon. First courses tend to be filling, including hearty cabbage-based soups and platters of steaming sausages with potatoes.

## SOUPE AU CHOU
### Cabbage and garlic soup

Followed by a platter of cheese and fruit, this rib-sticking soup makes a winter dinner. In the mountainous Jura region, where such rustic soups are common, the cheese might well be a local Comté, Morbier, or *reblochon.*

> 3 tablespoons minced garlic
> 8 cups Fond de Volaille (see page 32)
> 1 cup long-grain white rice
> 6 cups shredded savoy cabbage
> 1 teaspoon freshly ground pepper
> Kosher salt
> 12 Croutons (see page 16)
> 2 tablespoons minced parsley, for garnish

**1.** In a medium saucepan combine garlic, 2 cups of the stock, and rice. Bring to a boil over moderate heat; cover, reduce heat to maintain a simmer, and cook 20 minutes. Transfer to a blender or food processor, add 4 cups of the stock, and blend, in batches if necessary.

**2.** Return to saucepan and add the remaining 2 cups stock and cabbage. Simmer 15 minutes over moderately low heat. Add pepper and add salt if necessary. Place Croutons in individual soup bowls and ladle soup over. Garnish with parsley and serve immediately.

*Makes 6 generous cups, 6 servings.*

**Make-Ahead Tip**   Soup may be made up to 3 days ahead and kept in the refrigerator or frozen for up to 1 month.

## SAUCISSONS CHAUDS À LA LYONNAISE
### Poached sausages with warm potato salad

Typically served as a first course in Lyonnais bistros, this hearty combination could also make a light luncheon dish. Any European-style link sausage is suitable: Consider French *boudin noir* or *cervelas,* Italian *cotechino,* German bratwurst, or Polish kielbasa. If the sausage is fresh (not cooked or smoked), it must be slowly poached until it is cooked throughout. Cooking time will vary depending on the size of the links; cut into one to test for doneness. Precooked or smoked sausages need only be heated through. The cooking time specified in the following recipe is for fresh 4-ounce links.

> 1½ pounds red potatoes of similar size
> ¼ cup Dijon-style mustard
> 6 green onions, minced
>   Basic Vinaigrette (see page 31)
> ⅓ cup minced parsley
> ½ cup dry white wine
> 1½ pounds sausage (in 4-oz links)

**1.** In a large saucepan cover potatoes with salted water. Bring to a boil over high heat. Reduce heat to maintain a simmer and cook until potatoes are tender when pierced with a knife (20 to 25 minutes). Drain. When potatoes are just cool enough to handle, slice them about ¼ inch thick and place in a bowl. Add mustard and toss gently to mix. Add green onions and vinaigrette. Toss gently but well with your hands. Add ¼ cup of the parsley.

**2.** In a large skillet over high heat, bring wine and 2 cups water to a boil. Add sausages and cover. Reduce heat to maintain a simmer and cook until sausages are firm and hot throughout (about 15 minutes).

**3.** Transfer potato salad to a warm platter. Surround with poached sausages. Garnish with the remaining parsley. Serve immediately.

*Serves 6.*

## SALADE DE GRUYÈRE
### Gruyère salad

Serve this simple salad before a main course of red meat or poultry.

> 5 ounces Gruyère cheese
> 3 tablespoons minced shallot
>   Lemon-Chive Vinaigrette
>   (see page 31)
> 2 heads curly endive or escarole
> ¼ cup minced chives

**1.** Cut cheese into matchsticks about 2 inches long and ⅛ inch wide. In a medium bowl combine cheese, shallot, and vinaigrette. Marinate 1 hour at room temperature.

**2.** Wash and dry endive or escarole. Tear into bite-sized pieces and place in a salad bowl. Add cheese mixture and chives. Toss lightly but well. Serve immediately.

*Serves 6.*

## BETTERAVES EN SALADE
### Pickled beet salad

In a Lyonnais bistro, a beet salad such as this one might be part of a salad assortment including cucumbers dressed with oil and vinegar and celery root rémoulade (see page 34). Note that the beets should be made at least three days in advance.

> 8 medium beets
> 2 cups white wine vinegar
>   Grated zest and juice
>   of 1 lemon
> ½ cup sugar
>   Six sprigs thyme (each
>   3 in. long)
> 1 bay leaf
> 3 large cloves garlic, peeled
>   and left whole
> 1 cup thinly sliced onion
>   Kosher salt and freshly
>   ground pepper
> 2 small heads curly endive
> ½ cup olive oil
> 3 tablespoons minced chives,
>   for garnish

**1.** Scrub beets well. Place in a covered steamer and steam over boiling water until beets can be pierced easily with a knife (20 to 25 minutes). Add more water to steamer as necessary. Drain beets; when cool enough to handle, peel and slice into ¼-inch-thick rounds.

**2.** In a medium saucepan over high heat, bring vinegar, lemon zest, lemon juice, and sugar to a boil. Simmer 3 minutes. Add sliced beets, turn to coat with liquid, and cook 2 minutes. Transfer beets with a slotted spoon to a stainless steel, glass, or enamel bowl. Add thyme, bay leaf, garlic cloves, and onion.

**3.** Over high heat, reduce liquid in saucepan to 1 cup. Pour over beets and toss to coat. Cool to room temperature, then transfer to a covered container and refrigerate for at least 3 days or up to 2 weeks.

**4.** Remove beets from refrigerator 15 minutes before serving. Discard garlic, bay leaf, and thyme. Season to taste with salt and pepper. Wash and dry endive and separate into leaves. Line individual salad plates or a large serving platter with endive. Top with beets and onions. Drizzle salad lightly with beet liquid, then drizzle with olive oil and garnish with chives.

*Serves 6.*

*Sweet-and-sour beets and onions make a refreshing salad course that's best when made a few days ahead.*

81

## CHARCUTERIE: THE FRENCH APPROACH TO PORK

After stops at the bakery, the produce market, the cheese shop, and the butcher, the French shopper is likely to visit a favorite charcuterie before heading home. This specialty shop is the source of all the prepared pork products that the French adore.

In the United States, finding a French-style charcuterie is sometimes difficult. Government regulations prohibit the importation of most European pork products. Fortunately, some French-trained *charcutiers* (pork butchers) are now manufacturing products in this country, which you may be able to find in selected fine food stores.

In addition to sausages of all kinds, many made on the premises, the French charcuterie typically sells condiments such as mustards and vinegars; hams, both fresh and smoked; housemade pâtés and terrines; and prepared salads of celery root, potatoes, or beets.

It is said that the French use every part of the pig but the squeal. Here are a few of the many pork-based items you might find at a French charcuterie. A good charcutier in a large town will offer a much larger selection.

**Boudin noir**    Blood sausage is highly seasoned with onions and quatre-épices (see Note, page 61) and thickened with bread crumbs. These sausages are served hot, usually with sautéed apples, potatoes, or onions.

**Fromage de tête**    A highly seasoned terrine of chopped cooked head meat bound in natural gelatin, pork head cheese is sliced like a pâté and served with mustard or vinaigrette as a first course.

**Jambon de Bayonne**    This dry, smoked ham, comparable to Italian prosciutto, is served in the same way—in paper-thin slices with butter or melon.

**Jambon de Paris**    This mild, unsmoked ham is similar to American canned hams.

**Petit salé**    Similar to American salt pork but made from the leaner end of the pork belly, *petit salé* is often served in thick, hot slices with puréed lentils or white beans.

**Pieds de porc**    Pig's feet are sold cooked, boned, and rolled in butter and bread crumbs. At home, they are grilled and served as a first course with vinaigrette.

**Rillettes**    A delectable coarse spread of pork and pork fat, *rillettes* is served on toasts as an appetizer or spread on a baguette for a sandwich.

**Saucisses and saucissons**
Small and large sausages may be fresh (uncooked), cooked, or air-dried. The most popular fresh sausages are the small and spicy *chipolatas,* which in Bordeaux are sometimes served hot with raw oysters, and the *crêpinettes* (see page 83), flat sausage patties wrapped in caul fat. The best-known cooked sausage is probably the *saucisse de Toulouse,* made of coarsely ground pork. This is the sausage typically used in cassoulet (see page 109). A larger cooked sausage known as *cervelas* is boiled, sliced, and eaten with potato salad, or is wrapped in brioche dough, baked, and served as an hors d'oeuvre. Air-dried sausages, such as the garlicky *saucisson à l'ail,* are firm enough to slice thin. A platter of sliced dried sausage is often served as an hors d'oeuvre with bread, butter, and olives.

**A SPRING BRUNCH**

*Crépinettes à l'Ail*

*Salade de Pissenlits*

*Brioche Grillée*

*Soufflé aux Amandes*

*Sparkling Wine or
Iced Mint Tea*

---

*The concept of a large
late-morning meal is
unfamiliar in France, where
people rarely eat anything
substantial before noon.
Nonetheless, many authentic
French dishes seem right
at home at an American-
style brunch. Invite friends
to celebrate spring with
a menu of Rhône specialties.
Because even the host
shouldn't have to rise at
the crack of dawn, almost
everything in this menu
can be assembled ahead.
Menu serves six.*

## CRÉPINETTES À L'AIL
### Fresh pork and spinach sausage

The flat, hand-formed sausages known as *crépinettes* are a popular first course in the Rhône. Their name derives from the wrapper of caul fat (*crépine*) that holds the patties together and bastes them while they are fried, baked, or grilled. Made in large rounds, crépinettes are a knife-and-fork first course; made small, they can be a stand-up hors d'oeuvre accompanied by a glass of sparkling wine. Note that the mixture needs to rest at least three hours before cooking.

        2   tablespoons unsalted butter
        4   ounces chicken liver
        1   pound coarsely ground pork
        1   egg
        1   cup minced onion
        2   tablespoons minced garlic
        2   cups coarsely chopped, tightly
            packed fresh spinach leaves
        2   teaspoons minced fresh sage
            or 1 teaspoon dried sage
        2   tablespoons flour
        1   cup soft bread crumbs
        ½   teaspoon kosher salt
        1   teaspoon freshly ground
            pepper
            Pinch nutmeg
        ½   pound caul fat (see Note)
            Sage sprigs, for garnish

**1.** In a large skillet over moderate heat, melt butter. Add liver and sauté until lightly browned (about 1½ minutes on each side). Transfer liver to a plate. Add pork and sauté until it is no longer pink (about 3 minutes).

**2.** *To make in a food processor:* Transfer pork and liver to processor and process 2 seconds. Add egg, onion, garlic, spinach, sage, flour, bread crumbs, salt, pepper, and nutmeg. Pulse several times until blended. *To make by hand:* Chop pork and liver until finely minced. Transfer to a bowl and stir in egg, onion, garlic, spinach, sage, flour, bread crumbs, salt, pepper, and nutmeg. Refrigerate mixture at least 3 hours, or overnight.

**3.** Preheat oven to 375° F. Shape sausage into 6 large or 12 small patties. Cut caul into squares and wrap each patty in caul. Bake on htly oiled baking sheet until browned (10 to 15 minutes for small sausages, 25 minutes for large ones). Transfer to a warm platter and garnish with sage.

*Serves 6.*

<u>Note</u>   Caul fat is a lacy, netlike fat that surrounds a cow's stomach. Most specialty butchers can get it for you with a few days' notice.

## SALADE DE PISSENLITS
### Dandelion salad with soft-cooked egg

This salad is best made with young, tender dandelion leaves, which are peppery but not excessively bitter.

        1   pound dandelion greens
            (as young as possible)
        ½   pound thick-sliced bacon,
            cut in 1-inch pieces
        6   eggs
            Mustard Vinaigrette
            (see page 31)
            Freshly ground pepper
       18   warm Croutons à l'Ail
            (see page 114)

**1.** Wash and dry dandelion greens. Remove tough stems. In a skillet over moderate heat, render bacon until crisp. Drain on paper towels.

**2.** Fill a medium saucepan with salted water and bring to a boil over high heat. Add eggs and return to a boil. Reduce heat to maintain a simmer and cook 5 minutes. Drain eggs and run cold water over them immediately to stop cooking. Shell eggs.

**3.** Toss dandelion leaves with ½ cup Mustard Vinaigrette. Divide among 6 salad plates. Sprinkle with bacon. Halve eggs and arrange 2 halves on each plate. Spoon the remaining vinaigrette over eggs. Grind pepper over each salad. Garnish each plate with 3 croutons.

*Serves 6.*

*Pork and spinach sausages, toasted brioche, and a dandelion and egg salad make a festive spring brunch.*

## BRIOCHE GRILLÉE
### Toasted brioche

A butter-rich brioche dough baked in a loaf pan makes a bread that toasts beautifully. In this recipe, the dough is made entirely in the mixer. Note that the bread needs to be started about 12 hours ahead.

> ½ package active dry yeast
> ¼ cup warm milk (100° F)
> 2½ cups unbleached flour
> 4 eggs
> 1 tablespoon sugar
> ½ cup unsalted butter, very soft
> 2 tablespoons unsalted butter, melted

**1.** In large bowl of electric mixer, sprinkle yeast over milk. Stir with a fork to dissolve. Let stand 5 minutes. Add ½ cup of the flour and 1 egg. Stir well to blend. Sprinkle 1½ cups of the flour over mixture but do not stir in; cover with plastic wrap. Set aside in a warm place for 2 hours.

**2.** Add sugar, 2 eggs, and softened butter. Beat on medium speed for 3 minutes. Sprinkle dough with ¼ cup of the flour but do not stir in. Cover with plastic wrap and set aside in a warm place for 3 hours. Punch dough down with a spatula, stirring in flour on top. Cover with plastic wrap and refrigerate 45 minutes.

**3.** Spread work surface with 3 tablespoons of the flour. Transfer dough to floured surface and pat with lightly floured hands into a 12- by 9-inch rectangle. Fold in thirds to make a 4- by 9-inch rectangle. Sprinkle with the remaining 1 tablespoon flour. Cover with plastic wrap and refrigerate at least 4 hours or up to 4 days; dough may also be frozen for up to 1 month. To thaw, place frozen dough in refrigerator overnight.

**4.** Preheat oven to 400° F. Grease a 9-inch loaf pan with melted butter. Shape dough into a loaf and transfer to prepared pan. Cover loosely with plastic wrap. Let rise in a warm place for 45 minutes.

**5.** Lightly beat remaining egg. Brush surface of loaf with beaten egg and bake 10 minutes. Reduce heat to 350° F and continue baking until loaf is golden brown (25 to 30 more minutes). Transfer to a rack to cool. To serve, slice bread about ⅓ inch thick and toast in oven or toaster.

*Makes one 9-inch loaf.*

## SOUFFLÉ AUX AMANDES
### Cold almond soufflé

Almond desserts often go well with a glass of sweet wine, and this chilled soufflé is no exception. To accompany the soufflé, pass a bowl of peeled, halved, and sugared apricots marinated in the same dessert wine. If apricots are unavailable, poached cherries or halved poached peaches make a good substitute. The soufflé may be made one day in advance. Note that it needs to chill for three to five hours.

> 8 egg yolks
> ½ cup sugar
> ½ teaspoon kosher salt
> 3 ounces almond paste, broken into small pieces
> 1 envelope unflavored gelatin
> 5 tablespoons cold water
> ¼ cup almond-flavored liqueur
> ½ cup egg whites (from 3 to 4 eggs)
> 1 cup whipping cream
> 3 tablespoons toasted sliced almonds, for garnish

**1.** Prepare a paper collar for one 5- to 6-cup soufflé dish or individual collars for six 1-cup soufflé dishes: Cut a piece of parchment paper 4 inches wide and slightly longer than the circumference of the dish. Wrap collar around dish and secure with string, allowing paper to extend 2 inches above rim of dish.

**2.** In large bowl of electric mixer, beat egg yolks with sugar and ¼ teaspoon of the salt until mixture forms a ribbon when beaters are lifted (about 4 minutes). Add almond paste and blend 1 minute.

**3.** In the top of a double boiler, sprinkle gelatin over the cold water. Place over, not in, simmering water and cook, stirring, until gelatin is completely dissolved. Whisk in ¾ cup of egg yolk mixture, then transfer to mixer bowl. Stir in 2 tablespoons of the almond-flavored liqueur.

**4.** Beat egg whites with the remaining ¼ teaspoon salt until stiff but not dry. In a separate bowl whip cream to soft peaks, and stir in the remaining 2 tablespoons almond liqueur. Fold cream into yolk mixture, then gently fold in whites. Divide mixture among prepared soufflé dishes. Chill small dishes for at least 3 hours, a large one for at least 5 hours. Just before serving, remove paper collars and garnish tops with toasted almonds.

*Serves 6.*

# MAIN COURSES AND SIDE DISHES

To accompany their robust red wines, diners in the Rhône Valley and the nearby mountains turn to sturdy fare: garlicky chicken, boiled beef, and a wide range of variety meats, including liver, brains, and tripe. Among the most popular side dishes are the golden gratins (baked dishes with crusty toppings), such as potatoes in thick cream or artichokes layered with seasoned bread crumbs.

## TRIPES À LA LYONNAISE
### Braised tripe with onions

The abundance of onions marks this dish as a specialty of Lyon. Typically, the tripe would be served with a garnish of small boiled potatoes.

- 3 pounds ready-to-cook honeycomb tripe
- 2 tablespoons unsalted butter
- 2 tablespoons olive oil
- 4 medium onions, diced
- 2 teaspoons minced garlic
- ½ teaspoon kosher salt, plus salt to taste
- 1 teaspoon freshly ground pepper, plus pepper to taste
- 1 bay leaf
  Pinch nutmeg
- 1 cup dry white wine
- ¼ cup lemon juice
- ½ cup whipping cream
- ⅓ cup plus 1 tablespoon minced parsley

Cut tripe into 2- by ¼- by ¼-inch strips. In a large saucepan or dutch oven over moderate heat, heat butter and olive oil. Add onions and garlic and sauté 5 minutes. Add tripe and sauté 5 minutes. Add the ½ teaspoon salt, the 1 teaspoon pepper, bay leaf, nutmeg, and wine. Bring to a simmer, then cover and reduce heat to low. Cook 1¼ hours. Stir in lemon juice and cream and season to taste with salt and pepper. Stir in the ⅓ cup parsley. Transfer to a warm serving platter. Garnish with the remaining parsley.

*Serves 6.*

## FOIE DE VEAU À LA LYONNAISE
### Sautéed liver with creamy onions

Calves' liver takes well to a subtle sweet-and-sour treatment. In Lyon, cooks serve tender panfried liver on sweet, slow-cooked onions and spoon a sherry vinegar glaze on top. To complete the course, add fresh peas and a light red Côtes-du-Rhône.

- ¼ cup olive oil
- 8 large onions, chopped
- 1 tablespoon sugar
- ¼ cup whipping cream
- 1 cup flour
- 1 teaspoon kosher salt
- 1 teaspoon freshly ground pepper
- ½ teaspoon minced fresh thyme
- 2½ pounds calves' liver, cut in 6 pieces
- 3 tablespoons (approximately) clarified butter (see Note, page 87)
- ¼ cup sherry vinegar
- 3 tablespoons unsalted butter, cut in 6 pieces

**1.** In a large skillet over low heat, heat oil. Add onions and cook for 40 minutes, stirring occasionally. Add sugar and continue cooking for 20 minutes. Onions should just begin to caramelize. Stir in cream, then transfer onions to a warm platter.

**2.** Put flour, salt, pepper, and thyme in a paper bag and shake to blend. Pat liver dry, add to seasoned flour in bag, and shake bag to coat liver well; remove liver from bag and shake off excess flour. In the same skillet used for sautéing onions, heat 2 tablespoons of the clarified butter over high heat. Sauté liver, in batches as necessary, until lightly browned (about 2 minutes on each side). Transfer liver to platter with onions as it is done and add more clarified butter to skillet as needed.

**3.** When all liver is cooked, pour off any excess fat in skillet, add sherry vinegar to skillet, and cook over high heat until vinegar is reduced by half, stirring with a wooden spoon to dislodge any drippings stuck to bottom of skillet. Remove skillet from heat, add unsalted butter, and swirl skillet until butter melts. Spoon over liver and serve immediately.

*Serves 6.*

## POULET À L'AIL
### Baked chicken with garlic

Like their Provençal neighbors, Rhône Valley residents are fiends for garlic. Typically they tuck slices under the skin of chicken or insert slivers into a leg of lamb. Here, a creamy garlic paste flavors baked chicken thighs to make a rustic dish for a picnic or a simple dinner.

- 14 large cloves garlic, peeled
- 1 cup whipping cream
- 2 tablespoons minced fresh chervil or parsley
- 12 chicken thighs
  Kosher salt and freshly ground pepper
- 5 sprigs thyme (each 3 in. long)

**1.** In a small saucepan combine garlic cloves, cream, and 3 cups water. Bring to a boil over moderate heat, reduce heat to maintain a simmer, and cook, uncovered, until mixture is thick and creamy (about 1¼ hours). Place in a blender or food processor and blend until smooth. Add chervil and blend briefly.

**2.** Preheat oven to 350° F. Place 2 teaspoons garlic mixture under skin of each thigh, spreading it evenly over surface of meat. Lightly salt and pepper chicken. Place in roasting pan. Scatter thyme sprigs over chicken. Bake 30 minutes, basting after 20 minutes with pan drippings. Raise oven temperature to 400° F and bake an additional 10 minutes. Serve hot, warm, or at room temperature.

*Serves 6.*

**Make-Ahead Tip** Recipe may be prepared through step 1 up to 2 days in advance. Cover garlic mixture and refrigerate.

## POT-AU-FEU
### French boiled dinner

For the best pot-au-feu, the broth is painstakingly skimmed and each different vegetable is cooked only as long as required. Note that you will need a very large stockpot for simmering the beef and chicken and a moderately large one for the sausage and cabbage.

> 1 large bulb garlic
> 3 large onions
> 1 tablespoon olive oil
> 2 pounds meaty beef bones
> 2 pounds oxtail
> 2½ pounds beef short ribs
> 2 tablespoons peppercorns
> 3 cloves
> 3 sprigs parsley
> 3 bay leaves
> 1 chicken (3 to 4 lb), trussed
>   Kosher salt and freshly
>   ground pepper
> 6 small red potatoes
> 12 ounces turnips, peeled
>   and halved if large
> ½ pound small carrots, peeled
>   and left whole
> 1 pound green cabbage,
>   halved and cored
> 2 pounds smoked pork
>   sausage links
> 6 tablespoons dry red wine
>   Cornichons (see page 70)
>   Optional Accompaniments:
>   Croutons (see page 16), 2 cups
>   grated Gruyère cheese, Coulis
>   de Tomates (see page 94),
>   Basic Vinaigrette (see page
>   31), Aioli (see page 100)

**1.** Preheat oven to 450° F. Remove papery outer skin from garlic and from one onion but do not peel. Coat garlic and onion with oil, and roast in a baking dish for 45 minutes.

**2.** Place beef bones, oxtail, and short ribs in a large stockpot. Add water to cover. Bring to a simmer over moderate heat, then reduce heat to maintain a simmer and cook 5 minutes, carefully skimming any scum that rises to the surface. Add roasted onion and garlic. Tie peppercorns, cloves, parsley, and bay leaves together in a cheesecloth bag and add to stockpot. Cover partially and simmer 2 hours.

The pot-au-feu may be prepared up to this point, cooled, and refrigerated for up to 2 days. Lift off any congealed surface fat before continuing.

**3.** Add whole chicken and enough extra water to bring contents of pot at least three fourths of the way up sides of chicken. Bring to a simmer over moderately high heat, skimming any scum that rises to surface. Reduce heat to maintain a simmer and cook until chicken juices no longer run pink (about 1½ hours).

**4.** Remove roasted onion and garlic and cheesecloth bag from stock. Bring stock to a simmer and season to taste with salt and pepper. Peel the remaining 2 onions and trim root ends, but leave onions whole. Add onions to pot and simmer 15 minutes. Add potatoes and turnips and simmer 25 minutes, adding more water as needed to barely cover vegetables. When potatoes and turnips are almost tender, add carrots and cook for an additional 10 minutes. Taste stock again and reseason.

**5.** In a large stockpot over high heat, bring 4 quarts of salted water to a boil. Add cabbage and sausage. Cook until cabbage is tender and sausage is hot throughout (10 to 15 minutes). Transfer sausage to stockpot with beef and chicken. Drain cabbage and cut each half in thirds.

**6.** To serve, arrange short ribs, oxtails, sausages, and vegetables on a warm serving platter or platters. Untruss chicken, carve, and add to platter. Moisten platter with a little broth, cover loosely with aluminum foil, and place in a warm oven. In each of 6 warm soup bowls, place 1 tablespoon red wine. Ladle broth into each bowl and accompany (if desired) with croutons and cheese. Follow the broth with platter of boiled meats and vegetables, accompanied by Cornichons and, if desired, croutons; cheese; and one, two, or all three of the sauces.

*Serves 6.*

**Make-Ahead Tip** Pot-au-feu may be prepared through step 3, cooled, and refrigerated for up to 2 days. Lift off any congealed surface fat before continuing with step 4.

## CERVELLES DE VEAU PANÉES
### Panfried calves' brains

A bread-crumb jacket protects the brains during the rapid frying and forms a crisp coat that contrasts with the creamy interior. Note that the brains need to soak eight hours.

> 3 pounds calves' brains
> 2 tablespoons peppercorns
> 4 teaspoons kosher salt
> ¼ cup lemon juice
> 1 bay leaf
> 1½ cups clarified butter (see Note)
> 2 cups fine, soft bread crumbs
> 1 teaspoon freshly
>   ground pepper
>   Lemon wedges, for garnish

**1.** Put brains in a large bowl and cover with cold water. Refrigerate 8 hours, changing water three times. Drain brains and peel off outer membrane with fingers or a sharp knife.

**2.** Place brains in a saucepan with cold water to cover. Add peppercorns, 2 teaspoons salt, lemon juice, and bay leaf. Bring to a boil over moderate heat. Simmer 3 minutes. Drain in a colander and rinse with cold water until brains are cold.

**3.** Drain brains, pat dry, and slice ¼ inch thick. In a small saucepan over low heat, melt ¾ cup clarified butter. Season bread crumbs with pepper and the remaining salt, and place in a shallow dish. Dip brains first in butter, then in crumbs, coating all sides. Dry on a rack 5 minutes.

**4.** In each of 2 large skillets over moderate heat, heat 6 tablespoons of the clarified butter. When butter foams, add brains and sauté on both sides until brown (about 4 minutes per side). Serve with lemon wedges.

*Serves 6.*

**Make-Ahead Tip** Brains may be prepared through step 2 one day ahead. Refrigerate in cold water.

*Note* To clarify butter, melt it in a small pan over low heat. Skim off froth and carefully pour clear butter from pan, leaving the milky residue behind. One pound butter yields about 1½ cups clarified butter.

## GRATIN D'ARTICHAUTS
### Baked artichokes and bread crumbs

Layers of artichoke hearts, onions, and seasoned bread crumbs make a delectable dish to serve with roast or grilled lamb.

    12  small (egg-sized) artichokes
        Juice of 1 lemon
     1  cup soft bread crumbs
     1  clove garlic, halved
     6  tablespoons olive oil
     3  cups thinly sliced onions
     2  teaspoons kosher salt
     1  teaspoon freshly
        ground pepper
    ⅓  cup plus 2 tablespoons
        minced parsley

**1.** With a sharp, serrated knife, cut about ½ inch off top of each artichoke. Pull off and discard tough, dark green outer leaves to reveal pale green hearts. Trim dark stem end of each artichoke. Quarter artichokes. With a small spoon, scrape out any prickly inner leaves. Add lemon juice to a bowl of water and drop artichokes in to prevent browning.

**2.** Preheat oven to 350° F. Toast bread crumbs on a baking sheet, stirring once or twice, until lightly browned (about 10 minutes).

**3.** Rub an 8- by 12- by 1½-inch oval baking dish with halved garlic clove. Let dry 5 minutes. Brush dish with 1 tablespoon of the olive oil. In a large skillet over moderate heat, heat 3 tablespoons of the oil. Add onions and sauté 5 minutes. Add bread crumbs, stir to mix, and remove from heat. Stir in salt, pepper, and the ⅓ cup parsley.

**4.** Sprinkle one third of bread crumb mixture over bottom of baking dish. Drain artichokes and pat dry. Spread half the artichokes over bread crumbs. Add, in successive layers, half the remaining bread crumbs, the remaining artichokes, and the last of the bread crumbs. Drizzle with the remaining 2 tablespoons oil. Cover dish and bake 30 minutes. Uncover and bake until artichokes are tender when pierced with a knife (about 10 more minutes). Let cool 10 minutes before serving. Dust with the 2 tablespoons parsley just before serving.

*Serves 6.*

## GRATIN DAUPHINOIS
### Casserole of potatoes and cream

Some cooks argue that a true *gratin dauphinois* contains neither eggs nor cheese. Other cooks, equally adamant, use both. This recipe takes the middle road, producing a rich, creamy side dish for roast lamb or chicken.

    1½  pounds baking potatoes,
         peeled and sliced ⅛
         inch thick
     3   cups milk
    ½   teaspoon freshly grated
         nutmeg
     2   teaspoons kosher salt
     1   teaspoon freshly ground
         pepper
     1   clove garlic, halved
     4   tablespoons unsalted butter
    ¼   cup minced shallot
    ½   cup whipping cream
     2   eggs

**1.** Preheat oven to 375° F. In a medium saucepan combine potatoes, milk, nutmeg, salt, and pepper. Bring to a boil and boil 5 minutes.

**2.** Rub an 8- by 12- by 1½-inch baking dish with halved garlic clove. Let dry 5 minutes. Coat dish with 2 tablespoons of the butter. Sprinkle shallot over bottom of dish. Transfer potatoes with a slotted spoon to baking dish. Add 1½ cups seasoned milk to dish. Discard remaining milk or save for soup. Whisk cream and eggs together and pour over top. Dot surface with the remaining 2 tablespoons butter. Bake until custard is firm and golden (35 to 40 minutes). Serve hot.

*Serves 6.*

## SERVING FRENCH CHEESES

Winston Churchill once remarked that he couldn't imagine how one could govern a country that made 377 different cheeses. In fact, if one counts all the farmhouse cheeses sold only at local markets, the French surely make more than that.

In the minds of most French people, a meal is incomplete without a little cheese. At home, the cheese course may be no more than a wedge of Camembert. In restaurants, the cheese selection is typically presented on a platter or wheeled to the table on a cart, with diners encouraged to choose as many types as they would like to try. The waiter cuts appropriate portions and presents them on the same plate.

Cheese is almost never served before a meal in France. At a traditional lunch or dinner, the main course is followed by a small green salad, with the cheese course served after the salad. Fruit may be offered at the same time as the cheeses, but it is meant to be eaten afterward for good reason: The red French wines that go so beautifully with cheese are not compatible with fruit.

When planning a cheese course, bear in mind that it's fine to present just one or two perfectly ripe cheeses. If you'd like to offer a more varied platter, the important consideration is balance. Contrast soft cheeses with hard ones, pungent with mild, fresh cheeses with aged, cow's milk cheeses with goat's milk cheeses.

The following cheeses are among France's best known and are widely available in this country.

**Brie** A soft cow's milk cheese with a powdery white rind. A ripe Brie will be smooth and creamy throughout; underripe Brie is chalky in the middle. Texture should be soft but not excessively runny. Avoid Brie with an ammoniated odor.

**Camembert**  A soft cow's milk cheese with a powdery white rind, in small rounds. A perfectly ripe Camembert can have an aroma of mushrooms. Select as for Brie.

**Cantal**  A firm cow's milk cheese with a nutty flavor. Young Cantal is smooth and mellow; as it ages, the flavor gets sharper and the texture more crumbly.

**Chèvre**  The generic term for goat's milk cheese. *Chèvres* come in a nearly endless variety of shapes and flavors. When very young, they can be quite mild and creamy. As they age, they get sharper and drier. The French goat cheeses commonly found in this country include Montrachet, *bûcheron,* and Sainte-Maure. Goat's milk cheeses are delicious with the Loire Valley wines, such as Sancerre, Pouilly-Fumé, and Chinon.

**Comté**  A firm cow's milk cheese. The French equivalent of the Swiss Gruyère, Comté is an excellent mild grating cheese for use in cooking. Emmenthal is comparable to Comté.

**Époisses**  A small round cow's milk cheese from Burgundy. Époisses has a creamy, moderately pungent interior and a reddish rind washed with *marc de Bourgogne,* the brandy made from Burgundy wine.

**Fourme d'Ambert**  A blue cheese made from cow's milk. The classic Fourme d'Ambert is a cylinder about twice as high as it is wide; the rind is golden orange, the interior strong in flavor and slightly crumbly.

**Fromage des Pyrénées**  A generic name for cheeses from the Pyrénées region. Most of the *fromage des Pyrénées* exported to the United States is made of cow's milk, but sheep's milk cheeses are made in France. *Doux de montagne* is often found in the United States and has a semisoft interior and a mild, nutty flavor.

**Munster**  A soft cow's milk cheese from Alsace. Munster is superb with Alsatian Gewurztraminer or with beer; in France it is sometimes served with caraway or cumin seed. This round cheese has a yellow-gold rind and a pale, creamy interior; when fully ripe, it can be agreeably pungent.

**Petit-Suisse**  A fresh cow's milk cheese, usually packaged in single-serving plastic containers. *Petit-Suisses* are enjoyed throughout France as dessert cheeses; typically they are spooned out of their containers, sweetened with sugar, and eaten with fruit.

**Pont-l'Evêque**  A soft cow's milk cheese from Normandy. Pont-l'Evêque is fabricated in a small square; it has a powdery orange rind and a creamy, golden interior with a strong flavor. Enjoy it with cider or a full-bodied red wine.

**Reblochon**  A soft cow's milk cheese from the Savoy region. *Reblochon* is made in small rounds. Its rind is pale orange with a powdery white coat; the interior is pale, creamy, and full-flavored when ripe. Try it with Beaujolais, Chinon, or Bourgeuil.

**Roquefort**  A blue cheese made from cow's milk. To select a good Roquefort, look for a cheese that's creamy, pale, and well marbled with blue veins. Avoid cheeses that are excessively salty or crumbly. Some diners like to mute the pungent character of Roquefort by eating it with butter. On its own, the cheese is a challenge for wines. Sturdy red wines can work with it, but some say that the ideal match is a sweet Sauternes.

The local olive oil is the foundation of all Provençal cooking. Garlic, lavender, and such herbs as basil add pungent accents.

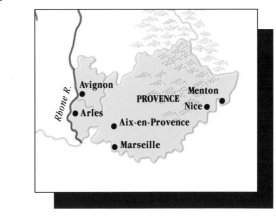

B lessed by sun, Provence is a land
where thyme and lavender blanket
the hillsides and tomatoes grow
to sweet perfection. Garlic pervades
Provençal cooking. It is essential to such
regional specialties as Bouillabaisse (see page
102), Bourride (see page 100), and Soupe
au Pistou (see page 95). Local anchovies and
olives garnish the classic Salade Niçoise
(see page 93), and fresh sea bass from the
Mediterranean is grilled over fennel branches
(see page 98). For a taste of this bounty,
prepare the tantalizing Summer Terrace
Dinner à la Provençale (see page 95).

# PROVENCE

The southern corner of France is a land blessed by the sun. Long, hot summer days and dependably mild winters ensure a lively produce market the year around. Sun-loving vegetables such as eggplant, zucchini, tomatoes, garlic, and green beans thrive in Provence and along the Côte d'Azur. (The spectacular Azure Coast, also known as the Riviera, falls within most definitions of Provence.) Figs and melons ripen in the region's summer warmth and winter brings lemons, oranges, and tangerines.

The nearby Mediterranean greatly influences the region's cuisine; local seafood is a major part of the coastal diet. In the outdoor markets, vendors hawk varieties of fish and shellfish that often have no counterpart in this country. Choice fish such as sea bass and tuna are grilled over fennel branches or poached and eaten cold with a dollop of heady aioli (garlic mayonnaise). The more humble denizens of the deep go to frugal home cooks who know how to turn them into delectable fish soups and stews. Silvery anchovies are harvested in profusion from the Mediterranean; some are sent to the fresh market but most are packed in salt for long keeping. Tinned anchovies add a salty pungency to Provençal sandwiches, spreads, and salads.

The Provençaux like their food aggressively seasoned. They give bouillabaisse a kick with a peppery *sauce rouille* and top vegetable soup with a spoonful of aromatic *pistou* (garlic and basil paste). Every household worth the Provençal name has a summer garden or at least a windowsill overflowing with basil. And when the herb supply threatens to run low, families head to the nearby hills to gather armloads of wild lavender and thyme.

Herbs are not the only aromatics to reign in the Provençal kitchen. Garlic is the king among seasonings in southern France. The local passion for this fragrant lily is unmatched elsewhere in France. Garlic is halved and rubbed on hot toasts, cut into slivers to scent a lamb leg, or

pounded to a paste and stirred into mayonnaise to make aioli. To the Provençal taste, there are few dishes—mashed potatoes included—that a garlic clove won't improve.

A first-time visitor to the Provençal countryside can't help but notice the olive orchards that blanket the rocky hillsides. The fruit of these gnarled trees is perhaps the most important crop in Provence. Fully ripened and then pressed, the olives yield a fruity olive oil that is the foundation of Provençal cooking. Visit an outdoor market anywhere in Provence and there will be vendors selling olives—green and black—from giant vats. It is the rare Provençal home that has no olives on hand to offer visitors at the hour of the apéritif.

The rough, rocky terrain of the countryside is inhospitable to cattle, but nimble goats and sheep thrive on the herb-covered hillsides. The Provençaux enjoy both young tender lamb and older mutton and swear that the meat is imbued with the thyme and lavender on which the sheep grazed. Many farmers keep small herds of goats and turn the extra milk into cheese for the local market. These farmstead goat cheeses—some fresh and mild, others aged until they are hard and strong—are among the never-exported treasures of the region.

## FIRST COURSES AND LUNCH DISHES

A garlicky vegetable soup, a tuna salad, and soft-scrambled eggs with croutons are among the savory ways that Provençaux begin their meals. At quick lunches and light suppers, these dishes often take center stage.

### PAN BAGNAT
#### *Provençal tuna sandwich*

*Pan bagnat* (bathed bread) is street food in Provence, purchased from mobile sandwich vans on city sidewalks or at the beach. To make it, brush a sturdy sandwich roll with vinaigrette, then stuff it with tomatoes, anchovies, peppers, tuna, and olives. It's the sort of sandwich that gets better if it sits for a while to let the juices soak into the bread.

- 2 French-style baguette loaves
- 1 clove garlic, peeled and halved
  Basic Vinaigrette (see page 31)
- 2 cans (6½ oz each) water-packed albacore tuna, drained
- 2 ripe tomatoes, sliced ⅓ inch thick
- 2 roasted red bell peppers, peeled and cut in ½-inch strips
- 1 large red onion, thinly sliced
- 3 hard-cooked eggs, halved and sliced
- ¼ cup capers
- 6 anchovy fillets
- ⅓ cup pitted Niçoise olives

Slice baguettes in half lengthwise. Rub cut sides with garlic, then brush liberally with vinaigrette. Combine remaining vinaigrette with tuna and stir with a fork to blend. Divide tuna between the two bottom baguette halves. Then layer ingredients in the following order: tomatoes, bell peppers, onion, eggs, capers, anchovies, and olives. Top with upper halves of baguettes and press down firmly. Wrap sandwiches in plastic wrap. Sandwiches may be made up to 4 hours in advance; refrigerate but bring to room temperature before serving. To serve, unwrap and cut each baguette in thirds.

*Serves 6.*

## SALADE NIÇOISE
### Provençal tuna and vegetable salad

In almost every cafe from Menton to Marseille, you'll find *salade Niçoise* on the menu. Purists insist that it should be made with raw vegetables only; most versions, however, contain cooked green beans, boiled potatoes, and, often, beets. Either way, the salad is a perfect summer lunch. Serve it with a chilled rosé wine from Provence or a Sauvignon Blanc.

¼ cup mixed fresh herbs (parsley, chives, basil)

2 recipes Basic Vinaigrette (see page 31)

½ pound green beans, ends trimmed

12 small red new potatoes

2 tablespoons olive oil

6 ripe plum tomatoes, halved or quartered

1 cucumber, peeled, halved, seeded, and sliced ¼ inch thick

1 bunch radishes, ends trimmed

2 cans (6½ oz each) canned water-packed albacore tuna, drained

3 hard-cooked eggs, peeled and halved or quartered

1 tin (2 oz) anchovy fillets in olive oil, drained, for garnish

1 red onion, thinly sliced, for garnish

⅔ cup Niçoise olives

1 head romaine lettuce (pale inner leaves only)

Croutons à l'Ail (see page 114)

**1.** In a medium bowl combine herbs and vinaigrette and whisk to blend. Set aside.

**2.** Bring a large pot of salted water to a boil over high heat. Add green beans and cook until barely tender (6 to 8 minutes). Drain and refresh under cold running water to stop cooking. Drain again and pat dry.

**3.** Bring a large pot of salted water to a boil over high heat. Add potatoes and cook until just tender when

pierced with a knife (8 to 10 minutes). Drain thoroughly and pat dry. Place in a small bowl and add olive oil. Toss to coat with oil.

**4.** On a very large platter, arrange beans, potatoes, tomatoes, cucumber, and radishes in neat mounds. Place tuna in center. Fill in spaces with hard-cooked eggs. Garnish with anchovies and onion slices. Scatter olives randomly. Tuck romaine around outside of platter. If platter is large enough, place croutons on platter; if not, serve alongside in a basket. Just before serving, drizzle salad with 1 cup of the vinaigrette. Pass the remaining vinaigrette separately.

*Serves 6.*

*The Provençal version of tuna salad—salade Niçoise—gives the cook a chance to design an eye-catching arrangement.*

93

*The aromatic basil-and-garlic topping called pistou is the crowning touch on this Provençal vegetable soup.*

### OEUFS BROUILLÉS AU COULIS DE TOMATES
**Scrambled eggs with fresh tomato sauce**

You'll almost never find eggs served for breakfast in France. Instead, eggs are a first course or the main event of a light supper. Scrambled eggs with fresh tomato sauce and garlic croutons might be served in a Provençal home on Sunday evening, followed by a green salad, some local goat cheese, and a baked apple.

  10  *eggs*
       *Kosher salt and freshly ground pepper*
    3  *tablespoons unsalted butter*
  ⅔  *cup Coulis de Tomates (see right)*
       *Croutons à l'Ail (see page 114)*

**1.** In a large mixing bowl, whisk eggs lightly. Season with salt and pepper. In a large skillet over moderately low heat, melt butter. Add eggs and scramble slowly until just set (5 to 8 minutes).

**2.** While scrambling eggs, heat tomato sauce in a small saucepan over moderately low heat. When eggs are cooked to desired doneness, turn them out onto a warm platter. Make a trough in the center and fill with tomato sauce. Arrange croutons around edge of platter or pass them separately.

*Serves 6.*

### COULIS DE TOMATES
**Fresh tomato sauce**

To make a great tomato sauce you need great tomatoes. Prepare this sauce in quantity when summer tomatoes are at the peak of flavor, and freeze several batches for future use.

  2  *tablespoons olive oil*
  ½  *cup minced shallot*
  1  *tablespoon minced garlic*
  3  *pounds ripe tomatoes, peeled, seeded, and coarsely chopped*
  1  *teaspoon minced fresh thyme*
  2  *teaspoons tomato paste*
  2  *tablespoons unsalted butter, softened*
  ¼  *cup minced fresh basil*
      *Kosher salt and freshly ground pepper*

**1.** In a large saucepan over moderate heat, heat olive oil. Add shallot and garlic and sauté until fragrant and slightly softened (about 3 minutes). Add tomatoes and thyme; reduce heat to moderately low and simmer, stirring occasionally, until reduced and thickened (20 to 30 minutes).

**2.** Add tomato paste, butter, and basil, and whisk until butter melts. Remove from heat and season to taste with salt and pepper.

*Makes about 2 cups.*

**Make-Ahead Tip** Tomato sauce may be refrigerated for up to 2 weeks or frozen for up to 1 year.

## SOUPE AU PISTOU
### Vegetable soup with basil purée

Stir a spoonful of Pistou—a purée of basil, garlic, and cheese—into a thick vegetable soup to make one of the best-loved dishes of the Provençal kitchen. Note that the white beans need to soak overnight.

- ½ cup small dried white beans
- 12 cups Fond de Volaille (see page 32)
- 1 onion, cut in ½-inch dice
- 1 leek (white part only), sliced ½ inch thick
- 1 stalk celery, cut in ½-inch dice
- ½ large potato, peeled and cut in ½-inch dice
- 2 carrots, cut in ½-inch dice
- 1 cup tomato, peeled, seeded, and coarsely chopped
- ¾ cup green beans, cut in 1-inch lengths
- 2 small zucchini, cut in ½-inch dice
- ½ cup dried macaroni
- 1 cup grated Gruyère cheese

### Pistou

- 2 tablespoons minced garlic
- 4 tablespoons olive oil
- 1 cup fresh basil leaves
- ½ cup grated Gruyère cheese

**1.** Put white beans in a bowl and cover by 1 inch with cold water. Let soak overnight. Drain.

**2.** In a large stockpot over moderate heat, bring stock to a boil. Add white beans, reduce heat to low, and simmer for 35 minutes. Add onion, leek, celery, potato, and carrots. Simmer 20 minutes. Add tomato, green beans, zucchini, and macaroni, and simmer until all vegetables are tender (about 20 minutes more). Serve in warm bowls; garnish each serving with 2 teaspoons Pistou. Pass extra Pistou and Gruyère at the table.

*Serves 6.*

**Pistou**  Place all ingredients in a blender or food processor and blend until smooth.

*Makes about ½ cup.*

---

# *menu*

## SUMMER TERRACE DINNER À LA PROVENÇALE

*Caviar d'Aubergines*

*Olives Noires Marinées*

*Fougasse*

*Soupe aux Poissons*

*Salade de Pois Chiches*

*Loup Grillé au Fenouil*

*Glace aux Abricots et au Miel*

*Sauvignon Blanc*

---

*In Provençal towns and cities, life is largely lived outdoors. The Provençaux often take dinner in sidewalk cafés or in the courtyards and on the terraces of their homes. The following menu is typical of a midsummer meal in Provence—zesty in flavor, relaxed in style, and based on seasonal produce. For a stand-up cocktail hour, fill an ice bucket with a couple of bottles of crisp white wine and set the hors d'oeuvres on a small table where guests can serve themselves. You can serve the same wine throughout the meal or switch to a rosé or a light-bodied red with the sea bass. Menu serves eight.*

---

## CAVIAR D'AUBERGINES
### Eggplant spread

A creamy eggplant purée to spread on warm Fougasse (see page 97) gets this dinner off to a delectable start. For an intriguing smoky flavor, cook eggplant over charcoal, turning often until flesh is soft and skin is blackened.

- 2 pounds (about 2 large) eggplant
- ½ large onion, peeled
- 1 clove garlic, peeled
- 2 tablespoons olive oil
- 1 tablespoon red wine vinegar
- 2 tablespoons lemon juice
  Kosher salt and freshly ground pepper
- ½ cup Coulis de Tomates (see page 94)
- 3 tablespoons minced fresh basil

**1.** Preheat oven to 350° F. With a small, sharp knife, cut a half-dozen slits in skin of each eggplant to allow steam to escape. Place eggplants on a baking sheet. Bake until very soft (about 1 hour).

**2.** When cool enough to handle, peel eggplants and place pulp in a food processor or blender with onion and garlic. Blend until smooth. Add oil, vinegar, and lemon juice, and pulse to blend. Transfer mixture to a bowl. Season to taste with salt and pepper. Stir in tomato sauce and basil.

*Makes about 4 cups, 8 servings.*

**Make-Ahead Tip**  This spread may be made up to 2 days ahead, omitting basil. Refrigerate, but bring to room temperature to serve. Just before serving, mince basil and stir it in; taste spread and adjust seasoning.

*Marinated Niçoise olives and a crisp white wine launch this Provençal summer dinner, with grilled sea bass and a chick-pea salad to follow.*

## OLIVES NOIRES MARINÉES
### Marinated Niçoise olives

Tiny black Niçoise olives are sold at specialty food stores and well-stocked supermarkets. Green *picholine* olives, another Provençal variety, can be substituted in whole or in part. Note that the olives should marinate for at least two days.

> 1 pound Niçoise olives, drained of all brine
> Lemon-Chive Vinaigrette (see page 31)
> Zest of 1 lemon, removed in large strips with a sharp vegetable peeler
> 2 large cloves garlic, halved
> 1 tablespoon fennel seed
> 1 bay leaf
> 2 tablespoons minced chives (optional)

In a large, clean glass jar, combine olives, vinaigrette, lemon zest, garlic, fennel seed, and bay leaf. Cover and shake to blend well. Refrigerate for at least 2 days or up to 1 month. To serve, transfer olives with a slotted spoon to a small serving bowl and sprinkle with chives (if desired).

*Makes 1 pound olives.*


## FOUGASSE
### Provençal flatbread

Long before there were baking pans and temperature-controlled ovens, there was *fougasse*, a flat bread baked on the floor of the hearth. A warm fougasse, brushed with olive oil and dusted with rosemary and salt, can be cut in small squares for an appetizer or in larger pieces as a partner for cheese or grilled meats. Note that the dough must rise for about three hours.

> 1 envelope active dry yeast
> 1½ cups cool (approximately 75° F) water
> 7 tablespoons olive oil, plus oil for greasing
> 3 cups bread flour, plus flour for kneading
> ½ cup whole wheat flour
> 3 teaspoons kosher salt
> 2 large cloves garlic, minced
> 1 teaspoon minced fresh rosemary

**1.** In a large bowl sprinkle yeast over the water and stir with a fork to dissolve. Let stand 5 minutes. Whisk in 4 tablespoons of the olive oil. In a separate bowl stir together the 3 cups bread flour, whole wheat flour, and 1 teaspoon of the salt; add flour, 1 cup at a time, to yeast mixture, stirring well after each addition. When dough begins to come away from sides of bowl, turn out onto a lightly floured surface. Knead in garlic and ½ teaspoon of the rosemary. Continue kneading, adding more flour as necessary, until dough is shiny, elastic, and no longer sticky (about 10 minutes).

**2.** Transfer dough to a lightly oiled bowl and turn to coat all sides with oil. Cover bowl with plastic wrap and set aside until dough triples in volume (about 2 hours).

**3.** Punch dough down and place in an oiled 9- by 13- by 1-inch baking sheet. Press and pat dough until it covers entire surface of pan. Cover with a towel and let rise until dough reaches top edge of sheet (about 45 minutes).

**4.** Preheat oven to 400° F. Just before baking, dimple dough with fingertips and drizzle surface with 2 tablespoons of the olive oil. Sprinkle with the remaining ½ teaspoon rosemary and the remaining 2 teaspoons salt. Transfer to middle rack of oven. Put an empty baking dish on lower rack. Quickly pour 1 cup boiling water into empty dish and close oven door. Bake until bread is golden and well risen (20 to 25 minutes). Remove bread from pan and place on a rack. Brush top surface with the remaining 1 tablespoon oil. Cut into squares and serve warm.

*Makes one 9- by 13- by 1-inch flatbread.*


## SOUPE AUX POISSONS
### Mediterranean fish soup

This aromatic soup has no visible pieces of fish—just the essence of fish, along with tomatoes, saffron, and fennel. A rock cod is simmered in broth until it gives up its flavor, then the soup is puréed and served over croutons.

> 1 whole rock cod or red snapper (2½ lb), head on
> ¼ cup olive oil
> ½ pound yellow onions, chopped
> 3 cloves garlic, minced
> 1 pound ripe tomatoes, coarsely chopped
> 1 teaspoon fennel seed
> 3 sprigs thyme or ½ teaspoon dried thyme
> 1 bay leaf
> ¼ to ½ gram (½ to 1 teaspoon) saffron threads
> Salt and freshly ground black pepper
> Croutons à l'Ail (see page 114)
> Aioli (optional; see page 100)

**1.** Clean fish well inside and out. Use a large, heavy knife or cleaver to cut fish into 6 or 8 pieces. Set aside.

**2.** In a large, heavy stockpot over moderate heat, heat olive oil. Add onions and garlic, and sauté for 3 minutes. Add tomatoes, fennel seed, thyme, and bay leaf. Sauté for 3 minutes. Raise heat to high and bring sauce to a rapid boil. Add fish, reduce heat to moderate, and simmer for 5 minutes. Raise heat to high and add 1 gallon water. Bring to a boil; reduce heat to moderate and boil, uncovered, for 30 minutes. Add ½ teaspoon saffron and cook for 1 minute; if saffron flavor is too subtle, add the remaining ½ teaspoon saffron and cook an additional minute. Remove from heat; discard bay leaf.

**3.** Purée soup in food mill, removing fish bones as necessary to allow mixture to pass through mill. Season to taste with salt and pepper. Return to a clean pot and reheat to serve. Serve with a basket of croutons to float in the soup and Aioli to spread on the croutons (if desired).

*Makes 8 cups, 8 servings.*

## SALADE DE POIS CHICHES
### Chick-pea salad

Chick-peas soak up the flavor of garlic, lemon, and mint in this cool and refreshing summer salad. Note that the chick-peas need to soak 24 hours.

> 2½ cups dried chick-peas
> 1 teaspoon baking soda
> 1 teaspoon freshly ground pepper, plus pepper to taste
> 1 bay leaf
> 2 cloves garlic, peeled
> ½ teaspoon minced fresh thyme
> 3 tablespoons olive oil
> ⅔ cup minced red onion
> 1½ tablespoons minced garlic
> ⅓ cup freshly squeezed lemon juice
> ½ cup dry white wine
> ½ cup minced fresh mint
> Kosher salt
> ¼ cup thinly sliced red onion

**1.** Place chick-peas in a saucepan with baking soda and cold water to cover by 2 inches. Soak 24 hours. Drain. Put chick-peas in a medium saucepan and cover with cold water. Add the 1 teaspoon pepper, bay leaf, garlic cloves, and thyme. Bring to a boil over high heat. Reduce heat to maintain a simmer, cover, and cook until peas are tender but not mushy (about 45 minutes). Drain; discard garlic and bay leaf. Cool chick-peas to room temperature.

**2.** In a large skillet over moderate heat, heat olive oil. Add minced onion and minced garlic and sauté for 3 minutes. Add lemon juice, wine, 1 tablespoon of the mint, and chick-peas. Cook until chick-peas are hot throughout (5 to 7 minutes). Season to taste with salt and pepper. Stir in all but 1 tablespoon of remaining mint. Cool chick-peas to room temperature.

**3.** Thirty minutes before serving, put cooled chick-peas, sliced red onion, and remaining 1 tablespoon mint in a serving bowl. Stir to blend. Serve at room temperature.

*Serves 8.*

**Make-Ahead Tip** Salad may be prepared through step 1 up to 3 days in advance. Refrigerate chick-peas in their cooking liquid. Drain before continuing with recipe.

## LOUP GRILLÉ AU FENOUIL
### Sea bass grilled over fennel

In the south of France, fresh fennel stalks are piled directly on burning coals to flavor the fish or meat cooked above them. Sometimes supermarkets trim bulb fennel for display; if yours does, ask the produce manager to save the stalks and feathery leaves for you.

> 8 sea bass fillets (about 8 oz each and at least 1 in. thick)
> 10 tablespoons olive oil
> 10 tablespoons freshly squeezed lemon juice
> 1 tablespoon kosher salt
> 1 teaspoon freshly ground pepper
> 2 large fennel stalks
> Fennel leaves, for garnish
> Lemon wedges, for garnish

**1.** Place fish on a large platter or in a glass baking dish. In a small bowl whisk together olive oil, lemon juice, salt, and pepper. Brush fish with half the mixture.

**2.** Prepare a very hot charcoal fire. Preheat grill over hot coals at least 5 minutes to keep fish from sticking. When coals are coated with gray ash, place fennel stalks directly on coals. Let smoke die down, then grill fish 3 to 4 minutes on each side or until done to your liking, basting occasionally with remaining marinade. Transfer to a warm serving platter or to individual plates. Garnish sea bass with feathery fennel leaves. Accompany with lemon wedges.

*Serves 8.*

## GLACE AUX ABRICOTS ET AU MIEL
### Apricot-honey ice cream

Lavender honey from Provence is prized throughout France, for spreading on a breakfast baguette or for sweetening ice cream. Note that the mixture needs to chill for at least 12 hours before freezing.

> 1 pound ripe apricots
> ½ cup plus 1 tablespoon lavender honey or other high-quality honey
> 1 tablespoon freshly squeezed lemon juice
> 2 cups milk
> 6 egg yolks
> 1 cup half-and-half
> ½ teaspoon kosher salt

**1.** *To make in a food mill:* Halve and pit apricots and purée them in mill, discarding skins. *To purée in a food processor or blender:* Apricots must be peeled first. If they are very ripe, skins may slip off easily. If not, bring a large pot of water to a boil over high heat. With a small, sharp knife, cut an *x* in end of each apricot. Blanch in boiling water 30 seconds, then drain and place in ice water. Skin should slip off easily. Halve and pit apricots. Purée in food processor or blender. You should have about 1 cup purée.

**2.** Transfer purée to a small bowl and stir in the 1 tablespoon honey and lemon juice.

**3.** In a large saucepan over moderate heat, heat milk and the ½ cup honey, stirring often, until honey dissolves and milk is just about to boil. In a medium bowl whisk egg yolks until pale and thick. Gradually whisk in 1 cup hot milk, then pour egg mixture into hot milk in saucepan, whisking constantly. Reduce heat to low and cook, stirring constantly, until mixture reaches 180° F. Do not boil.

**4.** Stir in half-and-half and salt. Strain custard through a sieve into a container. Cool, then stir in purée. Cover and chill 12 to 24 hours. Transfer to an ice cream freezer and freeze according to manufacturer's directions.

*Makes about 1½ quarts.*

## MAIN COURSES AND SIDE DISHES

What good is a main course without garlic? The saffron-scented fish stew, the Sunday leg of lamb, the lovingly simmered beef stew—in Provence, all get the benefit of a little garlic. Make that a lot of garlic.

### RATATOUILLE
#### *Mixed vegetable stew*

Eggplant, tomatoes, bell peppers, and zucchini are the stars of the Provençal summer garden. Combine them in one pot with the usual Provençal aromatics—garlic, basil, and thyme— and you have an authentic ratatouille. The dish travels well for picnics and flatters grilled lamb, chicken, or veal.

- 1 *large eggplant (about 1 lb)*
- 1 *tablespoon kosher salt, plus salt to taste*
- 2 *pounds ripe tomatoes, peeled, halved, and seeded*
- 11 *tablespoons olive oil*
- ½ *pound zucchini, sliced ½ inch thick*
- ½ *pound yellow crookneck squash, sliced ½ inch thick*
- 1 *green bell pepper, seeded, ribs removed, and cut in 1-inch squares*
- 1 *red bell pepper, seeded, ribs removed, and cut in ¼-inch-wide strips*
- 1½ *cups coarsely chopped onion*
- 1 *tablespoon minced garlic*
- 3 *sprigs thyme or ½ teaspoon dried thyme*
- 6 *tablespoons coarsely chopped parsley*
- 6 *tablespoons coarsely chopped fresh basil*
   *Freshly ground pepper*

**1.** Cut unpeeled eggplant into 1-inch cubes. In a medium bowl toss cubes and the 1 tablespoon salt, then transfer to a sieve or colander and allow to drain for 30 minutes.

**2.** Cut each tomato half in quarters and let drain in a colander or sieve for 30 minutes.

**3.** In a large skillet over moderate heat, heat 2 tablespoons of the oil. Add zucchini and crookneck squash, and sauté until lightly browned (about 5 minutes). Transfer to a bowl with a slotted spoon. Add 2 more tablespoons oil to pan and sauté bell peppers for 5 minutes; add to bowl.

**4.** Rinse eggplant, drain, and pat dry. Add 4 tablespoons of the olive oil to skillet; when oil is hot, add eggplant. Sauté, stirring often to prevent sticking, until eggplant is lightly colored and softened (about 7 minutes). Transfer to bowl with other vegetables.

**5.** Add the remaining 3 tablespoons oil to skillet. Sauté onion and garlic until garlic is fragrant (about 3 minutes). Add tomatoes, thyme, and 2 tablespoons parsley. Simmer 10 minutes. Return sautéed vegetables to skillet and simmer 10 minutes. Vegetables should be tender but not mushy. Remove from heat and gently stir in the remaining parsley and 4 tablespoons basil. Season to taste with salt and pepper. Serve warm, at room temperature, or cold. Add the remaining basil and adjust seasoning just before serving.

*Serves 6.*

*The famous vegetable stew of Provence, ratatouille, is delicious hot, warm, or at room temperature.*

## BOURRIDE
### Provençal fish soup with garlic mayonnaise

Leftover aioli is delicious on bread, sandwiches, cold vegetables, grilled chicken, and roast lamb.

- 3 tablespoons olive oil
- 1½ cups chopped onion
- 1 leek (white and pale green part), cleaned and cut into ½-inch rounds
- 1 stalk celery, chopped
- 1 carrot, chopped
- 3 pounds meaty fish bones
- 1 cup dry white wine
  Zest of ½ orange, removed with a sharp vegetable peeler
- 3 large sprigs thyme or ½ teaspoon dried thyme
- 3 bay leaves
- 1 teaspoon freshly ground pepper
- 1 teaspoon fennel seed
  Kosher salt
- 2½ pounds fish fillets (preferably a mixture: sea bass, cod, snapper, halibut), cut in 1½-inch cubes
  Croutons à l'Ail (see page 114)
- 3 tablespoons minced chives, for garnish

### Aioli

- 1½ tablespoons coarsely chopped garlic
- 1 teaspoon kosher salt, plus salt to taste
- 3 egg yolks
- 1 cup olive oil
- ½ cup safflower oil
  Lemon juice

**1.** In a large stockpot over moderate heat, heat olive oil. Add onion, leek, celery, and carrot. Reduce heat to low and cook gently until vegetables are soft (about 15 minutes). Add fish bones, wine, 2 cups water, orange zest, thyme, bay leaves, pepper, and fennel seed. Raise heat to moderate and bring mixture to a boil, skimming any scum that rises to the surface. Reduce heat to maintain a simmer and cook for 35 minutes. Strain soup into a clean pot. Season to taste with salt.

**2.** Return broth to a simmer over moderate heat. Add fish cubes. If using only one type of fish, add all at once; otherwise, add firm fish first, more delicate fish about 2 minutes later. Cook until fish just begins to flake (3 to 4 minutes total). Remove fish with a slotted spoon to a warm platter. Moisten with ¼ cup broth, cover, and keep warm in a low oven.

**3.** Put 1 cup of the Aioli in a medium bowl. Whisk in ½ cup hot broth. Whisk this mixture back into stockpot. Cook over low heat, stirring constantly with a wooden spoon, until visibly thickened (about 3 minutes). Do not allow soup to boil or it will curdle.

**4.** To serve, place 2 or 3 croutons in each of 6 warm soup bowls. Put a few cubes of fish in each bowl. Ladle broth into bowls. Garnish each serving with minced chives. Pass any extra croutons and the remaining 1 cup Aioli separately.

*Serves 6.*

**Aioli**   *To prepare by hand:* Combine garlic and the 1 teaspoon salt in a mortar and grind to a paste with pestle. Or, sprinkle salt over garlic on a cutting board and mince to a paste. In a small bowl whisk yolks together well. Begin adding olive oil to eggs drop by drop, whisking constantly. When mixture is thick and smooth, add oil faster, still whisking constantly. Whisk in safflower oil, then whisk in garlic paste. Season to taste with lemon juice, adding more salt if necessary. *To make in a food processor:* Process garlic, salt, and yolks until smooth. With motor running, begin adding oils drop by drop through feed tube. When mixture is thick and smooth, add oil faster. Transfer to a bowl and season to taste with lemon juice, adding more salt if necessary.

*Makes 2 cups.*

## GIGOT D'AGNEAU À LA PROVENÇALE
### Roast leg of lamb with garlic and lavender

The fragrant lavender that scents the hillsides of Provence is a particularly good partner to lamb. Serve the lamb with a drizzle of its own aromatic juices; accompany with Purée de Pommes de Terre à l'Ail (see page 103) and a bottle of red Côtes-de-Provence or Rhône wine. Note that the lamb needs to marinate at least six hours.

- 1 leg of lamb (7 lb), bone-in
- 3 cloves garlic, peeled and sliced thin lengthwise
- 3 tablespoons olive oil
- 1 tablespoon kosher salt
- 1 teaspoon freshly ground pepper
- ½ teaspoon fennel seed
- 1½ teaspoons dried ground lavender (see Note)
- ½ teaspoon minced dried orange peel (see Note)

**1.** With a small, sharp knife, make slits all over lamb and insert garlic slivers. In a small bowl whisk together olive oil, salt, pepper, fennel seed, lavender, and orange peel. Rub spice mixture all over lamb. Place lamb in a baking dish, cover with plastic wrap, and refrigerate for at least 6 hours or up to 1 day.

**2.** Preheat oven to 450° F. Place lamb on a rack in a large roasting pan and roast, fat side up, for 10 minutes. Reduce heat to 375° F and continue cooking until a meat thermometer inserted in thickest part of leg registers 120° F (about 1 hour) for rare lamb or 130° F (about 1 hour and 20 minutes) for medium lamb. Let stand 10 minutes before carving. Reserve any juices to spoon over meat.

*Serves 6.*

*Note*   Dried lavender can be purchased at specialty herb and spice stores. Dried orange peel is available in well-stocked supermarkets.

*A dollop of golden aioli (garlic mayonnaise) gives this traditional Provençal bourride its pungent character.*

## BOUILLABAISSE
### Provençal fish stew

What started as a humble soup made by fishermen's wives to use up fish too small or lowly to sell has become a dish that commands a high price in Provençal restaurants. Lobster, shrimp, and other expensive fish and shellfish can turn a rustic bouillabaisse into an extravagant main course. In the spirit of the original bouillabaisse, cooks who live near the ocean should try making the dish with local rockfish and crustaceans. The following version includes the traditional garnish of rouille, a spicy saffron mayonnaise.

- 3 pounds mixed fish fillets (bass, cod, halibut, snapper), cut in 4-ounce pieces
- 5 tablespoons olive oil
- 3 tablespoons Pernod or other anise-flavored apéritif
- 1 teaspoon kosher salt, plus salt to taste
- ½ teaspoon freshly ground pepper, plus pepper to taste
- 2 pounds fish bones (white fish only—no salmon)
- 2 cups coarsely chopped onion
- 6 cloves garlic, peeled and crushed with flat side of knife
- 1 cup coarsely chopped leek
- 1 pound ripe tomatoes, each cored and cut into 8 wedges
- ½ teaspoon dried thyme
- 2 bay leaves
- ½ teaspoon fennel seed, lightly crushed
- 3 strips orange zest (each 3 in. long)
- 4 sprigs parsley
- 1 bottle (750 ml) dry white wine
- 3 cups boiling potatoes, cut in ½-inch cubes
- 18 mussels, scrubbed and debearded
- 6 large shrimp, in shells
- 6 cooked crab claws, cracked
- ½ to ¾ grams (1 to 1½ teaspoons) saffron threads
  Croutons (see page 16)

### Rouille

- 3 egg yolks
- ¼ teaspoon dry mustard
- 1½ tablespoons minced garlic
- 1½ cups olive oil
- ½ gram (1 teaspoon) saffron threads
- 1 tablespoon warm fish broth from Bouillabaisse
- ¼ teaspoon cayenne pepper, or more to taste
- 1 teaspoon Pernod or other anise-flavored apéritif
  Kosher salt
  Lemon juice

**1.** Place fish fillets on a large platter. In a small bowl whisk together 2 tablespoons of the olive oil, 2 tablespoons of the Pernod, the 1 teaspoon salt, and the ½ teaspoon pepper. Brush mixture on fillets and set aside.

**2.** In a large stockpot over moderate heat, heat the remaining 3 tablespoons olive oil. Add fish bones and stir to coat with oil. Sauté 3 minutes. Add onion, garlic, leek, tomatoes, thyme, bay leaves, fennel seed, orange zest, and parsley. Sauté, stirring, for 3 minutes. Add wine and 9 cups water and bring to a boil. Reduce heat to low and simmer for 25 minutes.

**3.** Transfer soup to a food mill, discarding fish heads and large bones. Purée soup directly into a large, clean pot. Bring to a simmer. Add potatoes and cook for 7 minutes. Add firm-fleshed fish such as bass, cod, or halibut. Return soup to a simmer and cook for 3 minutes. Add mussels, shrimp, crab claws, and saffron. Return to a simmer and cook for 2 minutes. Add delicate fish such as snapper and cook for 3 minutes. Stir in the remaining 1 tablespoon Pernod and cook until all fish and potatoes are done (about 3 more minutes). Season to taste with salt and pepper. Bouillabaisse should be quite peppery.

**4.** To serve, put a crouton into each of 6 warm bowls. Ladle soup over croutons. Pass Rouille separately.

*Serves 6.*

**Rouille**   Put egg yolks, mustard, and garlic in a blender or food processor. Blend 30 seconds. With motor running, begin adding oil drop by drop. When mixture is thick and smooth, oil may be added faster. Continue adding oil in a steady stream until all is used. Dissolve saffron in broth. Add to blender along with cayenne and Pernod. Pulse just to mix. Transfer to a bowl and stir in salt and lemon juice to taste.

*Makes 2 cups.*

## DAUBE DE BOEUF À LA PROVENÇALE
### Provençal beef stew

Garlic, thyme, and orange zest mark this as the Provençal version of beef stew. Like most such stews, the best *daubes* are made with an inexpensive, gelatinous cut of meat, cooked very slowly and allowed to mellow for a day before serving. Buttered noodles are the traditional accompaniment. Note that the meat needs to marinate at least 12 hours.

- 3 pounds beef chuck
- 1⅓ cups white wine vinegar
- 4 tablespoons olive oil
- 1 teaspoon kosher salt
- ½ teaspoon freshly ground pepper
- 1 bay leaf
- 2 cloves garlic, peeled and crushed with flat side of knife
- 1 teaspoon minced fresh thyme or ½ teaspoon dried thyme
- 2 narrow strips orange zest
- 2 cups dry red wine
- 2 tablespoons minced parsley, for garnish

**1.** Trim meat of excess fat and cut into 2-inch cubes. In a large bowl whisk together vinegar, 2 tablespoons of the oil, salt, pepper, bay leaf, garlic, thyme, and orange zest. Add meat, cover bowl with plastic wrap, and refrigerate for 12 to 18 hours. Drain meat, reserving marinade. Pat meat dry with paper towels.

**2.** In a dutch oven or large skillet with lid over moderately high heat, heat remaining 2 tablespoons olive oil. Brown meat well on all sides. Add wine and reserved marinade. Bring to a simmer and cook, uncovered, for 3 minutes. Reduce heat to maintain a bare simmer. Cover and cook until meat is meltingly tender (about 3 hours). For best flavor, allow daube to cool to room temperature, then refrigerate, covered, overnight. Reheat gently to serve. Ladle stew into warm soup bowls, over buttered noodles if desired, and garnish each serving with parsley.

*Serves 6.*

**Make-Ahead Tip** Stew may be made up to 2 days in advance and refrigerated.

## PURÉE DE POMMES DE TERRE À L'AIL
### *Garlic mashed potatoes*

Mashed potatoes don't get any better than this!

- 2 bulbs garlic
- 2 tablespoons olive oil
- 2 sprigs thyme
- 3 pounds (about 4 large) potatoes, peeled and cut into eighths
- ½ cup whipping cream
- 4 tablespoons unsalted butter, softened
  Kosher salt and freshly ground pepper
- 2 tablespoons minced fresh chervil (optional)

**1.** Preheat oven to 350° F. Remove outermost papery leaves from garlic but do not break bulbs apart or remove thin paper sheath covering each clove. Rub garlic bulbs with olive oil and wrap together in a loose aluminum foil packet; tuck thyme sprigs into packet. Place packet in a baking dish and roast until garlic is very tender (about 1½ hours). When cool enough to handle, peel garlic and squeeze soft cloves into a bowl.

**2.** Place potatoes in a large saucepan and cover by 1 inch with cold salted water. Bring to a boil over moderately high heat. Cover and cook until potatoes are tender (15 to 20 minutes). Drain. Purée potatoes in a food mill or potato ricer, or mash with a potato masher (do not use a food processor). Return to a clean saucepan; stir in cream, butter, and garlic cloves, and beat well. Season to taste with salt and pepper. Transfer to a warm bowl and garnish with minced chervil (if used).

*Serves 6.*

*You know you're in Provence when the beef stew is scented with strips of orange zest.*

Southwest France supplies
Bordeaux wine and Roquefort
cheese; in the Basque country,
cooks make heavy use of
cornmeal and sweet peppers.

# The Southwest

Bordeaux
PÉRIGORD    LIMOUSIN    Lyon
Dordogne R.
GUYENNE
Cahors
Garonne R.
Avignon
GASCONY    Arles
Toulouse
LANGUEDOC
BÉARN
Espelette  Bayonne

Although the town of Bordeaux is the commercial center for the region's world-famous wines, the most distinctive food of the southwest is found in the countryside. There, beans and cabbage lend substance to a hearty duck stew (see Garbure, page 108) and the local mussel soup (see Mouclade, page 106) is laced with Cognac. In the Basque region, peppers both sweet and hot dominate the cooking. Specialties include red pepper soup (see Soupe de Piments d'Espelette, page 116) and spicy chicken with tomatoes and peppers (see Poulet à la Basquaise, page 119). The Basques are also known for their distinctive cornmeal cookies (see Biscuits au Maïs, page 120) and cornmeal cakes (see Gâteau au Maïs, page 120).

# BORDEAUX AND ITS NEIGHBORS

Bordeaux, a major wine and shipping center, is a town of considerable wealth. The food served in the local *restaurants de luxe* and at the tables of the great chateaux bears little resemblance to the rustic food of the countryside.

Bordeaux cooking is refined and sophisticated, designed to flatter the region's elegant wines. Outside of Bordeaux, however, and in the southwest regions of Périgord, Limousin, Gascony, and Guienne, the cooking is rustic, without finesse but with great vitality. This is agricultural country, where hearty eating is the norm and where the cook has abundant and varied resources.

Raising duck is the preoccupation of many farms in this region. Every part of the duck is valued, from feathers to fat. Duck breasts are sautéed or grilled; duck livers are used in pâtés; and duck legs are preserved for long keeping with salt, herbs, and a layer of clear fat.

From the sea come oysters and mussels for grilling and steaming. Mussel soup with Cognac (see Mouclade, right) is a regional specialty. The woods yield wild mushrooms and aromatic black truffles, along with abundant game birds and animals. Orchards produce top-quality prunes, peaches, apples, and pears; the local fruits are eaten fresh, made into fruit compotes, or preserved in the local brandy.

Hard outdoor work leads to hearty appetites. It's little wonder, then, that this area of France is responsible for such filling dishes as garbure (see page 108), cassoulet (see page 109), and *mique sarladaise* (see page 110). The local vineyards yield wines that go wonderfully with such rustic food—namely, the full-bodied red wines from the region of Quercy and its capital, Cahors. These are intense, sturdy wines, which also happen to be excellent partners for the southwest's best-known cheese—the pungent, blue-veined Roquefort.

## SOUP AND SALAD

Cooks in southwestern France don't have to look far to find good material for soups and salads: Atlantic mussels, locally raised ducks, and Cognac from the region's distilleries find their way into many traditional dishes.

### MOUCLADE
### Mussel and saffron bisque

A dash of brandy perks up the mussel soup from Charente, the French *département* where Cognac is made.

> 6 pounds mussels
> 2 cups dry white wine
> ¾ cup minced shallot
> ½ teaspoon freshly ground pepper, plus pepper to taste
> 1 bay leaf
> 1 clove garlic, peeled and crushed
> 2 tablespoons lemon juice
> ½ cup whipping cream
> 3 egg yolks
> 1 teaspoon kosher salt, plus salt to taste
> 1 tablespoon unsalted butter
> ¼ gram (½ teaspoon) saffron threads
> 2 tablespoons Cognac

**1.** Scrub mussels well under cold running water. Pull out hairy beard that protrudes from shell. In a large stockpot over high heat, bring mussels, wine, ½ cup of the shallots, the ½ teaspoon pepper, bay leaf, and garlic to a boil. Cover and steam until mussels open, shaking pot occasionally (3 to 5 minutes). Check pot occasionally and remove mussels to a large bowl as they open. Discard any mussels that refuse to open after 5 minutes.

**2.** Remove and discard top half of each mussel shell. Place mussels in a large bowl and sprinkle with lemon juice. Cover bowl and transfer to a low oven to keep warm.

**3.** Strain cooking liquid through dampened cheesecloth. In a small bowl whisk together cream, egg yolks, and the 1 teaspoon salt. In a large stockpot over low heat, sauté the remaining ¼ cup shallots in

butter for 3 minutes. Add strained mussel liquid and saffron. Cook for 1 minute. Whisk in cream mixture. Stir constantly over low heat for 3 minutes. Add Cognac and cook for another 2 minutes; do not allow soup to boil. Season to taste with salt and pepper. Divide mussels among 6 warm soup bowls. Ladle hot soup over mussels.

*Makes 6 cups, 6 servings.*

### SALADE DE CANARD AUX CRAQUELINS
### Duck salad with duck cracklings

This easy and elegant salad makes a lovely spring lunch. Add oven-crisped baguettes and a bottle of chilled white Zinfandel; for dessert, offer Sorbet de Framboises à la Menthe (see page 114) and store-bought wafer cookies. Note that the duck needs to sit overnight.

> Boneless duck breasts (5 oz each), skin removed and reserved
> 1 tablespoon kosher salt
> 3½ cups Fond de Volaille (see page 32)
> ½ cup dry red wine
> Mustard Vinaigrette (see page 31)
> 1 tablespoon capers
> 1 bunch radishes, thinly sliced
> ⅔ cup celery, cut in ½-inch dice
> 2 bunches watercress

**1.** Sprinkle duck breasts with salt. Thread breasts loosely together using a larding needle and kitchen string. (String makes it easier to lift breasts in and out of poaching liquid, but you may eliminate this procedure.) Place duck breasts in a baking dish, cover, and refrigerate overnight. Bring to room temperature before continuing.

**2.** Preheat broiler. Broil duck skins on a rack in broiler pan until crisp (about 8 minutes). Drain on paper towels, then slice into ¼-inch-wide strips with a sharp knife.

**3.** In a large saucepan over moderate heat, bring stock and wine to a boil. Reduce heat to maintain a simmer and cook for 5 minutes. Wipe salt off duck breasts with a paper towel. Add breasts to stock and simmer to desired doneness (about 4 minutes for rosy meat, 5 minutes for medium). Remove breasts from stock.

**4.** In a small bowl whisk together vinaigrette and capers. Combine radishes and celery in a medium bowl, add 2 tablespoons of the vinaigrette, and toss to coat.

**5.** Wash and dry watercress, removing any large stems. Arrange watercress on a large serving platter or on individual plates. Spoon celery and radishes on top of watercress. Slice duck breasts neatly against the grain and arrange attractively on platter. Drizzle remaining vinaigrette over salad and garnish with cracklings. Serve immediately.

*Serves 6.*

## MAIN COURSES AND SIDE DISHES

The gastronomic renown of southwestern France is based on rustic farmhouse specialties such as garbure, cassoulet, and *confit d'oie*.

### JARRET D'AGNEAU À L'AIL
*Lamb shanks with garlic sauce*

Meaty shanks, cooked slowly, are one of the most succulent cuts of lamb. To accompany this garlicky dish, try roast potatoes or buttered noodles and a robust red Côtes-du-Rhône.

> 6 *lamb shanks (about 1 to 1⅓ lb each), sawed into 3 or 4 pieces*
> 2 *bulbs garlic, separated into unpeeled cloves*
> 6 *large tomatoes, cored*
> 3 *tablespoons olive oil*
> 1 *tablespoon kosher salt*
> 1½ *teaspoons freshly ground pepper*
> ½ *cup minced shallots*
> 4 *large sprigs fresh thyme or 1 teaspoon dried thyme*
> 1½ *cups dry red wine*

**1.** Preheat oven to 325° F. Trim shanks of any visible fat; reserve. In a large roasting pan, drizzle garlic cloves and tomatoes with oil. Roast, uncovered, for 45 minutes. Transfer tomatoes and garlic to a bowl. When cool enough to handle, peel tomatoes and garlic. Chop tomatoes coarsely.

**2.** Raise oven temperature to 400° F. Season shanks with salt and pepper. Roast 30 minutes; turn shanks, add shallots, and cook for 15 minutes.

**3.** Spoon off all but 2 tablespoons fat. Add tomatoes, garlic, thyme, and red wine to pan. Cover and bake for 30 minutes. Uncover and continue baking for 30 minutes. Turn shanks and continue cooking until they are fork-tender (20 to 30 more minutes). Remove from oven; discard thyme.

**4.** Transfer shanks to a warm platter, cover loosely with aluminum foil, and keep warm in a low oven. Pour contents of pan into a measuring cup and let settle 5 minutes. Spoon off any fat that floats to surface. Place contents of cup in a blender or food processor and blend until smooth and silky. Reheat sauce and spoon over and around shanks.

*Serves 6.*

*Garlic perfumes the tomato sauce for these tender lamb shanks in a preparation typical of the cooking of southwest France.*

*The pride of southwest France, the rustic cassoulet, is a dish for cold weather and hearty appetites.*

## GARBURE
### *Country soup of preserved duck, beans, and cabbage*

The composition of this hearty soup varies from cook to cook, but beans and cabbage are a constant and preserved duck is common. Note that the dried beans, if you use them, need to soak overnight.

>   3   *pounds fresh fava beans or 2 cups dried white beans*
>   3   *legs Confit de Canard (see page 109)*
>   2   *ham hocks*
>   6   *cups shredded green cabbage*
>   6   *medium leeks (white part only), cut in 1-inch lengths*
>   6   *small carrots, peeled*
>   3   *tablespoons fat from Confit de Canard (see page 109)*
>   1   *tablespoon minced garlic*
>   1½  *cups diced onion*
>   1   *cup diced celery*
>   ¼   *cup minced parsley*
>   2   *red bell peppers, roasted, peeled, seeded, and cut into ¼-inch strips*
>   1   *bunch (about 10 oz) Swiss chard, coarsely chopped*
>       *Kosher salt and freshly ground pepper*

**1.** If using dried white beans, cover them with cold water and let soak overnight. The next day, bring duck legs to room temperature. Let excess fat drip off into a container. Separate drumsticks from thighs.

**2.** In a stockpot combine hocks and 1 gallon water. Bring to a boil over high heat. Reduce heat to maintain a simmer and cook 3 hours. Add cabbage, leeks, carrots, and dried beans (if using). Simmer 1 hour.

**3.** In a large skillet over moderate heat, melt the 3 tablespoons duck fat. Add garlic, onion, and celery, and sauté for 10 minutes. Stir in parsley and remove from heat. Add to soup along with duck legs and fresh fava beans (if using). Simmer for 30 minutes. Add roasted peppers and chard, and simmer for 30 minutes.

**4.** Remove ham hocks; slice meat off of hocks and return to pot. Soup should be quite thick. Season to taste with salt and pepper, then serve in warm soup bowls, making sure that each portion includes either a drumstick or a thigh.

*Serves 6.*

## CASSOULET
### Casserole of preserved duck, pork, and beans

Not a dish for dainty eaters, a hearty cassoulet tastes best when the weather is brisk and appetites lively. This rib-sticking, garlic-laced mixture of meats and beans needs only a simple green salad (see page 31) and a fruit compote (see page 111) for dessert. Note that the beans must soak over-night. Cassoulet may be made up to two days in advance and refrigerated.

    2 pounds small dried
      white beans
    1 teaspoon dried thyme or 2
      teaspoons minced fresh thyme
    2 onions, peeled and halved,
      each half stuck with a clove
    1 bay leaf
    1 bulb garlic, halved crosswise
    2 ham hocks
    2 teaspoons freshly ground
      pepper
      Kosher salt
    6 legs Confit de Canard
      (at right)
    2 tablespoons fat from
      Confit de Canard (at right)
    2 cups coarsely chopped onion
    1 tablespoon minced garlic
    2 pounds garlic pork sausage
      links, cut into 2-inch chunks
    ½ cup day-old bread crumbs

**1.** Cover beans with cold water and soak overnight. Drain beans and place in a large stockpot. Add thyme, onion halves, bay leaf, garlic bulb, ham hocks, and black pepper. Add cold water to cover by 1½ inches. Bring to a simmer over moderately high heat. Reduce heat to low and cook for 2 hours, adding water as necessary to keep beans barely covered. Taste beans and add salt if necessary. Remove onion halves and garlic bulb. Transfer beans, bay leaf, and ham hocks to a large earthen-ware casserole.

**2.** Bring duck legs to room tempera-ture, letting excess fat drip off. Wipe duck legs with paper towels.

**3.** Preheat oven to 325° F. In a medium skillet over low heat, melt the 2 tablespoons fat. Add chopped onion and minced garlic and sauté for 10 minutes. Add to beans along with sausage and duck legs. Cover loosely with aluminum foil and bake for 1¼ hours. Uncover and sprinkle with bread crumbs. Bake for 30 minutes.

*Serves 6.*

## CONFIT DE CANARD
### Preserved duck

Throughout southwestern France, cooks are experts at *confit*, the fat-sealed preserves of pork, goose, duck, and sausage. The unusual cooking process renders the meats especially tender and tasty and prepares them for long keeping. The following duck confit may be used in Cassoulet (at left) and Garbure (see page 108). Or you can scrape off most of the fat, sauté the duck legs, and serve them with panfried potatoes. The garlic cloves may be added to a potato purée or squeezed out of their papery shells and served with toast. Use leftover duck fat for cooking potatoes and omelets. Note that the duck legs must marinate 36 hours.

    3 whole fresh ducks, with
      gizzards
    ¼ cup kosher salt
    1 teaspoon freshly ground
      pepper
    1 bay leaf, crumbled
    2 cloves garlic, minced
    2 tablespoons minced shallot
    2 tablespoons minced parsley
    3 cups rendered poultry fat
      or lard, plus fat as needed
    1 bulb garlic, halved crosswise

**1.** Remove excess fat from ducks and reserve. Cut off legs above thigh and set aside with gizzards. Cut off breasts and reserve for another use (see pages 106 and 113). Pull skin off backs and reserve. Save carcasses for stock (see page 32), if desired.

**2.** In a large bowl stir together salt, pepper, bay leaf, minced garlic, shal-lot, and parsley. Add duck legs and gizzards and toss to coat with season-ings. Cover and refrigerate 36 hours.

**3.** In a deep, heavy pot, combine reserved duck skin and fat with 2 tablespoons water and melt over low heat. Cook until fat is completely rendered. Combine with the addi-tional 3 cups rendered fat. Pat duck legs and gizzards dry with paper towels, then add to melted fat along with halved garlic bulb. Add fat as necessary to keep duck pieces im-mersed. Cook over low heat until duck is very tender (about 1½ hours). Remove pot from heat and let con-tents come to room temperature.

**4.** With a slotted spoon, transfer duck legs, gizzards, and halved garlic bulb to a 1-quart crock. Bring fat to a simmer over moderate heat, skim-ming off any scum that forms on the surface. Simmer for 5 minutes. Spoon clear fat into crock, leaving any residue in pot. Confit should be cov-ered in fat by 1 inch. If not, melt additional fat and add to crock. Refrigerate. When cool, cover crock with plastic wrap. Confit may be stored in the refrigerator for up to 2 months.

**5.** To use confit, bring crock to room temperature. Gently lift out as many pieces of duck and gizzard as neces-sary and cook as recipe directs.

*Makes 1 quart confit.*

## MIQUE SARLADAISE
### Southwestern boiled dinner with steamed dumpling

In the region surrounding Sarlat, a town in southwest France, *la mique sarladaise* is a traditional winter dish. The name refers not only to the entire dish of boiled meats and vegetables, but also to the giant steamed dumpling that differentiates this pot-au-feu from others. Begin this dish at least one day ahead.

- 2 pounds oxtail
- 1 bulb garlic, halved crosswise
  Bouquet garni (2 bay leaves, 4 sprigs parsley, and 1 sprig thyme)
- 1 cup thickly sliced onion
- 1 tablespoon cracked peppercorns
- 1 large roasting chicken (about 4 lb)
- 3 eggs
- ¼ cup half-and-half
- 3 green onions, minced
- 1 teaspoon kosher salt
- ½ teaspoon freshly ground pepper
- 2 cups bread cubes (½ in.)
- 1½ teaspoons baking powder
- 1 cup flour
- 1 sheet caul fat (about 12 by 18 in.; see Note, page 83)
- 6 medium carrots, peeled
- 2 large turnips, peeled
- 1 whole celery heart, washed
- 1 green cabbage, cut in half
- 12 small boiling onions, peeled
  Dijon-style mustard and Cornichons (see page 70), for accompaniment
  Sauce Gribiche (see page 40; optional)

**1.** At least 1 day in advance, place oxtail, garlic, bouquet garni, sliced onion, and peppercorns in a large pot. Cover with cold water by 1 inch. Bring to a simmer over moderate heat, skimming off any skum that rises to surface. Reduce heat to maintain a simmer and cook for 2 hours. Add chicken and enough additional cold water to cover. Raise heat to moderate and bring to a simmer, then reduce heat to maintain a simmer and cook for 45 minutes. Remove from heat and let cool to room temperature. With a slotted spoon, transfer chicken and oxtails to a plate. Cover with plastic wrap and refrigerate overnight. Cover stock and refrigerate overnight.

**2.** Lift off congealed fat from surface of stock and reserve 2 tablespoons of fat. In a large bowl whisk eggs to blend. Whisk in half-and-half, green onions, reserved fat, salt, and pepper. Stir in bread cubes and let rest 15 minutes. Combine baking powder and flour, and stir into egg mixture. Let dough rest another 15 minutes.

**3.** Lay caul fat out on a flat surface and place dumpling dough on it. Pat dough out into a round about 1 inch thick. Wrap with caul and slide onto a plate.

**4.** In a large pot over moderate heat, bring stock to a simmer. Add oxtails, chicken, carrots, turnips, celery, cabbage, and boiling onions. When stock returns to a simmer, slide in dumpling. Add boiling water to cover if dumpling is not completely covered by liquid. Reduce heat to low, cover, and cook for 1 hour.

**5.** Uncover pot and transfer dumpling to a warm serving platter with a large flat strainer or slotted spoon. Cut chicken into serving pieces and arrange on a second serving platter, surrounded with pieces of oxtail. Remove vegetables from stock with a slotted spoon. Cut carrots in 2-inch lengths, quarter turnips, cut celery heart into 6 wedges, and cut each cabbage half into 3 wedges. Arrange vegetables on serving platter with dumpling. Moisten both platters with a little warm stock. Accompany with mustard, Cornichons, and, if desired, Sauce Gribiche. Cut dumpling into wedges to serve.

*Serves 6.*

## ESCAROLE BRAISÉE
### Braised escarole

Crisp, slightly bitter escarole is one of the most popular salad greens in France. Like cabbage and other sturdy greens, it also stands up well to braising and makes a delicious side dish for roast pork or roast duck (see page 75).

- 1 tablespoon oil
- 1 shallot, minced
- 1 tablespoon minced garlic
- 1 large head escarole, washed, dried, and coarsely chopped
- ½ teaspoon dried thyme or 1 teaspoon minced fresh thyme
  Kosher salt and freshly ground pepper
  Juice of ½ lemon

In a large skillet over moderate heat, heat oil. Add shallot and garlic, and sauté for 3 minutes. Add escarole and stir to coat with oil (about 30 seconds). Add thyme. Cover, reduce heat to maintain a simmer, and cook for 10 minutes. Uncover, raise heat to high, and cook until any remaining liquid has evaporated. Season to taste with salt, pepper, and lemon juice. Transfer to a serving bowl and grind fresh pepper over top.

*Serves 6.*

## CÔTE DE BOEUF GRILLÉE AU ROQUEFORT
### Grilled rib-eye steaks with Roquefort butter

Pungent Roquefort cheese, aged in the caves of Roquefort-sur-Soulzon, adds a delightful tang to the butter for these thick grilled steaks. Pommes Frites (see page 114) and a red Cahors wine or an inexpensive Bordeaux would be good accompaniments.

- 6 rib-eye steaks (about 1 in. thick)
- 6 tablespoons olive oil
- 2 tablespoons freshly ground pepper

#### Roquefort Butter

- ½ cup Roquefort cheese
- 2 tablespoons sour cream
- 4 tablespoons unsalted butter, softened
- 1 tablespoon minced chives

Prepare a hot charcoal fire. Trim all excess fat from steaks and bring meat to room temperature. Brush steaks with olive oil and sprinkle both sides with pepper. Grill steaks, turning once, until done to your liking (2 to 3 minutes per side for rare). Transfer steaks to warm dinner plates and put a spoonful of Roquefort Butter on top of each. Pass any remaining Roquefort Butter separately.

*Serves 6.*

**Roquefort Butter**   Combine all ingredients in a small bowl. Beat with a wooden spoon until smooth. Transfer to a crock and serve at room temperature.

*Makes 1 scant cup.*

### MARRONS BRAISÉS
### *Braised chestnuts*

Look for fresh chestnuts in the market from November through January; select those that feel firm and heavy for their size. Braised chestnuts are a holiday treat in France and are served with the Christmas duck, pheasant, or goose.

> 2  *pounds fresh chestnuts*
> 5  *ounces lean salt pork, cut in ¼-inch dice*
> 3  *tablespoons minced shallot*
> 1½ *cups Fond de Volaille (see page 32)*
> ½  *cup dry red wine*
>    *Kosher salt and freshly ground pepper*
> 2  *tablespoons minced chives, for garnish*

**1.** Preheat oven to 400° F. With a small, sharp knife, cut an *x* in flat side of each chestnut. Transfer chestnuts to a rimmed baking sheet or a roasting pan and bake for 12 minutes. Remove from oven; when just cool enough to handle, peel chestnuts.

**2.** In a large skillet over moderate heat, render salt pork until lightly browned (about 5 minutes). Add shallot and sauté for 3 minutes. Add stock, wine, and peeled chestnuts. Reduce heat to maintain a simmer,

cover, and cook until chestnuts are tender and most of the liquid has evaporated (about 1 hour). Season to taste with salt and pepper. Transfer to a warm serving bowl and garnish with chives.

*Serves 6.*

## DESSERTS

The best finale to a hearty meal is a fruit dessert, such as the classic *clafoutis Limousin* or a colorful compote.

### COMPOTE DE FRUITS AU SAUTERNES
### *Compote of fruit in Sauternes*

After the rich meals typical of southwest France, a fruit compote makes a welcome dessert. Note that fruit needs to marinate for at least six hours.

> 2½ *cups Sauternes or other sweet white wine*
>    *Zest of 1 lemon, cut in julienne strips*
> 6  *prunes*
> 4  *fresh or dried figs*
> 2  *large green apples, cut into eighths and cored*
> 2  *tablespoons sugar*
> 1  *cinnamon stick*
> ½  *cup walnut halves*
> ½  *teaspoon vanilla extract*

In a medium mixing bowl, combine wine, lemon zest, prunes, and dried figs (if using). Let marinate at room temperature at least 6 hours, or overnight. Transfer to a medium saucepan and add apples, sugar, cinnamon stick, and walnut halves. Bring to a simmer and cook for 5 minutes. If using fresh figs, halve or quarter them (depending on size) and add to saucepan. Simmer another 5 minutes. Remove from heat and cool slightly; stir in vanilla, then cool to room temperature. Serve at room temperature or chill slightly. Remove cinnamon stick before serving.

*Serves 6.*

**Make-Ahead Tip**   Compote may be made up to 3 days in advance and refrigerated. Remove from refrigerator 30 minutes before serving.

### CLAFOUTIS LIMOUSIN
### *Baked cherry pudding*

The Limousin region, northeast of Bordeaux, is the birthplace of *clafoutis*, a rustic pudding-cake made with the local cherries or prune plums. Apricots, blueberries, or brandy-soaked prunes can also be used. Offer guests a small glass of kirsch with this fresh cherry version.

> 2½ *cups pitted fresh cherries*
> 2  *tablespoons kirsch or other cherry brandy*
>    *Grated zest of 1 lemon*
> ½  *cup sugar*
> 1  *cup whipping cream*
> ½  *cup milk*
> 4  *eggs*
> 1  *teaspoon vanilla extract*
> ¼  *teaspoon freshly grated nutmeg*
> ½  *cup flour*
> 2  *tablespoons unsalted butter, for greasing pan*
>    *Crème Fraîche (see page 22) or storebought ice cream (optional)*

**1.** Preheat oven to 350° F. In a small bowl combine cherries and kirsch. Let marinate at room temperature for 30 minutes. In a food processor or blender, combine lemon zest and sugar. Process until you can no longer see bits of yellow zest (about 10 seconds). Add cream, milk, eggs, vanilla, and nutmeg, and process briefly to blend. Add flour and pulse briefly to blend.

**2.** Grease a 9-inch-diameter pan with butter. Transfer cherries and any accumulated juice to pan. Pour batter over top. Bake until well browned and puffy (about 30 minutes). Transfer to a rack to cool for at least 10 minutes. Clafoutis is best served warm. Serve in squares, garnished with Crème Fraîche or ice cream (if desired).

*Serves 6.*

*For a dinner to flatter a red Bordeaux wine, consider a first course of sautéed wild mushrooms and a second course of grilled duck breast with crisp french fries.*

## DUCK DINNER FOR FOUR

*Cèpes à la Bordelaise*

*Magrets de Canard Grillés*

*Pommes Frites*

*Salade de Frisée aux
Croûtons au Roquefort*

*Sorbet de Framboises à la Menthe*

*Red Bordeaux*

*This autumn menu is best
suited to a casual occasion,
with guests who won't mind
when you disappear to do
some quick, last-minute
cooking. The mushrooms
must be sautéed just before
you sit down to eat them;
the best solution is to invite
guests into the kitchen for
a glass of wine while you
stir and season. The duck
breasts don't need to go
on the grill until you've
finished the first course;
however, you'll need a helper
then to watch the duck
while you fry the potatoes.
A red Bordeaux would be
a good choice to partner the
earthy, uncomplicated
flavors of both mushrooms
and duck.*

## CÈPES À LA BORDELAISE
### *Sauteed mushrooms with garlic and parsley*

Fresh *Boletus edulis* are available in specialty produce markets in the late fall and winter. Sometimes the mushrooms are labeled by their French name (cèpes) or Italian name ( *porcini* ). They are always expensive; substitute cultivated mushrooms if you prefer. To soak up the delectable juices, be sure to offer plenty of warm French bread.

- *1 pound fresh cèpe mushrooms*
- *1 tablespoon minced garlic*
- *3 tablespoons olive oil*
- *1 tablespoon unsalted butter*
- *1 teaspoon minced fresh thyme or ½ teaspoon dried thyme*
- *2 tablespoons lemon juice*
- *2 tablespoons minced parsley*
- *Kosher salt and freshly ground pepper*

**1.** Clean mushrooms well with a damp paper towel or mushroom brush. Remove stems and mince them. Combine minced stems and garlic. Cut mushroom caps into ¼-inch-thick slices.

**2.** In a large skillet over moderate heat, heat oil and butter. Add mushroom stems and sauté for 2 minutes. Add mushroom caps and gently mix to coat with oil. Add thyme, reduce heat to low, and cook until moisture evaporates (10 to 12 minutes). Add 1 tablespoon of the lemon juice and continue cooking for 5 minutes. Stir in parsley and the remaining 1 tablespoon lemon juice. Season to taste with salt and pepper. Transfer to warm plates and serve immediately.

*Serves 4.*

## MAGRETS DE CANARD GRILLÉS
### *Grilled duck breasts*

A grilled duck breast, with its dark meat and full flavor, tastes almost like a juicy beefsteak. Take care not to overcook it or the lean meat will be dry. Note that the duck needs to marinate at least one day.

- *1 tablespoon minced garlic*
- *1 tablespoon minced shallot*
- *1 tablespoon kosher salt*
- *1 teaspoon freshly ground pepper*
- *1 tablespoon minced chives*
- *1 tablespoon minced parsley*
- *4 boneless duck breast halves*
- *2 bay leaves*
- *2 tablespoons red wine*

**1.** In a small bowl stir together garlic, shallot, salt, pepper, chives, and parsley. Pat mixture onto both sides of duck breasts. Put a bay leaf on skin side of 2 breasts. Cover each with another breast, skin side down. Press together and place breasts in a stainless steel, glass, or enamel bowl. Sprinkle with wine and cover bowl with plastic wrap. Refrigerate for at least 1 day or up to 48 hours. Remove breasts from refrigerator 45 minutes before cooking.

**2.** Prepare a medium-hot charcoal fire. Discard bay leaves and pat breasts dry with paper towels. With a small, sharp knife, slash skin of each breast in 4 places to prevent breast from curling as it cooks. Grill breasts, skin side down, for 1 minute. Turn and cook until breasts are springy to the touch (3 to 5 minutes). Remove from grill and let rest for 3 minutes before carving. To serve, hold a knife at a 45-degree angle and carve wide slices against the grain.

*Serves 4.*

## POMMES FRITES
### French fries

For crisp french fries, dry the potatoes well before frying and fry in small batches to keep the oil temperature constant (see opposite page).

> *Safflower oil or vegetable oil, for deep-frying*
> 3 *large baking potatoes*
> *Kosher salt*

**1.** Put at least 3 inches of safflower oil in a deep fryer, deep skillet, or wok. Heat to 375° F. Peel potatoes and cut into matchsticks (see Perfect French Fries, page 115). Transfer to a bowl of cold water immediately after cutting to prevent browning.

**2.** Dry potatoes thoroughly in dish towels, drying only as many as you plan to fry at one time. Fry potatoes in small batches until golden brown (3 to 5 minutes). Drain thoroughly, then sprinkle with salt and transfer to a paper-towel–lined, ovenproof platter. Keep french fries warm in a 200° F oven. When all potatoes are fried, transfer to a clean serving platter or napkin-lined basket.

*Serves 4.*

## SALADE DE FRISÉE AUX CROÛTONS AU ROQUEFORT
### Chicory salad with Roquefort toasts

The chicory family includes curly endive, Belgian endive, escarole, and radicchio. Any of those greens, or a combination of them, could be used in this salad.

> 2 *small* or 1 *large head curly endive*
> *Basic Vinaigrette (see page 31)*
> 2 *ounces Roquefort cheese, crumbled*
> 8 *Croûtons à l'Ail (at right) Freshly ground pepper*

Wash curly endive, dry it well, and tear it into bite-sized pieces. In a small bowl whisk together vinaigrette and 1 tablespoon of the crumbled Roquefort. Spread one side of each crouton with about 1 teaspoon Roquefort. In mixing bowl, toss curly

114

endive with vinaigrette. Add croutons and toss. Divide among 4 serving plates. Crumble remaining Roquefort over salads and grind pepper on top.

*Serves 4.*

## CROÛTONS À L'AIL
### Garlic croutons

Use these thin toasts for garnishing soups or as a foundation for creamy cheeses or spreads.

> *8-inch length of French baguette*
> ¼ *cup olive oil*
> 2 *tablespoons unsalted butter*
> 1 *clove garlic, peeled and crushed*

Preheat oven to 350° F. Slice baguette on the diagonal about ¼ inch thick. In a small saucepan over medium heat, heat olive oil, butter, and garlic until butter melts. Lightly brush both sides of bread with mixture and bake until golden brown (about 5 minutes).

*Makes about 30 croutons.*

## SORBET DE FRAMBOISES À LA MENTHE
### Raspberry mint ice

Fresh mint gives this berry ice its clean, refreshing flavor. Note that the sorbet needs to chill at least eight hours before freezing.

> 1¼ *cups dry red wine*
> 6 *tablespoons sugar*
> 2 *tablespoons lemon juice*
> ½ *cup loosely packed mint leaves*
> 2 *pints raspberries*

**1.** In a medium saucepan, combine red wine, sugar, lemon juice, and mint leaves. Bring to a simmer over moderate heat. Add raspberries, then crush berries lightly with a wooden spoon. Return to a simmer and cook 2 minutes. Remove from heat and cool to room temperature.

**2.** Transfer mixture to a blender or food processor and blend until smooth. Strain through a fine sieve. Cover and refrigerate at least 8 hours or up to 1 day. Transfer to an ice cream freezer and freeze according to manufacturer's directions.

*Serves 4.*

# THE BASQUE COUNTRY

The Basque language, which bears no evident relation to other European tongues, has helped preserve the distinctive culture of this corner of southwest France. In some ways, the Basques are a nation within a nation, with their own habits, customs, and approaches to food.

Basque cooking, with its heavy use of tomatoes, sweet peppers, onions, ham, and garlic, is more Spanish in flavor than French. It is a rustic, straightforward cuisine, suited to the tastes and rugged lifestyles of shepherds, fishermen, and farmers.

The Basques make good use of the fish and shellfish from the nearby gulf, but they also have a fondness for salt cod. Oddly, they are the only people in France to have taken a liking to corn. They grow maize and use cornmeal in breads, pastries, and Italian-style polenta dishes.

The mountainous region is not suited to cattle, but raising sheep is a major enterprise. The Basques are highly skilled shepherds, and milk from Basque sheep is made into a variety of cheeses enjoyed throughout France. Pigs are also important to the local gastronomy; the cured hams of Bayonne are world-famous.

## FIRST COURSES

Artichokes, clams, red peppers, saffron—ingredients that dominate the cooking of Spain to the southwest—are beloved among the residents of the *pays basque* (Basque country).

## ARTICHAUTS, SAUCE BÉARNAISE
### Artichokes with béarnaise sauce

A warm, sweet artichoke knows no better accompaniment than tarragon-scented *sauce béarnaise.*

> ½ *cup lemon juice*
> 6 *large artichokes*

### Sauce Béarnaise

- ¼ cup dry white wine
- ¼ cup tarragon vinegar or white wine vinegar
- 1 tablespoon minced shallot
- 2 teaspoons minced fresh tarragon
  Pinch cayenne pepper
- 3 egg yolks
- 1 cup unsalted butter, cut into small pieces
  Kosher salt and freshly ground white pepper

**1.** Put ¼ cup of the lemon juice in a large stainless steel or glass mixing bowl. Add cold water to fill bowl. Using a serrated stainless steel knife, cut 2 inches off top of each artichoke. Pull off and discard small tough leaves at base of artichoke. Cut off stem at base. Using scissors, snip off top ¼ inch of each leaf to remove pointed tip. Drop artichokes into acidulated water to prevent browning.

**2.** Bring a large pot of salted water to a boil over high heat. Add artichokes and the remaining ¼ cup lemon juice. Cover, reduce heat to maintain a simmer, and cook until artichokes are tender (about 30 minutes). A leaf will pull out easily when artichokes are done. Drain artichokes upside down on paper towels for 2 minutes.

**3.** Using your fingers, carefully spread back center leaves just enough to allow you to remove the choke—the prickly inner leaves and the hairy fibers at base of artichoke. Use a small spoon to scrape out hairy fibers. Place artichokes on individual serving plates and divide Sauce Béarnaise among them, spooning it into center of each artichoke. Serve immediately.

*Serves 6.*

**Sauce Béarnaise**  Put wine, vinegar, shallot, 1 teaspoon of the tarragon, and cayenne in the top of a double boiler. Set directly over high heat and boil until liquid is reduced to 3 tablespoons. Strain through a fine sieve and return to top of double boiler. Whisk in egg yolks, then place over barely simmering water and continue whisking until mixture begins

to thicken slightly. Begin whisking in butter bit by bit, adding more only when the previous addition is thoroughly incorporated. Sauce must not be allowed to become too hot or it will break; if necessary, remove pan from heat and continue whisking in butter. Whisk in the remaining 1 teaspoon tarragon. Season to taste with salt and pepper and serve immediately.

*Makes 1 cup.*

---

### PALOURDES AU SAFRAN
#### Clams with saffron

For a more substantial dish, serve these clams over spaghetti tossed in olive oil. Note that clams need to refrigerate for six hours.

- 6 pounds small clams
- 2 tablespoons cornmeal
- 1 tablespoon unsalted butter
- 1 tablespoon olive oil
- 1½ tablespoons minced shallot
- 1 teaspoon minced garlic
- 1 cup peeled, seeded, and chopped tomatoes
- ¼ gram (½ teaspoon) saffron threads
- 1 cup dry white wine
  Pinch cayenne pepper
  Freshly ground pepper

**1.** Wash clams well, discarding any that refuse to close when pressed. Place clams and cornmeal in a large stainless steel bowl. Cover with water and refrigerate for 6 hours. Drain.

**2.** In a pot big enough to hold all the clams, heat butter and oil over moderate heat. Add shallot and garlic and sauté for 3 minutes. Add tomatoes, saffron, wine, and pepper; reduce heat to low and simmer for 5 minutes. Raise heat to high; add clams and cover. Steam clams until they open (5 to 7 minutes). Check pot occasionally and remove any opened clams to a large, warm bowl. Discard any clams that refuse to open after 7 minutes. Distribute clams among individual warm soup bowls. Pour pan juices over clams and serve immediately.

*Serves 6.*

### PERFECT FRENCH FRIES

**1.** *Peel potatoes and cut into matchsticks. Transfer to a bowl of cold water immediately after cutting to prevent browning.*

**2.** *Dry potatoes thoroughly in dish towels, drying only as many as you plan to fry at one time.*

**3.** *Fry potatoes in small batches until golden brown (3 to 5 minutes). Drain thoroughly, then sprinkle with salt and transfer to a paper-towel–lined platter.*

## SOUPE DE PIMENTS D'ESPELETTE
### Red pepper soup from Espelette

Each year, the tiny Basque town of Espelette holds a colorful pepper festival to celebrate its best-known crop. To approximate the slightly piquant flavor of the Espelette red pepper, the following recipe uses sweet red bell peppers and a dash of cayenne.

- ¼ cup olive oil
- 1½ cups chopped onion
- 2 leeks (white part only), chopped
- 1 tablespoon minced garlic
- 4 cups peeled, seeded, and coarsely chopped tomato
- 4 cups neatly diced red bell pepper
- 1 cup shredded green cabbage
- 3 cups Fond de Volaille (see page 32)
- 1 tablespoon tomato paste
- ½ cup dry red wine
- ¼ teaspoon cayenne pepper, or more to taste
  Kosher salt
- 6 slices (1 in. thick) dense country-style bread
- ¾ cup freshly grated Romano cheese

**1.** In a large stockpot over moderately low heat, heat olive oil. Add onion, leeks, and garlic, and sauté for 5 minutes. Add tomato and bell peppers and sauté for 5 minutes. Add cabbage, stock, tomato paste, wine, and the ¼ teaspoon cayenne. Bring to a simmer, reduce heat to maintain a simmer, and cook for 15 minutes. Season to taste with salt.

**2.** Remove soup from heat. Transfer 2 cups of soup to a blender or food processor and blend until smooth. Stir purée back into pot. Reheat soup; add salt and cayenne to taste. Soup should be very spicy.

**3.** Preheat broiler. Arrange bread slices on a baking sheet, sprinkle each with 2 tablespoons of the cheese, and broil until bubbly (about 4 minutes). Serve soup in warm bowls and float a slice of bread on top.

*Serves 6.*

## CREPAZES
### Savory crêpe cake

Saffron often turns up in traditional Basque dishes, probably due to Spanish influence. Here, saffron-flavored crêpes are layered with cheese, ham, and chard to make an unusual appetizer or brunch dish.

- 3 tablespoons unsalted butter
- 2 cups chopped onion
- 3 cups cooked, drained, and chopped Swiss chard
- 2 eggs, lightly beaten
- 1 cup ricotta cheese
  Kosher salt and freshly ground pepper
- 3 ounces prosciutto, thinly sliced
- 6 tablespoons grated Parmesan cheese
- 2 tablespoons olive oil

#### Saffron Crêpes

- 3 eggs
- 2 cups milk
- ½ gram (1 teaspoon) saffron threads
- 1½ cups flour
- ½ cup plus 2 tablespoons water
- 2 tablespoons olive oil
- 1 teaspoon kosher salt
- ½ teaspoon freshly ground pepper
- 2 tablespoons minced green onion
- 1 tablespoon (approximately) unsalted butter, melted

**1.** In a large skillet over low heat, melt 2 tablespoons of the butter. Add onion and sauté for 10 minutes. Add chard and sauté for 3 minutes. Remove from heat and let cool 5 minutes. Stir in eggs. Add ½ cup of the ricotta. Season to taste with salt and pepper.

**2.** Preheat oven to 350° F. To assemble crêpe cake, grease a 9-inch-diameter cake pan with the remaining tablespoon butter. Place 1 crêpe, cooked side down, on bottom. Cover with one third of the prosciutto slices. Top with a crêpe, cooked side down. Spread with one third of the remaining ricotta. Top with a crêpe, cooked side down. Spread with one third of the chard mixture. Top with a crêpe, cooked side down. Sprinkle with 2 tablespoons Parmesan, then repeat layering process twice, beginning with prosciutto slices.

**3.** Drizzle cake with olive oil. Cover loosely with aluminum foil, so that foil does not touch top of cake but is sealed around sides of pan. Bake 1 hour. Uncover and bake 10 minutes. Remove from oven and cool 10 minutes. Invert cake onto a warm serving plate. Present whole, then slice into wedges to serve.

*Serves 6.*

**Saffron Crêpes** In a food processor or blender, combine eggs, milk, saffron, flour, the water, olive oil, salt, and pepper. Blend until smooth. Transfer to a bowl and whisk in green onions. Let batter rest 20 minutes; it should resemble pancake batter. If too thick, thin with cold water. To cook, heat a nonstick, 9-inch frying pan or crêpe pan over moderate heat. Brush very lightly with some of the melted butter. Using about ¼ cup batter per crêpe, pour batter into pan and swirl to coat bottom of pan evenly. Cook until crêpe sets (about 1 minute). Turn out onto a dry surface. Repeat until batter is used up, buttering pan only as necessary to keep batter from sticking. When completely cool, stack crêpes, wrap in plastic wrap, and refrigerate for up to 3 days.

*Makes ten 9-inch crêpes.*

## MAIN COURSES

Onions, sweet peppers, and tomatoes
are essential to the Basque kitchen.
This aromatic trio is stirred into
scrambled eggs, spooned atop grilled
rockfish, or used as a braising medium for rice and chicken.

### PIPÉRADE DU PAYS BASQUE
### *Scrambled eggs with tomatoes and peppers*

Onions, peppers, tomatoes, and the
locally raised ham turn basic scrambled eggs into a memorable dish.

- ⅓ *pound prosciutto, thinly sliced*
- 2 *to 3 tablespoons olive oil*
- ¾ *cup chopped onion*
- 1 *tablespoon minced garlic*
- 3 *cups coarsely chopped tomato*
- 2½ *cups neatly diced red bell pepper*
- 2½ *cups neatly diced green bell pepper*
- 2 *teaspoons tomato paste (if needed)*
- *Kosher salt, freshly ground black pepper, and cayenne pepper*
- 8 *eggs, lightly beaten*

**1.** Trim any fat from prosciutto. In
a large skillet over moderate heat,
heat 2 tablespoons of the olive oil
and prosciutto fat. If prosciutto
doesn't yield at least 1 tablespoon fat,
use an additional tablespoon olive
oil. Add onion and garlic, and sauté
for 3 minutes. Add tomato, reduce
heat to low, and simmer for 15
minutes. Add 1 cup of the red pepper
and 1 cup of the green pepper; cover
and cook for 20 minutes. Peppers
should be quite soft.

**2.** Remove skillet from heat. Pass
mixture through a food mill; or,
purée mixture thoroughly in a
blender or food processor, then press
through a sieve. Return mixture to
skillet. If tomatoes lack flavor and
color, stir in tomato paste. Season
mixture highly with salt, black pepper, and cayenne. Add remaining bell
peppers and bring to a simmer. Reduce heat to low, add eggs, and
scramble gently until curds are firm
but not dry (about 4 minutes). Serve
in shallow soup bowls, garnished
with sliced prosciutto.

*Serves 6.*

*Pipérade, one of the best-
known Basque dishes,
combines scrambled eggs
with peppers, tomatoes,
and ham.*

*Pairing a grilled rockfish with sweet peppers and capers is typical of Basque cuisine.*

## CALMARS À LA BASQUAISE
### *Squid with tomato, garlic, and anchovy*

Offer plenty of crusty French bread for sponging up the delicious sauce. To make a heartier entrée, this preparation can be tossed with well-drained spaghetti.

- 2 pounds squid
- 3 tablespoons olive oil
- 2 cups chopped onion
- 4 cups peeled, seeded, and chopped tomato
- 1 tablespoon plus 1 teaspoon minced garlic
- 2 tablespoons minced anchovies
- 4 tablespoons minced parsley
- ⅓ cup dry red wine
  Kosher salt and freshly ground pepper

**1.** Clean squid, separating tentacles from bodies. Leave tentacles whole if small; cut in half if large. Cut bodies into 1-inch-wide rings.

**2.** In a large skillet over moderate heat, heat olive oil. Add squid rings and sauté for 3 minutes. Add onion and sauté for 3 minutes. Add tomato, the 1 tablespoon garlic, anchovies, 2 tablespoons of the parsley, and wine. Bring to a simmer. Cover partially, reduce heat to maintain a simmer, and stew until squid is tender (about 25 minutes). Season to taste with salt and pepper. Combine the remaining 2 tablespoons parsley and the 1 teaspoon garlic. Serve squid in warm bowls, garnishing each portion with parsley-garlic mixture.

*Serves 6.*

## POISSON DE ROCHE GRILLÉ AUX POIVRONS ROUGES
### Grilled fish with bell pepper and capers

Oven-roasted potatoes and a bottle of dry white Bordeaux wine turn this easy dish into a complete dinner. If they're available, consider substituting a green and a yellow bell pepper for two of the reds.

- 3 red bell peppers
- 7 tablespoons olive oil
- 1 teaspoon minced fresh thyme
- 1½ tablespoons minced garlic
- 2 tablespoons capers
  Kosher salt, freshly ground black pepper, and cayenne pepper
- 2 tablespoons lemon juice
  Pinch hot-pepper flakes
- 6 fillets (6 to 8 oz each) rock cod or other firm-fleshed white fish

**1.** Halve bell peppers, remove stems, ribs, and seeds, and cut into ¼-inch-wide strips. In a large skillet over moderate heat, heat 4 tablespoons of the olive oil. Add peppers and stir to coat with oil. Add thyme and cover. Stew peppers for 10 minutes. Uncover, add garlic and capers, and raise heat to high. Sauté for 30 seconds, stirring. Remove from heat. Season to taste with salt, black pepper, and cayenne. The dish should be spicy.

**2.** Prepare a hot charcoal fire. Thirty minutes before fire is ready, whisk together the remaining 3 tablespoons olive oil, lemon juice, and pepper flakes. Brush fish with some of the mixture. Let stand at room temperature until ready to cook. Salt and pepper fish lightly, then grill to desired doneness (8 to 10 minutes per inch of thickness), basting occasionally with remaining marinade. You do not need to turn fish. Serve immediately on warm dinner plates, topping each portion with warm peppers.

*Serves 6.*

**Make-Ahead Tip** Recipe may be prepared through step 1 up to 1 day in advance. Cover and refrigerate. Rewarm gently to serve.

## POULET À LA BASQUAISE
### Spicy chicken with tomatoes and bell peppers

Serve steamed rice and a full-bodied red wine with this saucy dish.

- 3 tablespoons olive oil
- 2 chickens (3 lb each), cut into 6 pieces each
- 2 bay leaves
- 2 strips (3 in. long) orange peel
- ¾ pound chorizo sausage, loose or removed from casing
- 1 cup chopped onion
- 4 cups peeled, seeded, and chopped tomato
- 2 cups red bell pepper, cut in 1-inch squares
- 2 cups green bell pepper, cut in 1-inch squares
- ¼ teaspoon cinnamon
- ½ teaspoon minced fresh thyme
- ¼ teaspoon cayenne pepper
  Kosher salt and freshly ground pepper
- 2 tablespoons minced parsley, for garnish

**1.** In each of two large skillets over moderate heat, heat 1½ tablespoons of the olive oil. Pat chicken pieces dry with paper towels, then brown on all sides, in batches if necessary. To each skillet, add ½ cup water, a bay leaf, and a strip of orange peel. Cover, reduce heat to low, and cook until chicken is almost tender (about 20 minutes).

**2.** In a large dutch oven or a roasting pan big enough to hold all the chicken, sauté chorizo for 3 minutes over moderate heat, breaking up sausage with a wooden spoon. Add onion, reduce heat to low, and sauté for 3 minutes. Add tomato, bell peppers, cinnamon, thyme, and cayenne. Sauté for 20 minutes.

**3.** Transfer chicken to pan with tomato sauce, cover, and continue cooking until chicken is done throughout (about 10 more minutes). Season to taste with salt and pepper. Transfer to a warm platter or individual plates and garnish with parsley.

*Serves 6.*

**Make-Ahead Tip** This dish may be prepared up to 3 days in advance and refrigerated. Undercook slightly to allow for reheating.

## RIZ À LA BASQUAISE
### Rice with sausage, bacon, and peppers

The Basque region is one of the few areas in France where rice dishes are common. A typical preparation involves steamed rice with spicy peppers, tomatoes, bacon, and sausage.

- ¼ pound bacon, cut in 3-inch lengths
- 1 cup red bell pepper, cut in ½-inch squares
- 1 cup green bell pepper, cut in ½-inch squares
- 2 tablespoons olive oil
- ½ pound spicy sausage links
- 1½ cups minced onion
- 1 small jalapeño chile, seeded and minced
- 1½ cups long-grain white rice
- 3 cups hot Fond de Volaille (see page 32)
- 2 cups cored, seeded, and diced tomato
- 3 tablespoons minced parsley
  Kosher salt and freshly ground black pepper

**1.** In a large skillet over moderately low heat, cook bacon until most of the fat is rendered. Add peppers, cover, and cook for 10 minutes.

**2.** In another large skillet over moderate heat, heat olive oil. Add sausage and brown lightly on all sides. Add onion and jalapeño, and reduce heat to low. Sauté for 10 minutes. Add rice and stir to coat with fat. Add stock and bring to a boil. Cover tightly and cook over low heat for 18 minutes.

**3.** Lift sausage out of rice and slice into rounds. With a fork, stir sausage back into rice. Drain excess fat from bacon, then stir bell pepper and bacon into rice. Combine tomato and parsley. Add to rice and toss well with a fork. Season to taste with salt and pepper. Transfer to a warm serving bowl and serve immediately.

*Serves 6.*

## POLENTA AU COULIS DE TOMATES
### Polenta with fresh tomato sauce

Polenta, coarse-ground cornmeal, is as popular in the Basque country as it is in northern Italy. Cooked polenta makes a satisfying light supper when topped with fresh tomato sauce; for a heartier meal, add a platter of grilled sausages.

- 4 tablespoons olive oil
- 1 tablespoon minced garlic
- 6 cups water
- 1½ teaspoons kosher salt, plus salt to taste
- 1½ cups polenta
  Coulis de Tomates (see page 94)
- 2 tablespoons red wine vinegar
  Fresh basil leaves, for garnish

**1.** In a large saucepan over moderate heat, heat 2 tablespoons of the olive oil. Add garlic and sauté for 3 minutes. Add the water and the 1½ teaspoons salt, raise heat to high, and bring mixture to a boil. Add polenta in a slow, steady stream, whisking constantly. Reduce heat to low and cook for 15 minutes, stirring often to prevent sticking or lumping. Whisk in the remaining 2 tablespoons oil. Remove from heat and pour into an oiled 9- by 13-inch baking dish. Let stand at least 10 minutes to firm up, or cover and refrigerate for up to 24 hours.

**2.** Cut firm polenta into squares or diamonds. If polenta was refrigerated, cover dish with aluminum foil and reheat in a preheated 350° F oven until hot throughout (about 20 minutes).

**3.** In a saucepan over moderate heat, bring tomato sauce to a simmer. Divide polenta among warm dinner plates. Spoon about ⅓ cup sauce over each portion, drizzle with red wine vinegar, and garnish with torn basil leaves.

*Serves 6.*

## DESSERTS

Among French pastry makers, only the Basques occasionally use cornmeal in desserts. The following two examples are not terribly sweet, which makes them just right for accompanying a glass of dessert wine.

## BISCUITS AU MAÏS
### Basque cornmeal raisin rounds

Cornmeal sweets are a specialty of Basque bakeries. Try these with a winter fruit compote (see page 111) or as an afternoon snack. Note that the dough must be refrigerated overnight. These cookies may be frozen for up to one month.

- ¼ cup golden raisins
- 1 tablespoon rum
- ½ teaspoon vanilla extract
- ¼ cup unsalted butter, softened, plus butter for greasing
- ¼ cup sugar
- 2 tablespoons honey
- 1 large egg
- ½ cup polenta (coarse-ground cornmeal)
- ¾ cup flour, plus flour for dusting
- ¼ teaspoon cinnamon
- ½ teaspoon salt

**1.** In a small bowl combine raisins, rum, and vanilla. Stir and let stand for 20 minutes.

**2.** In a medium bowl cream butter. Add sugar and honey, and cream well. Beat in egg. Add polenta gradually and beat to blend. In a separate bowl, stir together flour, cinnamon, and salt. Add gradually to creamed mixture. Stir in raisins.

**3.** Pat dough into a 6-inch square, wrap in plastic, and refrigerate overnight.

**4.** Preheat oven to 375° F. Roll dough out ¼ inch thick on a lightly floured surface. Cut out rounds with a 1½-inch cookie or biscuit cutter. Gather scraps and reroll. Place rounds on a lightly buttered baking sheet. Bake until lightly browned (18 to 20 minutes). Cool on rack.

*Makes about 2 dozen rounds.*

## GÂTEAU AU MAÏS
### Cornmeal cake with peaches

Berries or a winter fruit compote (see page 111) could take the place of the sugared peaches.

- 1 cup sweet white wine
- ⅓ cup golden raisins
  Butter, for greasing pan
- 1 cup yellow cornmeal, plus 1 tablespoon cornmeal for dusting pan
- 3 cups milk
- 1 teaspoon kosher salt
- ¼ cup sugar
- 4 large eggs, separated
- ¼ cup olive oil
  Pinch salt
- 4 ripe peaches, peeled, sliced, and sugared to taste

**1.** In a small bowl combine wine and raisins and let stand for 30 minutes. Butter a 10-cup bundt or tube pan. Dust with the 1 tablespoon cornmeal, shaking out excess.

**2.** Preheat oven to 350° F. In a large saucepan combine milk, salt, and sugar. Bring to a boil over moderate heat, stirring to dissolve sugar. Reduce heat to low and add the 1 cup cornmeal in a slow, steady stream, whisking constantly. Cook for 2 minutes, whisking. Add wine and raisins. Cook for 2 minutes, whisking. Remove from heat.

**3.** In a medium bowl whisk egg yolks and olive oil until blended. Whisk into cornmeal mixture.

**4.** In a large bowl beat egg whites with a pinch of salt until stiff but not dry. Gently but thoroughly fold egg whites into cornmeal mixture. Transfer to prepared pan. Batter will fill pan. Bake until golden and firm to the touch (about 40 minutes). Cool on a rack. Cake will have risen over top of pan but will fall again as it cools. Refrigerate for 2 hours. Invert cake and remove pan. Cut cake into wedges and serve cold, with sliced peaches alongside.

*Makes one cake.*

## TARTE AUX POIRES À LA BASQUAISE
### *Pear tart with cornmeal crust*

Poached, sliced pears in a custard base make a handsome tart to end an autumn dinner.

> Zest of 1 lemon
> 2 tablespoons lemon juice
> ½ cup honey
> 2½ cups water
> ½ cup dry white wine
> 1 cinnamon stick
> 2 cloves
> ½ vanilla bean, split
> 2 large ripe pears, peeled, halved, and cored
> 3 large eggs
> ¾ cup whipping cream
> ¼ teaspoon freshly grated nutmeg

### Cornmeal Tart Dough

> 1 cup flour, plus 2 tablespoons flour if necessary
> ⅓ cup yellow cornmeal
> 2 tablespoons sugar
> ½ teaspoons kosher salt
> 6 tablespoons chilled unsalted butter, cut in small pieces
> 1 large egg, beaten with 1 tablespoon water

**1.** In a large pot combine lemon zest, lemon juice, honey, the water, wine, cinnamon, and cloves. With the tip of a small, sharp knife, scrape vanilla seeds into liquid, then add bean to pot. Bring mixture to a simmer over moderate heat. Add pears and poach just until a knife can be slipped in and out easily (15 to 25 minutes depending on size and ripeness). Cool in liquid.

**2.** With your fingers, press Cornmeal Tart Dough into a 9-inch-diameter tart tin, covering bottom and sides. Prick dough all over with a fork. Chill 45 minutes.

**3.** Preheat oven to 375° F. Cut each pear half in half lengthwise. Arrange pear neatly in tart shell, with one of the cut sides facing down. In a medium bowl whisk together eggs, cream, ¼ cup of the pear poaching liquid, and nutmeg. Carefully pour mixture around and over pears. Bake

until custard is firm to the touch and lightly browned (about 35 minutes). Cool on rack. Serve at room temperature.

*Makes one 9-inch tart.*

### Cornmeal Tart Dough

**1.** *To prepare in a food processor:* Place the 1 cup flour, cornmeal, sugar, and salt in work bowl of processor. Process until mixed (about 3 seconds). Add butter and process until blended (about 4 seconds). Add egg-water mixture and process until dough barely forms a ball. Turn out onto a lightly floured surface. *To prepare by hand:* Stir together the 1 cup flour, cornmeal, sugar, and salt. Cut in butter with a pastry blender or 2 knives until mixture resembles coarse crumbs. Add egg-water mixture and toss with a fork.

**2.** Turn out onto a lightly floured surface; knead lightly to form a ball, sprinkling with up to 2 more tablespoons flour if necessary. Pat into a square, cover with plastic wrap, and refrigerate at least 1 hour or up to 1 day (if more than 2 hours, remove from refrigerator 20 minutes before pressing out).

*A glass of Sauternes or sweet Muscat would complement this custard-filled pear tart.*

*Salt cod–stuffed peppers star in this Basque-inspired buffet, accompanied by a salad, Basque corn bread, and Pyrénées cheese.*

**AUTUMN BUFFET FOR 16**

*Poivrons Farcis à la Morue*

*Pain de Maïs*

*Salade Verte (Green Salad)*

*Fromage des Pyrénées (Pyrénées cheese)*

*Compote de Fruits au Sauternes (see page 111)*

*Beaujolais*

*Entertaining a large gathering is easy with a buffet meal that can be entirely made ahead. The following menu of Basque specialties fits the bill: The peppers can be stuffed in the morning and slipped into the oven just before guests arrive; the corn bread and compote can be made hours before. With a fresh green salad (see Basics, page 31), a half-wheel of Doux de Montagne or other Pyrénées cheese, and several bottles of Beaujolais, you have an easy, festive, and informal meal for a crowd. Be sure to triple the compote recipe, so there will be plenty to go around.*

## POIVRONS FARCIS À LA MORUE
### Salt cod–stuffed peppers

Stuffed with a creamy, garlicky mixture of potatoes and salt cod, these baked peppers hold up well on a buffet table. Note that the cod must soak for 24 hours.

- 3 pounds salt cod
- 5½ cups milk
- 3 tablespoons olive oil
- 1 medium red onion, thinly sliced
- 6 cloves garlic, thinly sliced
- 1½ cups whipping cream
- 1 pound potatoes, peeled and diced
- 3 tablespoons red wine vinegar
- ¾ teaspoon cayenne pepper
- 6 tablespoons capers
- 6 tablespoons minced parsley
- 1 large bunch green onions, chopped
- 8 green bell peppers
- 8 red bell peppers

**1.** Cover cod with cold water. Refrigerate 24 hours, changing water 3 times. The last time, add 4 cups of the milk to water. Drain and cut cod into 5-ounce pieces.

**2.** Preheat oven to 350° F. In a large skillet over moderate heat, heat oil. Add onion and garlic and toss to coat with oil. Add salt cod, the remaining 1½ cups milk, cream, and potatoes. Bring to a simmer, reduce heat to low, and cook for 5 minutes, turning fish occasionally. Remove fish to a bowl with a slotted spoon. Cover skillet and simmer until potatoes are tender (8 to 10 minutes longer).

**3.** Lightly break fish apart with a fork. When potatoes are tender, add contents of skillet to bowl, along with vinegar, cayenne, capers, parsley, and green onions. Stir to blend.

**4.** Cut tops off peppers and reserve. Remove seeds and cut out ribs. Stuff each pepper with ¾ cup salt cod mixture. Replace tops of peppers. Place peppers in a roasting pan, cover with aluminum foil, and bake until soft (30 to 35 minutes). Serve hot or warm.

*Serves 16.*

## PAIN DE MAÏS
### Basque corn bread

Christopher Columbus brought corn to the Old World in the fifteenth century, and thanks to some of Columbus's Basque crew, corn breads took hold in the *pays basque* and are still produced in local bakeries. Note that dough needs to rise for at least three hours.

- ¼ cup honey
- 3 cups warm (100° F) water
- 1½ packages active dry yeast
- 4½ cups (approximately) bread flour
- 1 cup polenta (coarse-ground cornmeal)
- 2 cups yellow cornmeal, plus cornmeal for baking sheet
- 1 tablespoon salt
- ¼ cup olive oil, plus oil for bowl
- 1 egg, beaten with 1 tablespoon milk

**1.** In a large mixing bowl, whisk together honey and the water. Whisk in yeast and let stand for 10 minutes. Add 1 cup of the bread flour, polenta, and cornmeal. Stir well. Cover bowl and let dough rise for 1½ hours.

**2.** Stir in salt, oil, and 3 cups bread flour. Stir until mixture comes away from sides of bowl. Turn out onto a lightly floured surface and knead, adding up to ½ cup flour to keep dough from sticking. Knead until smooth and elastic (about 10 minutes). Transfer to a large, lightly oiled bowl; turn to coat all sides with oil. Cover and let dough rise 1 hour.

**3.** Preheat oven to 350° F. Punch dough down, cover, and let rise for 35 minutes. Cut dough in half and shape each half into a round or loaf. If rounds, transfer to a heavy baking sheet dusted with cornmeal. If loaves, transfer to two buttered 9-inch loaf pans. Let dough rest, covered loosely with a towel, for 20 minutes. Brush dough with egg-milk mixture. Bake until breads are browned and sound hollow when tapped on the bottom (about 50 minutes). Remove from pans and cool on rack.

*Makes 2 round or 9-inch loaves.*

# INDEX

*Note: Page numbers in italics refer to photographs separated from recipe text.*

## U.S./METRIC MEASURE CONVERSION CHART

| | | Formulas for Exact Measures | | | | Rounded Measures for Quick Reference | |
|---|---|---|---|---|---|---|---|
| | Symbol | When you know: | Multiply by: | To find: | | | |
| **Mass (Weight)** | oz | ounces | 28.35 | grams | 1 oz | | = 30 g |
| | lb | pounds | 0.45 | kilograms | 4 oz | | = 115 g |
| | g | grams | 0.035 | ounces | 8 oz | | = 225 g |
| | kg | kilograms | 2.2 | pounds | 16 oz | = 1 lb | = 450 g |
| | | | | | 32 oz | = 2 lb | = 900 g |
| | | | | | 36 oz | = 2¼ lb | = 1,000 g (1 kg) |
| **Volume** | tsp | teaspoons | 5.0 | milliliters | ¼ tsp | = ¹⁄₂₄ oz | = 1 ml |
| | tbsp | tablespoons | 15.0 | milliliters | ½ tsp | = ¹⁄₁₂ oz | = 2 ml |
| | fl oz | fluid ounces | 29.57 | milliliters | 1 tsp | = ⅙ oz | = 5 ml |
| | c | cups | 0.24 | liters | 1 tbsp | = ½ oz | = 15 ml |
| | pt | pints | 0.47 | liters | 1 c | = 8 oz | = 250 ml |
| | qt | quarts | 0.95 | liters | 2 c (1 pt) | = 16 oz | = 500 ml |
| | gal | gallons | 3.785 | liters | 4 c (1 qt) | = 32 oz | = 1 liter |
| | ml | milliliters | 0.034 | fluid ounces | 4 qt (1 gal) | = 128 oz | = 3¾ liters |
| **Temperature** | °F | Fahrenheit | $\frac{5}{9}$ (after subtracting 32) | Celsius | 32° F | | = 0° C |
| | °C | Celsius | $\frac{9}{5}$ (then add 32) | Fahrenheit | 68° F | | = 20° C |
| | | | | | 212° F | | = 100° C |